DATE DUE

NOV 16 1995

WOMEN OF THE ASYLUM

WOMEN OF THE ASYLUM

VOICES FROM BEHIND THE WALLS, 1840–1945

Written and Edited by

Jeffrey L. Geller and Maxine Harris

Foreword by Phyllis Chesler

ANCHOR BOOKS
DOUBLEDAY
NEW YORK LONDON TORONTO SYDNEY AUCKLAND

AN ANCHOR BOOK

PUBLISHED BY DOUBLEDAY
a division of Bantam Doubleday Dell Publishing Group, Inc.
1540 Broadway, New York, New York 10036

ANCHOR BOOKS, DOUBLEDAY,
and the portrayal of an anchor are trademarks of
Doubleday, a division of Bantam Doubleday
Dell Publishing Group, Inc.

Library of Congress Cataloging-in-Publication Data

Women of the asylum : voices from behind the walls, 1840–1945 / written and edited by
Jeffrey L. Geller and Maxine Harris ; foreword by Phyllis Chesler.—1st ed.
p.   cm.
Includes bibliographical references.
1. Mentally ill women—United States—Biography.   2. Psychiatric hospital patients—
United States—Biography.   3 Psychiatric hospital care—United States—History—Sources.
4. Psychiatry—United States—History—Sources.   5. Women—United States—Social
conditions.   I. Geller, Jeffrey L.   II. Harris, Maxine.
RC451.4.W6W6567   1994
362.2'1'082—dc20   93-42478   CIP

BOOK DESIGN BY CLAIRE NAYLON VACCARO
ISBN 0-385-47422-9

PRINTED IN THE UNITED STATES OF AMERICA
July 1994

1   3   5   7   9   10   8   6   4   2

FIRST EDITION

For Daniel and Suzanne, there from the beginning

—JEFFREY GELLER

For my grandmother Molly Ozone,
may these voices speak for you as well

—MAXINE HARRIS

Acknowledgments

This book would not have been possible without the courageous women who wrote of their experiences and documented their ordeals. To them we owe a great debt.

Many libraries, guardians of the written record, generously assisted this project. We would like to give special thanks to the following libraries: American Antiquarian Society, Amherst College Library, Boston Public Library, Brattleboro Retreat Library, Cambridge City Library, Clark University Library, Countway Medical Library, Duke University Library, Forbes Library, Institute of Living Library, Library of Congress, Moody Bible Institute Library, National Library of Medicine, New York Academy of Medicine Library, New York Public Library, New York State Library, Payne Whitney Library, Quincy Public Library, Smith College Library, Stockbridge Public Library, University of Massachusetts Library, University of Pittsburgh Library, University of Texas Library, and Widener Library.

The Smithsonian Institution and the Costume Institute of

ACKNOWLEDGMENTS

the Metropolitan Museum of Art extended access to their collection of photographs and provided needed assistance.

Several people provided technical support for which we are grateful. Susan Azarin, Valerie Buffone, Helen Robitaille, and Janice Quinn assisted with typing the manuscript. Susan Azarin, Andrea Stevenson, and K. J. Williams spent many hours obtaining much needed data. Valerie Buffone carefully and thoughtfully coordinated the administrative aspects of the project.

Helen Bergman, Sara Harris, and Mark Smith read earlier versions of the manuscript and provided valuable commentary.

Phyllis Chesler graciously agreed to write the moving and impassioned foreword which accompanies this book.

We are especially grateful to our agent, Leslie Breed, who believed in this project and brought it to a successful outcome with skill and care. We would also like to thank Martha Levin of Anchor Books for seeing merit in this project.

Finally, we would like to thank our spouses, Merle Brandzel and Mark Smith, for providing loving support and genuine interest throughout a project that was at times emotionally draining.

Contents

CONTENTS

Preface

For years, the women whose stories are presented here had their voices silenced behind asylum walls. Once published, their first-person accounts of life in mental hospitals gathered dust in the attics of hospital or university libraries or in the back rooms of secondhand bookstores.

To be able to present even one or two stories would be significant. To be able to present in this one volume twenty-six first-person accounts of what it was like for a woman to be a mental patient is a rare privilege.

Although these women lived in different parts of the country, spanned two centuries of history, and wrote with very different and unique voices, they were indeed soulmates. Most saw their struggles with "mental illness" and subsequent forced incarceration into hospitals in both personal and political terms. They wanted to right the wrongs they saw being perpetuated by what they perceived to be autocratic families, domineering physicians, unfeeling attendants, and misguided lawmakers.

Theirs were not the only voices that emanated from behind

the asylum walls. Hospital physicians and superintendents wrote prolifically about the conditions inside asylums and about the latest treatments for the insane. In some cases, the views of these professionals agreed in substance if not in tone with these women's first-person accounts. In many cases, however, they did not; treater and treated experienced very different realities. To fully know what it was like to be a woman and a mental patient in the century between 1840 and 1945, we must listen to the women themselves.

To help understand both the importance and the historical context of these accounts, we are fortunate in having been able to draw on the groundbreaking work of several women scholars. Phyllis Chesler (whose foreword to this book follows), Barbara Ehrenreich, Elaine Showalter, and Carroll Smith-Rosenberg have all written about the complex and many-layered meaning of illness in the lives of women and about the sometimes confusing, adversarial, and often unhealthy tone that has characterized women's relationships to their physicians. We are grateful to them and to others for establishing a climate of inquiry in which these current first-person accounts of asylum care can be published and read.

Jeffrey Geller, M.D., M.P.H.
Maxine Harris, Ph.D.
June 1993

Foreword

Women of the Asylum is a true companion volume to my own *Women and Madness*, first published in 1972. I applaud Drs. Jeffrey Geller and Maxine Harris for bringing this anthology into being. These twenty-six first-person accounts are lucid, sometimes brilliant, always heartbreaking, and utterly principled, even heroic. Incredibly, these women were not broken or silenced by their lengthy sojourns in hell. They bear witness to what was done to them—and to those less fortunate than themselves, who did not survive the brutal beatings, near drownings, and force-feedings, the body restraints, the long periods in their own filth and in solitary confinement, the absence of kindness or reason, which passed for "treatment." These historical accounts brought tears to my eyes.

Whether these *Women of the Asylum* were entirely sane, or whether they had experienced postpartum or other depressions, heard voices, were "hysterically" paralyzed or disoriented; whether the women were well educated and well-to-do or members of the working poor; whether they had led relatively privileged lives or had been beaten, raped, abandoned, or victimized in other ways; whether the women accepted or could no longer cope with their narrow social roles; whether they had been idle for too long or had worked too hard for too long and were fatigued beyond measure—none were treated with any kindness, sympathy, or medical or spiritual expertise.

Elizabeth T. Stone (incarcerated 1840–42, in Massachusetts) describes the mental asylum as "a system that is worse than slavery"; Adriana Brinckle (1857–85, in Pennsylvania) describes the asylum as a "living death," filled with "shackles," "blackness," "handcuffs, straight-jackets, balls and chains, iron rings, and . . . other such relics of barbarism"; Tirzah Shedd (1865, in Illinois) tells us, "This . . . seems to me to be more a place of punishment, than a place of cure. . . . 'a wholesale slaughter-house!' "; Clarissa Caldwell Lathrop (1880–82, in New York) writes, "We could not read the invisible inscription over the entrance, written in the heart's blood of the unfortunate inmates, 'Who enters here must leave all hope behind.' " Female patients were routinely beaten, deprived of sleep, food, exercise, sunlight, and all contact with the outside world, and were sometimes even murdered. Their resistance to physical (and mental) illness was often shattered. Sometimes the women tried to kill themselves as a way of ending their torture.

I am amazed, and saddened, that I was able to complete my formal education *and* write *Women and Madness* without knowing more than a handful of the stories gathered here.

In 1969 I helped found the Association for Women in Psychology (AWP). I was a brand-new Ph.D., a psychotherapist-in-training, an assistant professor, and a researcher. Inspired by the existence of a visionary and radical grassroots feminist movement, I was conducting a study on women's experiences as psy-

chiatric and psychotherapeutic patients, and on sex role stereo-
typing in theory and practice. I planned to present some
preliminary findings at the annual convention of the American
Psychological Association (APA) in 1970, in Miami.

I read psychiatric, psychological, and psychoanalytic texts,
and historical, mythological, and fictional accounts of women's
lives. I located the stories of European women who'd been condemned as witches (including Regine Pernoud's book on Joan
of Arc) and, from the sixteenth century on, psychiatrically diagnosed and imprisoned. I read the nineteenth-century American
heroine Elizabeth Packard (whose words are contained here)
and about some of Freud's patients, most notably Anna O, who
became the feminist crusader Bertha Pappenheim, and Dora,
whose philandering and syphilitic father, in Freud's words, "had
handed [Dora] over to [a] strange man in the interests of his
own [extramarital] love-affair."

I learned that some well-known and accomplished women—
Zelda Fitzgerald, Virginia Woolf, Frances Farmer, Sylvia Plath,
and the fictionally named "Ellen West"—had been psychiatrically labeled and hospitalized. Based on numerous statistical, academic, and case studies, and on interviews with female ex-
mental and psychotherapy patients, I began to document what
patriarchal culture and consciousness had been doing to women
for thousands of years, including psychiatrically and "therapeu-
tically" in the twentieth century in the United States. I was also
charting the psychology of human beings in captivity who, as a
caste, did not control the means of production or reproduction
and who were routinely abused and shamed: sexually, economically, politically, and socially. I was trying to understand what a
struggle for freedom might entail, both politically and psychologically, when the colonized group was female.

In the midst of this work, I attended the 1970 APA convention. Instead of delivering an academic paper, on behalf of AWP, I asked the assembled APA members for one million dollars "in reparations" for those women who had never been helped by the mental health professions but who had, in fact, been further abused: punitively labeled, ordered to "adjust" to their lives as second- and third-class citizens, and blamed when they failed to do so, overly tranquilized, sexually seduced while in treatment, hospitalized, often against their will, given shock and insulin coma therapy, or lobotomies, straitjacketed, both physically and chemically, and used as slave labor in state mental asylums. "Maybe AWP could set up an alternative to a mental hospital with the money," I suggested, "or a shelter for runaway wives."

Two thousand of my colleagues were in the audience; they seemed shocked. Many laughed. Loudly. Nervously. Some looked embarrassed, others relieved. Quite obviously, I was "crazy." Afterward, someone told me that jokes had been made about my "penis envy." Friends: this was 1970, not 1870. And I was a colleague, on the platform, and at the podium.

Women and Madness was published in 1972. It was embraced, instantly, by other feminists and by many women in general. However, my analysis of how diagnostic labels were used to stigmatize women and of why more women than men were involved in "careers" as psychiatric patients was either ignored, treated as a sensation, or sharply criticized by those in positions of power within the professions. My statistics and theories were "wrong," I had "overstated" my case regarding the institutions of marriage and psychiatry, I'd overly "romanticized" archetypes, especially of the Goddess and Amazon variety. Moreover, I (or my book) was "strident," "hated men," and was "too angry." Like so many feminists before me, I became a "dancing dog" whom no university ever tried to hire. Luckily, I was just about to gain tenure at a university; luckily, no father, brother, or husband was able to psychiatrically imprison me because my ideas offended them.

It is conceivable, outrageous, but that is *all* Elizabeth T. Stone and Elizabeth Packard (1860–63, in Illinois) did: express views that angered their brothers or husbands. Phebe B. Davis's (1850–53) crime was daring to think for herself in the state of New York. Davis writes, "It is now twenty-one years since people found out that I was crazy, and all because I could not fall in with every vulgar belief that was fashionable. I never could be led by everything and everybody." Adeline T. P. Lunt notes that within the asylum the female patient must cease thinking or uttering any original expression. She must "study the art of doffing [her] true character . . . until you cut yourself to [institutional] pattern, abandon hope." Spirited protest, or disobedience of any kind, would only result in more grievous punishment. In fact, in 1861, Susan B. Anthony and Elizabeth Cady Stanton wrote:

> Could the dark secrets of those insane asylums be brought to light . . . we would be shocked to know the countless number of rebellious wives, sisters and daughters that are thus annually sacrificed to false customs and conventionalisms, and barbarous laws made by men for women.

In her work on behalf of both mental patients and married women, Elizabeth Packard proposes, as her first reform, that "no person shall be regarded or treated as an Insane person, or a Monomaniac, simply for the expression of opinions, no matter how absurd these opinions may appear to others." Packard was actually trying to enforce the First Amendment on behalf of women! Packard also notes, "It is a crime against human progress to allow Reformers to be treated an Monomaniacs . . . [W]ho will dare to be true to the inspirations of the divinity within them, if the Pioneers of truth are thus liable to lose their personal liberty . . . ?" Phebe B. Davis is more realistic. She writes that "real high souled people are but little appreciated in this world—they are never respected until they have been dead two or three hundred years."

The talented and well-connected Catherine Beecher (1840s–1850s) and the feminist writer Charlotte Perkins Gilman (1887) wanted "help" for their overwhelming fatigue and depression. Beecher, after years of domestic drudgery, and Gilman, after giving birth, found themselves domestically disabled. Gilman couldn't care for her infant daughter; Beecher could no longer sew, mend, fold, cook, clean, serve, or entertain. Beecher writes, "What [my sex] had been trained to imagine the highest earthly felicity [i.e., domestic life], was but the beginning of care, disappointment, and sorrow, and often led to the extremity of mental and physical suffering. . . . there was a terrible decay of female health all over the land." Nevertheless, both women blamed themselves; neither viewed her symptoms as possibly the only way she could (unconsciously) resist or protest her traditional "feminine" work—or overwork.

Beecher and Gilman described how they *weren't* helped—or how their various psychiatric cures damaged them even further. In Gilman's words, Dr. S. Weir Mitchell ordered her to

> "live as domestic a life as possible. Have your child with you all the time." (Be it remarked that if I did but dress the baby it left me shaking and crying—certainly far

from a healthy companionship for her, to say nothing of the effect on me.) "Lie down an hour after each meal. Have but two hours' intellectual life a day. And never touch pen, brush or pencil as long as you live."

This regime only made things worse. A desperate Gilman decided to leave her husband and infant to spend the winter with friends. Ironically, she writes, "from the moment the wheels began to turn, the train to move, I felt better."

Adjustment to the "feminine" role *was* the measure of female morality, mental health, and psychiatric progress. Adeline T. P. Lunt writes that the patient must "suppress a natural characteristic flow of spirits or talk . . . [she must] sit in ladylike attire, pretty straight in a chair, with a book or work before [her], 'inveterate in virtue,'" and that this will result in "being patted panegyrically on the head" and pronounced "better." According to Phebe B. Davis:

> Most of [the doctors] that are employed in lunatic asylums do much more to aggravate the disease than they do to cure it. . . . a patient who will not minister to the self-love of the physicians, must expect to be treated with great severity. . . . It is a pity that great men [the asylum doctors] should be susceptible of flattery; for . . . when there is a real mind, that will flatter no one, then you will see the Doctor's revengeful feelings all out.

Margaret Starr (1901–2, in Maryland) writes, "I am making an effort to win my dismissal. I am docile; I make efforts to be industrious."

How did these women of the asylum get *into* the asylum?

The answer is: most often against their will and without prior notice. Here is what happened. Suddenly, unexpectedly, a perfectly sane (or a troubled) woman would find herself being arrested by a sheriff: removed from her bed at dawn or "legally kidnapped" on the streets in broad daylight. Or her father, brother, or husband might ask her to accompany him to see a friend to help him with a legal matter. Unsuspecting, the woman would find herself before a judge and/or a physician, who certified her "insane" on her husband's say-so. Often, the woman was not told she was being psychiatrically diagnosed or removed to a mental asylum. Why did this happen?

Battering, drunken husbands had their wives psychiatrically imprisoned as a way of continuing to batter them; husbands also had their wives imprisoned in order to live with or marry other women. Tirzah Shedd writes that "there is one married woman [here] who has been imprisoned seven times by her husband, and yet she is intelligent and entirely sane? When will married women be safe from her husband's power?" Lydia A. Smith (1865–71, in New York and Michigan) writes:

> It is a very fashionable and easy thing now to make a person out to be insane. If a man tires of his wife, and is befooled after some other woman, it is not a very difficult matter to get her in an institution of this kind. Belladonna and chloroform will give her the appearance of being crazy enough, and after the asylum doors have closed upon her, adieu to the beautiful world and all home associations.

Alice Bingham Russell (1883, 1903–6, in Minnesota) was legally kidnapped by a sheriff on her husband's orders. After obtaining her own release, Russell spent twelve years trying to document and "improve the conditions of the insane." Russell describes many women whose husbands psychiatrically imprisoned them in order to gain control of their wives' property. Russell describes a woman who refused to

> sell her property to suit the caprice of her husband. . . . this young and capable woman who has been doing, up to the very hour before [she was legally kidnapped], all her housework, including the care of two children, leaves a good home and property worth $20,000, to become a public charity and mingle and associate continuously with maniacs.

At thirty-two, the unmarried Adriana Brinkle conducted an economic transaction on her own: she sold some furniture she no longer needed. Charges were brought against her for selling furniture for which she had not fully paid. For the crime of embarrassing her father's view of "family honor," Brinckle's physician-father and his judge-friend "sentenced" Brinckle to *twenty-eight years* in a psychiatric hospital. Russell tells us of a woman "who [had] been wronged out of some property [and who was] about to take steps to recover it when she [was] falsely accused and sent to the asylum by fraud."

Any sign of economic independence or simple human pride in a woman could be used against her, both legally and psychiatrically. Russell describes the following:

> A woman and her husband quarrel; the wife with independence accepts a position as janitress, hoping her absence will prove her worth at home. She returns to se-

cure some clothing, and learning from a neighbor that a housekeeper is in possession, and being refused admittance, she, in her haste to get justice, takes some of the washing from the clothes line, including some of the husband's and housekeeper's to give evidence of their living together. That evening she is arrested, but has not the least fear but that she can vindicate herself. To her surprise she is without friends or counsel committed to the St. Peter asylum.

Some women of the asylum evolve rather clear-minded views on the subject of marriage and husbands. Like Catherine Beecher, Anna Agnew (1878–85, in Indiana) believed something was truly "wrong" with her ("nervous prostration") when she could no longer perform her domestic duties. Anna Agnew suffered doubly when her family "charged [her] with . . . feigning insanity to evade the responsibilities of [her] home duties." Mrs. Agnew's husband finally had her institutionalized; but he did not visit her for nine months. Of that first visit, Mrs. Agnew writes:

> My husband had come, and he did care something for me after all. After I had entered the room, and closed the door, he stood looking at me, but not speaking a word until I said, "For heaven's sake, don't stand there staring at me in such a manner as that; sit down and say something to me. . . ." "Were you insane when you were married?" Not one single, little word of kindness or gesture of tenderness, not the shadow of a greeting; simply this cruel, calculating question. Evidently, he had even then formed the determination that I should never

leave that asylum alive. . . . [I answered] "I was not insane when we were married." I have changed my opinion since then, materially, and willingly admit I was insane, and my most pronounced symptom was that I married him.

Some asylum women did not speak; some spoke and made no sense. Some wept incessantly; some were violent. However, most women in asylums did not start out—or even become—insane. According to Adeline T. P. Lunt:

A close, careful study and intimacy with these patients [finds] no irregularity, eccentricity, or idiosyncrasy, either in language, deportment, or manner, than might be met with in any society of women thrown together, endeavoring to make the most of life under the most adverse and opposing circumstances.

The women of the asylum feared, correctly, that they might be driven mad by the brutality of the asylum itself, and by their lack of legal rights as women, and as prisoners. As Adeline Lunt writes, "INSANE ASYLUM. A place where insanity is made." Sophie Olsen (1862–64, in Illinois) writes, "O, I was so weary, weary; I longed for some Asylum from 'Lunatic Asylums'!" According to Mrs. L. C. Pennell (1880, in Maine), "The enforcement of the rules of the institution is the surest way in the world to prevent recovery." Jane Hillyer notes that asylum conditions "were so far removed from normal living that they actually aided my sense of cleavage, rather than cleared it up, as they are supposed to do." Margaret Isabel Wilson (1931–37) says, "I was afraid of incarceration; I had seen too much of the deadly effects of institutionalization."

Are these women of the asylum exaggerating or lying? Are they deluded? Obviously not. Each account confirms every other account. Each woman says, quite simply, that she, and *every other woman she ever met in the asylum*, were psychologically degraded, indentured as servants, and physically tortured by male doctors and especially by female attendants.

Some women of the asylum believe that their inability to function *deserved* a psychiatric label and a hospital stay. Two of these twenty-six women feel they were helped in the asylum and afterward, by a private physician. Lenore McCall (1934–38) writes that she recovered *because* of the insulin coma therapy. She also attributes her recovery to the presence of a nurse who had "tremendous understanding, unflinching patience [and whose] sole concern was the good of her patient." After Jane Hillyer was released from the asylum, she consulted a private doctor whom she feels rescued her from ever having to return.

McCall and Hillyer are decidedly in the minority. Twenty-four women of the asylum document that power is invariably abused: that fathers, brothers, husbands, judges, asylum doctors, and asylum attendants will do anything that We, the people, allow them to get away with; and that women's oppression, both within the family and within state institutions, remained constant for more than a century in the United States. (It exists today still, and in private offices as well as in private and state institutions.)

Do these accounts of institutional brutality and torture mean that mental illness does not exist, that women (or men) in distress don't need "help," or that recent advances in psychopharmacology, or insights gained from the psychoanalytic process, or from our treatment of sexual and domestic violence victims, are invalid or useless? Not at all. What these accounts document is that many women in asylums were not insane; that "help" was not to be found in doctor-headed, attendant-staffed, and state-run patriarchal institutions, neither in the nineteenth century nor in the twentieth; that what we call "madness" can *also* be caused or exacerbated by injustice and cruelty, within the family, within society, and in asylums; and that personal freedom, radical legal reform, and political struggle are enduringly crucial to individual mental and societal moral health.

These twenty-six accounts are documents of courage and integrity. The nineteenth-century women of the asylum are morally purposeful, philosophical, often religious. Their frame of reference, and their use of language, are romantic-Christian and Victorian. They write like abolitionists, transcendentalists, suffragists. The twentieth-century women are keen observers of human nature and asylum abuse—but they have no universal frame of reference. They face "madness" and institutional abuse alone, without God, ideology, or each other.

What do these women of the asylum think helped them or would help others in their position? Friends, neighbors, and sons sometimes rescued the women; however, many of the nineteenth-century women obtained their freedom only because laws existed or had recently been passed that empowered men who were *not* their relatives to judge their cases fairly. Therefore, for them, obtaining and enforcing their legal rights was a priority. Elizabeth Packard became a well-known and effective crusader for the rights of married women and mental patients; Mrs. L. C. Pennell also suggested reforms, as did Mrs. H. C. McMullen (1894–97 in Minnesota), who, while imprisoned, wrote some model "Laws for Protection of the Insane." As noted, Alice Bingham Russell documented the stories of still-imprisoned women and helped them obtain their freedom. Mrs. Pennell proposed that "every doctor after being called to examine a person for insanity shall immediately notify the proper authorities." Mrs. McMullen proposed that "all rules and laws for the protection of the hospital inmates should be posted up and enforced, it would be a relief of mind to know what rights they can demand."

In addition to legal reform, and the liberty to leave an abusive husband or an abusive asylum, what else proved helpful, or invaluable, to the women of the asylum? Phebe B. Davis writes that "kindness [has] been my only medicine"; Kate Lee (1899–1900, in Illinois) proposes that "Houses of Peace" be created, where women could learn a trade and save their money, after which they could "be both allowed and required to leave." Lee suggests that such Houses of Peace "operate as a home-finder and employment bureau . . . thus giving each inmate a new start in life [which] in many cases [will] entirely remove the symptoms of insanity." Margaret Isabel Wilson says that "Nature was my doctor." *Leaving* the asylum helped Wilson: "There were no maniacal shrieks to make me shudder; no attendants to yell out orders; no nurses to give me arsenic and physics; no doctors to terrify me."

I'd like Phebe B. Davis to have the last word about why women become "excitable" and about why psychiatric hospitalization is an especially painful and outrageous form of punishment. Davis writes:

I find that active nervous temperaments that are full of thought and intellect want full scope to dispose of their energy, for if not they will become extremely excitable.

Such a mind cannot bear a tight place, and that is one great reason why women are much more excitable than men, for their minds are more active; but they must be kept in a nut-shell because they are women.

Phyllis Chesler, Ph.D.

WOMEN OF THE ASYLUM

Introduction

In 1842 page one of the first volume of the *Asylum Journal* featured the following poem by an unnamed woman inmate.

SCENE IN A PRIVATE MAD-HOUSE

Stay, jailor, stay, and hear my woe!
  She is not made who kneels to thee,
For what I'm now, too well I know,
  And what I was, and what should be.
I'll rave no more in proud despair,
  My language shall be mild, though sad;
But yet I'll firmly, truly swear,
  I am not mad, I am not mad!

My tyrant husband forged the tale
  Which chains me in this dismal cell;
My fate unknown my friends bewail—
  Oh, jailer, haste that fate to tell!

Oh, haste my father's heart to cheer!
  His heart at once will grieve and glad,
To know, though kept a captive here,
  I am not mad, I am not mad!

He smiles in scorn and turns the key!
  He quits the grate—I kneel in vain!
His glimmering lamp still, still, I see!
  'Tis gone—and all is gloom again.
Cold! bitter cold—no warmth! no light!
  Life, all thy comforts once I had!
Yet here I'm chained this freezing night,
  Although not mad! no, no, not mad!

'Tis sure some dream—some vision vain!
  What! I, the child of rank and wealth!
Am I the wretch who clanks this chain?
  Bereft of freedom, friends and health!
Ah! while I dwell on blessings fled,
  That never more my heart must glad,
How aches my heart, how burns my head—
  But 'tis not mad! no, tis not mad!

Hast thou, my child, forget ere this,
  A mother's face, a mother's tongue?
She'll ne'vr forget your parting kiss,
  Nor round her neck how fast you clung;
Nor how with me you sued to stay,
  Nor how that suit your sire forbade;
Nor how—I'll drive such thoughts away—
  They'll make me mad—they'll make me mad!

His rosy lips, how sweet they smiled—
 His mild blue eyes, how bright they shone;
None ever bore a lovelier child—
 And art thou now forever gone?
And must I never see thee more,
 My pretty, pretty, little lad?
I will be free—unbar the door—
 I am not mad, I am not mad!

O hark—what mean those dreadful cries?
 His chains some furious madman breaks—
He comes—I see his glaring eyes—
 Now, now, my dungeon grate he shakes—
Help—help—he's gone. Oh fearful woe,
 Such screams to hear, such sights to see!
My brain, my brain—I know, I know
 I am not mad, but soon shall be.

Yes, soon—for lo, now—while I speak,
 Mark how yon demon's eyeballs glare!
He sees me—now with dreadful shriek,
 He whirls a serpent high in air!
Horror—the reptile strikes his tooth
 Deep in my heart, so crushed and sad!
Aye, laugh, ye fiends—I feel the truth—
 Your task is done—I'm mad, I'm mad![1]

The cries of this anonymous author echo the laments and the concerns of the twenty-six women whose first-person accounts of their psychiatric hospitalizations make up the main body of *Women of the Asylum*. Many of the women whose stories are excerpted here speak of the injustices that brought them to the asylum. Some were the victims of cruel and misguided fathers or husbands; others were punished for holding unpopular beliefs; still others behaved in ways unbecoming for women of their generation. Even those who felt that their hospitalizations were beneficial and justified longed for the freedoms that they had left behind, and they often failed to understand the convoluted and idiosyncratic process whereby release might be obtained.

In addition to their individual accounts of how and why their own hospitalizations occurred, some of the women tell the stories of sister inmates who did not or could not write on their own behalf. All of the women describe life in the asylum. Some focus on the therapies they received; most, however, talk of the meals, the crowding, the lack of privacy, and the often brutal and inhuman treatment by the ward attendants. What is telling is that these accounts of the "nontherapeutic" environment are remarkably consistent across the hundred-year time span 1840–1945 covered by the accounts in this book.

Just who were these twenty-six women who chose to make public their very personal accounts of life in the madhouse? It would not be too simplistic to say that they were "everywoman." Only four—Catherine Beecher, Charlotte Perkins Gilman, Elizabeth Packard, and Frances Farmer—achieved prominence either during their lifetime or subsequently. The rest were wives, mothers, daughters, and workers who spent from months to decades locked inside public asylums for the insane. Unlike some of the other inmates to whom they refer, all the women were educated and literate enough to write detailed and lengthy accounts; yet none save Charlotte Perkins Gilman could be considered a professional writer. Each of the twenty-six eventually secured her release from the institution and it was as a free person that she published her story. Most felt secure enough, or rash enough, to write of their trials using their own names.

It was the intent of each woman that her account be published and read by as many interested people as possible. None of the accounts excerpted here was written as a private journal or was given to a trusted friend in confidence. In several cases, the women published their stories at their own expense and sold copies on street corners or at public meetings to recoup their financial outlay.

The reasons women wanted to publish these first-person accounts were many and varied. Some women clearly wrote in the reform tradition of the turn of the century; they intended that their experiences be used to assist the efforts to improve conditions within asylums and to change the laws that kept men and women incarcerated against their will. Others intended their stories to serve as personal warnings to those who might fall prey to a similar fate. Still others wrote to further their own healing and recovery. Although the act of chronicling years of torment was often painful, some women felt that their writing was necessary if they were to still their inner unrest once and for all.

Some women felt it was their duty to write not only for themselves but for the many women who were locked away and who did not have the means to tell their own stories. Although many women denied writing to get even with family members or hospital superintendents, some clearly took pains to mention cruel attendants or heartless physicians by their full names. In the case of Charlotte Perkins Gilman, she specifically wanted her physician, S. Weir Mitchell, to read of her experience and of the harmful effects of what she believed to be his misguided methods. Some women wrote because they felt they had a story to tell.

Since the detailed study of a single case has a respected place within the discipline of psychiatry, one might expect that the first-person account of one individual's experience might be similarly well received. After all, what is a first-person account but a case study written by the patient rather than the doctor? But therein lies the crucial distinction and the reason that first-person accounts have been relatively ignored. In fact, first-person accounts have been denounced since they achieved public notice in the mid-nineteenth century. In a pointed correspondence dated 1864, psychiatrist Isaac Ray warned reformer Dorothea Dix against taking the accounts of the insane as truth.[2]

Until recently, these accounts have been ignored for several reasons. In general, our histories have been written from the perspective of those who held institutional power. We have just begun to appreciate that the diaries of midwives,[3] the journals of slaves, and the letters of women who made the continental westward journey[4] are valuable records of our past. Similarly the accounts of women who were treated in asylums tell us much about the history of psychiatry and about the constraints under which women in society lived their lives.

First-person accounts have also been questioned because they are subjective reports often designed to present the writer and her experiences in the best possible light.[5] While this may be true for some of the women whose accounts are presented here, others apologize for their behavior and speak of their shame, guilt, and loss of control. These women hardly seem guilty of attempting to manipulate their audiences. Moreover, this same charge of "self-serving" reporting might just as well be levied against the scores of practitioners and administrators who present cases and program descriptions in a light designed not only to inform but also to enhance the reputation of those doing the reporting. Even when outside observers report on the work of independent clinicians, they bring certain assumptions and values to the process of recording "truth."

Yet the first-person accounts of asylum inmates are subject to an added test. The very nature of psychiatric illness, which causes both thought and mood to be altered, renders the accounts of ex-patients suspect. Can there be any truth in an account told by a woman whose very sanity is at issue? An apocryphal story provides one response to this query:

A motorist was stopped outside of the walls of the hospital with a flat tire. He carefully removed the lug nuts from the wheel and placed them by the side of the road. As he was pulling on the tire, the four lug nuts rolled down the road into a sewer. The man raged and screamed but the bolts were gone.

As the man sat down to consider what to do next, he noticed an inmate of the hospital who had been quietly watching over the hospital wall. The inmate called to the motorist, "Just borrow one bolt from each of the other three tires and you'll be able to secure the tire well enough to drive to a gas station."

"Brilliant," cried the motorist, "but wait. What are you doing in a mental hospital?"

"I may be crazy, but I'm not stupid," replied the inmate as he walked away.

Even if all twenty-six of the women whose accounts are presented here suffered from a diagnosable mental illness, which seems highly questionable, they were still keen observers of their environments, meticulous chroniclers of their own experiences, and often poetic and witty recorders of their subjective mental and emotional state.

One way to evaluate first-person accounts is to understand the historical context in which these women wrote. To that end we have divided the time between 1840 and 1945 into four periods: 1840–1865, 1866–1890, 1891–1920, and 1921–1945. These roughly equal time segments maintain the integrity of major historical events. Each set of first-person accounts is introduced by a narrative which describes the historical context in which the women whose accounts follow wrote their stories.

In constructing the context, we paid particular attention to two separate questions: what was it like to be a woman during that time period, and what was happening within the psychiatric profession? These specific questions are important for several reasons. Many women who wrote believed, as scholars Phyllis Chesler[6] and Elaine Showalter[7] have aptly demonstrated, that the very fact of their hospitalizations as well as the manner and nature of their incarcerations was due at least in part to their being women. Each age defines "acceptable" or "ideal" womanhood in a particular way, and women who do not conform to those standards often find themselves ostracized or punished in some way. Regrettably "treatment" in asylums for the insane was one way of dispensing with some women who did not fit the mold of acceptability.[8] Consequently, for each historical period covered in this book it is important to know just what the ideal images of womanhood were and how much latitude was given to individual women to veer off in a different direction. What options, if any, were available to women who felt frustrated with their roles and their circumstances? In some eras, for example, a well-articulated reform agenda gave women ample legitimate means for expressing their frustration and their dissatisfaction with their marriages, the state of their families, and their role in society. Because many of the women felt additionally oppressed by their lack of legal rights and recourse, it is useful to know the status of the women's rights movement during each of the periods considered.

Since all of the women who wrote first-person accounts commented on the actual treatment they received, it is important to know the standards of psychiatric practice at the time. In the century during which the excerpts in this book were written, not only did standards of acceptable treatment change but the role of the asylum shifted and basic understandings of what caused and constituted psychiatric illness evolved as well. What is most significant for this book is that both the psychiatric treatment and the causes of psychiatric illness were different for men and for women. General therapies such as the use of mechanical restraints and wet packs could be applied equally to patients regardless of gender; specific treatments, however, like the rest cure and the removal of ovaries were designed specifically for women. These gender-differentiated treatments derived from unique ideas about what caused mental illness in the first place. The mere possession of a female body was thought to increase one's vulnerability to madness, and women who could not or would not adapt to their life circumstances were especially at risk. Some of the treatments directed at women seem so bizarre that it would be easy to dismiss descriptions of these as the rantings of madwomen if we did not have the concurrent reports of practicing psychiatrists who describe the very same therapies.

The narratives at the beginning of each time period are designed to set the historical context within the limited parameters described above. Major political, economic, and international events are discussed only insofar as they impact on the role of women or the history of psychiatry. War and economic depression, for example, shift role expectations for men and women, redefining at least for a time what constitutes acceptable or allowable behavior.

Finally, a word needs to be said about how the excerpts contained within this volume were constructed. Most of the women wrote rather lengthy accounts of their hospitalizations, desiring to give as many details about the asylum, their treatment, and their emotional state as they could remember. Because most were not professional writers, they paid more attention to recording the facts than to the style or flow of their stories. In order to make these first-person accounts more accessible to the modern reader, we have excerpted sections from noncontiguous parts of the account and put them together into one continuous narrative. The breakpoints have not been identified. In no instances have we distorted the intent, the spirit, or the meaning of the woman's words. The only times in which actual words were altered was to bring grammatical construction in line with modern usage. Our purpose was to produce a coherent essay that spoke to each woman's own understanding of her experiences and that also captured the interest of the reader.

We have chosen not to interpret the material presented by individual women or to comment on their particular stories. These women chose to write of their experiences because they wanted their stories—not someone else's—to be told. We have chosen to let the women speak for themselves. Whether they were rebels, social misfits, visionaries, or madwomen is left for the reader to decide.

PERIOD I

1840–1865

WOMEN'S LIVES

*D*espite the groundbreaking efforts of a small number of feminists at the Seneca Falls Convention in 1848, the prevailing image of the mid-nineteenth-century woman was that of the True Woman.[1] Although Mary Vaughn, at a Daughters of Temperance meeting in 1852, called the image of the True Woman a masculine idealization, Vaughn was equally aware of the power this image had in the lives of women who were eager and willing to mold themselves to its carefully drawn outline.[2]

Who was the True Woman? The True Woman was delicate, timid, and in need of protection. Her dependence on her husband went beyond economic support and included guidance and leadership as well. The True Woman was modest, sweet, and charming; a child/woman who maintained that persona despite assuming great responsibility within her home. When she acted to fulfill the domestic agenda of running a good home and caring for her children, she was motivated by purity and piety. For women in the mid-nineteenth century, the message was clear: stay within the domestic sphere and be adored and loved, venture outside and be despised.[3] The path to idealization was clearly marked; women only had to follow its signposts.

The newly established publishing industry, in a series of advice and popular fiction books for women, did much to perpetuate the image of True Womanhood. These books often followed a simple formula: a young woman would meet a handsome man; she would marry and set up housekeeping; within her home, she would assume a position of subservience; eventually, however, she would find some quiet and unobtrusive way to assert power and influence.[4] The story of the passive and submissive woman who achieved some limited status within her home was a popular one for women in the mid-nineteenth century. *Godey's Lady's Book*, one of the first women's magazines, also popularized this image of the True Woman as being dependent, submissive, and charming.[5]

The True Woman's very existence was a sign of her husband's economic success.[6] As a member of the household who made no obvious economic contribution, she could exist only in a marriage where the man had achieved financial success and status. Consequently, the True Woman served as a symbol of her husband's achievement in the world. Her economic subservience testified to the stature of her husband. Her economic dependence was essential to both her literal survival as a wife and her symbolic elevation as an image. Regrettably, that which gave her a roof over her head also contributed to her powerlessness.

It would seem that since economic accomplishment on the part of husbands was intimately tied to True Womanhood on the part of wives, the idealized image of the True Woman might have had little relevance in the lives of poor women. Such was not the case, however. Just as poor women in 1990 fantasize about the lives of soap opera stars, so, too, did poor women 150 years ago long to be like the idealized images of True Womanhood. In fact, medical practitioners and the psychiatric establishment believed that one of the causes of insanity in poor women was the struggle to live up to the idealized domestic agenda without the requisite economic resources.[7]

Regardless of whether she was rich or poor, the True Woman was first and foremost "the mother." Motherhood defined her very being and was also the source of her influence and power.[8] By producing many children, especially many sons, she was able to influence the developing society. In the public, political arena her influence did not result from her own input and direct participation; rather, she exerted her power indirectly through the actions of her sons. These young men, powerful in their own right, would reflect and carry into the public domain their mothers' particular values and beliefs. They would become a public reflection of her good mothering.

Ironically, biological mothering, so central to a woman's identity as a True Woman, was also implicated as one of the causes of insanity in nineteenth-century women. According to reports from the 1850s, one in eleven insane women suffered a nervous breakdown either during or after pregnancy; something about the biological and psychological activities associated with birthing purportedly made women crazy.[9] One hypothesis linked insanity with lactation. In this scenario, a woman with many children, who nursed her children for an extended period, would eventually suffer physical and emotional exhaustion.[10] While it seems obvious that such a life pattern might well be draining and exhausting for a woman, it is surprising that medical specialists concluded that this exhaustion led to insanity. Women begin to experience a disconcerting double bind as the very image of idealized womanhood itself becomes seen as one of the causes of psychic breakdown and insanity.

The True Woman was defined by her greater moral superiority. She was considered to be closer to God than were her brothers, husbands, and sons. Consequently, she was not to allow any intellectual or literary pursuits to interfere with this relationship to God.[11] It was her duty to cultivate her moral nature; paradoxically, this moral superiority became one legitimate way in which she might exert some direct influence over the men in her life and escape the image of the demure, powerless woman.

While the True Woman's aura of piety was a potential source of both real and imagined power, it is easy to see how any woman who might feel unable to live up to the ideal of spiritual superiority might feel outcast and despairing. Poor women who were driven to prostitution might feel doubly destitute if they believed they had failed to maintain the moral high ground. If a True Woman was moral and godly, what, then, was a woman who was unable to live up to these ideals? Insane, perhaps?

It is not surprising that the idealization of the domestic and moral woman went hand in hand with the idea that the world was divided into two separate and opposing spheres: the masculine sphere, which was public, competitive, and active, and the feminine sphere, which was passive, homebound, and private.[12] The home, which was known as the empire of the mother, was considered to be safe and civilized. Women were encouraged to stay within their own home base and to leave dealings with the world to the men in their lives. When women stepped outside of this rather narrow province, not only did they risk losing the support, love, and adoration of the important men in their lives but, according to one nineteenth-century theory, they also risked going insane. When women attempted traditionally masculine activities, they courted "brain strain," the exhaustion and eventual insanity brought on by attempting intellectual and active pursuits beyond their native capacity.[13] According to prevailing theory, these particular activities were not in and of themselves "crazy-making"; they only resulted in insanity when attempted by persons who did not have the natural endowments to pursue active intellectual activities. Consequently, a woman was ensured of staying not only safe and protected but also sane if she remained within her circumscribed and limited world.

One consequence of the division of the world into male and female spheres was the relatively limited contact that men and women had with one another.[14] In carrying out the domestic agenda, women associated only with other women; it was often the case that a woman would begin to have contact with a man only when she was married. Courting was conducted under the watchful eye of a chaperone, so that a young man and a young woman might well have had no private time until their wedding day. We can certainly speculate that both young men and women experienced marriage as a rather radical role change, which sometimes resulted in stressful and even disastrous consequences for both parties. Young men who felt that they had made a mistake might decide to undo the marriage by removing their new brides to asylums; some young women who felt unable to cope with the demands of married life might well experience some of the exhaustion and despair described in the early case histories of hospitalized women.

Despite the power of the idealized image of woman and the separation of male and female behavior into distinct spheres, the mid-nineteenth century nonetheless did offer women some opportunities in which the bounds of the domestic realm could be stretched and expanded. During the Civil War, women were actively involved in the antislavery movement. Given their acknowledged moral superiority, it was only natural that women should be outraged by the conditions under which slaves lived and by the institution of slavery itself. The National Women's Loyal League collected 400,000 signatures demanding an end to slavery.[15] While the righteous content of their cause was certainly in keeping with the idealization of the True Woman as a superior being, the activity itself allowed women to venture beyond the bounds of their homes and to interact in the world at large. During the Civil War, the Sanitary Commission, a central agency established in the North to supply troops with food, clothing, and bandages, became the special province of women. Hundreds of thousands of women actively raised money, cared for soldiers, and prepared bandages. Historian Donald Meyer has labeled the activities of women on behalf of the Sanitary Commission as the largest effort at social mothering up to that time.[16] In that sense, this foray beyond the bounds of the home was in keeping with the idealized image of the True Woman.

The westward migration, in which thousands of families moved across the country, also gave women an opportunity to expand the bounds of acceptable female behavior. On the overland trail, women were called upon to engage in activities that fell outside their traditional role, such as chopping wood and loading and unloading wagons. But even on the westward journey, women attempted to maintain some semblance of the female sphere and the domestic agenda.[17] It was their special task to stabilize and maintain their families and to perform the womanly functions of the journey; they cooked, washed, and visited the sick while moving their families and belongings across the country. Moreover, they maintained a close bond with other women on the journey. Their attachment to a traditional and idealized female agenda coexisted with their successful execution of more traditionally masculine tasks.

The mid-nineteenth century also saw the beginnings of a labor movement in which women participated and which took them once again beyond their idealized role. Labor shortages and economic necessity forced the textile and shoe industries to employ young women in stitching and in other activities. The lady shoe stitcher, romanticized as a moral and upright woman who took part in Christian and genteel activities when she was finished with her work in the factory, became an acceptable role for a young woman. The Women's Union for Christian Work was a middle-class effort to ensure that these young workingwomen would maintain their True Womanhood while working outside a woman's traditional sphere. Members of the Women's Union for Christian Work taught Bible classes, established reading rooms, and maintained a list of acceptable boardinghouses where young women entering the factories might find lodging.[18]

The most dramatic expansion of a woman's role beyond home and domestic agenda was the American Female Moral Reform Society. Following in the wake of the Second Great Awakening, a religious revival that converted large numbers of women, the American Female Reform Society attacked male economic greed and male sexuality.[19] Initially, this reform movement focused on putting an end to prostitution and the exploitation of vulnerable women at the hands of lustful and out-of-control men. Its early efforts were aimed at converting prostitutes to Christianity. However, the reform mission quickly expanded beyond the behavior of prostitutes to encompass the behavior of men and developed into a concerted effort to control male behavior. The idealized image of the True Woman gave women permission to assert their moral superiority. After all, the True Woman was pious, moral, and more in touch with godliness than were men. It was, therefore, a legitimate expansion of the female role for women to apply their greater moral consciousness to the behavior of both fallen women and out-of-control men.

During the Second Great Awakening, evangelical women were militant in their condemnation of male irreligiosity; these women urged men to triumph over their sinful and lustful behavior. Believing that many of society's ills were due to male sexuality and intemperance, reform-minded women sought to control male behavior, thereby making both their homes and the larger society safe and secure. The American Female Moral Reform Society movement was widespread, and its weekly periodical had 16,000 subscribers.[20] The magazine published attacks on male sexual and predatory behavior. Eventually, the society adopted a more broad-based feminist agenda, attacking low wages and the economic exclusion of women. These economic ills were seen as the cause of prostitution, and reformers believed that only when women had more economic rights and more independence would they be safe from sexual violation.[21]

The American Female Moral Reform Society allowed women several opportunities to expand their influence beyond the home. Primarily, it gave them a legitimate forum for expressing their dissatisfaction with their limited domestic role. Because anger and frustration were couched in the language of moral superiority and domestic security, women were allowed to give vent to feelings and beliefs that would otherwise have been unacceptable. After all, if women were moral and virtuous, it was reasonable for them to express that virtuous and spiritual sentiment. However, when one reads some of the diatribes that are leveled against men, one sees the extent of female anger and frustration. Some of this same anger and frustration makes its way into the writings of women who were locked away in asylums, a number of whom felt that they were being persecuted for expressing their moral and religious sentiments. While expanding their role into the realm of moral reform was tolerated for some women, women who went further than their husbands or communities deemed acceptable might well have been punished, even incarcerated, for their opinions and their passion. Many female reformers spoke in an evangelical language that might well have sounded hysterical and ranting, and therefore could be used in building a case for their being judged insane.

Any discussion of a woman's role in the mid-nineteenth century must address the all-important Seneca Falls Convention. This 1848 gathering of women in Upstate New York marked the beginning of the women's rights and feminist movements. This gathering took place in a legal climate in which the law of coverture dominated domestic relations. An extension of British common law, coverture declared that a husband and wife were one person under the law. Consequently, married women had no legal standing independent of their husbands; they had no property rights and no rights of any kind.[22] At the 1852 convention, Lucy Stone commented that many states ranked married women, insane persons, and idiots together in terms of their legal rights.[23]

The Seneca Falls Convention produced the Declaration of Sentiments, which was the equivalent of a female Bill of Rights. The declaration asserted that women have the right to own property, to control their own wages, to obtain a divorce, and to engage in free speech. It also declared that women should have equal opportunities in commerce, trade, the professions, and education; that they should be allowed to share in political offices and honors; that they should have the right to make contracts, testify in court, sue and be sued. The convention concluded with the declaration that women should also have the right to vote.[24]

In every year but one between 1850 and 1860, a women's rights convention was held reaffirming the Declaration of Sentiments set forth in the first Seneca Falls Convention. This first group of feminists challenged the way men and women thought about themselves. Many of the leaders of the convention began speaking on the lecture circuit, spreading the concerns about women's rights. Although there was a temporary cessation of the female agenda during the Civil War, when the rights of male slaves took precedence, the agenda was never forgotten. The women's rights movement was an attack on the domestic agenda and on the separation of male and female spheres. It was a declaration of equality and a plea for inclusion in the political process. Not surprisingly, the media attacked the Seneca Falls feminists as "old maids and hens that crow," despite the fact that many of the women who participated were married women with children.[25] The assumption persisted that since these women were violating their traditional roles, they must lie outside of acceptable womanhood.

Some of these early feminists realized that some hospitalized women were being persecuted by their husbands for holding beliefs with which the husbands disagreed. In 1860 Susan B. Anthony helped a mother and child escape from the woman's husband, who had previously committed her to an insane asylum. Anthony likened the plight of some hospitalized women to that of fugitive slaves.[26]

THE PSYCHIATRIC ESTABLISHMENT

In the mid-nineteenth century, psychiatry was a fledgling profession, in the throes of defining its mission and claiming its turf. Asylum superintendents formed an association which was to become the American Psychiatric Association, and specialists, known as alienists, engaged in heated debates about the causes of insanity.

Regardless of its cause, insanity was considered by mid-nineteenth-century practitioners as "an impaired action of the mind, instincts, and sentiments."[27] The insane person was someone who failed to make accurate judgments and perceive reality clearly. People believed that an insane person acted without the necessary forethought, making his or her actions appear impulsive rather than rational.[28]

While they might have concurred as to who was and who was not insane, specialists disagreed about what caused the disorder. There was a split between those who believed the cause of insanity to be physical and those who saw the cause as "moral." Thus began a theoretical debate that persisted for 125 years and has only recently been resolved by the emergence of causal models that integrate biological, psychological, and social influences.

The strict physicalists believed that insanity was a disease of the brain brought on by head trauma, liver disease, nervous system irritation, or some other clearly defined physical process.[29] The moralists, on the other hand, believed that insanity resulted from the exaggeration of certain normal feelings. Proponents of this view believed that particular social and psychological "exciting causes" disposed a person to behave in ways that were delinquent and out of control.[30] An 1860 survey of the causes of mental disease in more than 12,000 psychiatric patients reported that in 23 percent of the cases, the insanity was caused by an exaggeration of depressing emotions, with grief and disappointment prevailing. In 8 percent, the "exciting cause" came from some religious belief or experience. In 7 percent of the cases, it was worries about property that brought on the insanity, and in 5.5 percent it was general excessive mental action.[31]

Women, who were seen to be more emotional, sentimental, and impulsive than men, were thus likely victims of insanity. In fact, some practitioners suggested that the training women received, which emphasized their "delicate sensibilities" at the expense of their "reasoning faculties," might subject women to "hysterical, hypochondriacal, and maniacal" disorders.[32]

In addition to these general physical and moral causes of insanity, the medical establishment saw some particular conditions of female life as being especially conducive to producing insanity. Once again, these causes were divided along physical and moral lines. The gender-specific physical cause of insanity was believed to be a defect in the ovarian or uterine system which produced secondary symptoms of disorganization and hysteria.[33] In particular, hysteria, which was defined as a greater susceptibility to impressions and a tendency to "capricious motives and mutable feelings," was believed to derive from an excitement of the uterine system.[34] Similarly, the very processes of menstruating, giving birth, and lactating were identified as primary causes of secondary insanity in women.[35] The exhaustion that women experienced in trying to maintain their homes, the strain they felt in trying to balance their many responsibilities, and the duress they purportedly experienced in attempting strenuous mental activities were seen as the more psychosocial causes of insanity.[36] Excessive study, disappointment, and grief were considered to be direct causes of female insanity.[37]

Given these dichotomies between physical and social/psychological causes of mental illness, it is not surprising that the treatments that were proffered also split between physical and chemical interventions on the one hand and what became known as moral treatment on the other.

Based on the belief that insanity was caused by some irritation to the nervous or uterine system, many of the chemical treatments were intended to soothe an inflamed organ. Various vegetable and mineral tonics and narcotics were prescribed to help calm an agitated system.[38] Opiates were especially popular during this time as drugs that calmed irritability, soothed pain, and restored sleep.[39]

During the middle part of the nineteenth century, certain more aggressive physical interventions such as bloodletting, purging, and pouring cold water from the height of four feet onto the patient's head continued to be used.[40] Some of the physical treatments took the form of mechanical restraints; practitioners wrote justifications for the use of muffs, mittens, straight-waist coats, tranquilizing chairs, and in extreme cases, manacles and chains.[41]

Moral treatment, in contrast, was designed to repair the insane person's confidence, to engage him or her in pleasant social intercourse, and to allow the individual to engage in productive labor.[42] Kindness and gentleness were the order of the day.[43] Medical specialists believed that the establishment of regular habits was essential for promoting self-control. Consequently, many of the asylum treatments were designed to provide patients with regularly scheduled, rational employment for both the mind and the body.[44] Engaging in reading, writing, and working was an essential part of moral treatment. Interestingly, some specialists believed that marriage was one way in which both men and women could insulate themselves from the ravages of insanity, because marriage provided the right amount of ritualized and habitual activity needed for recovery.[45]

Both the moral and the physical treatments were often administered inside of an asylum. Many practitioners believed that recovery from insanity was impossible without the removal of the patient from the home. Moral treatment proponents propounded the belief that the influences of the home had become perverted and that family members were engaging in hurtful "indulgences and concessions" to the sick party. Therefore, the only way to protect the individual from some of these seemingly "pernicious effects" of family life was to remove her from the home completely.[46] At the asylum, a woman would be restored to health and would also be kept away from those who might be injured by her irrational and sometimes dangerous behavior.

In addition to being places that provided treatment for the insane person and safety for the community, asylums were seen as places in which incurably insane persons could receive lifelong comfort and care.[47] Even at their inception, insane asylums held out the possibility that a particularly recalcitrant inmate might become a lifetime resident. This fear of permanent incarceration is a theme that appears throughout the writings of women who have shared their first-person accounts of hospitalizations.

Much of the psychiatric writing of the period attempts to define the character and nature of the asylum. Many practitioners felt that asylums should consist of several buildings that might be arranged by the type of insane person who inhabited the building. There was a call for a separation of the sexes in different buildings within the same asylum.[48] This was ostensibly to protect female residents from receiving any visitors without the approval of a seemingly nurturing and responsible female attendant. Furthermore, the separation of male and female patients was designed to avoid what were called "pernicious influences."[49] In a similar vein, practitioners suggested that females should only be attended by female hospital workers and that males should similarly only be attended by men.[50] Furthermore, the hospital was to be located in close proximity to the community from which its patients came. Close proximity to home not only would aid in recovery but also would encourage family members to make the initial placement of an insane person in the institution.[51] Relatives might be reluctant to make an appropriate placement if the institution was far from home.

The optimal size of the hospital was determined to be somewhere between 150 and 200 patients; anything in excess of 200 was thought to be unmanageable.[52] In public hospitals, additional safety features were to be put in place. The public hospitals needed strong walls, strong doors, guarded windows, and a large corps of attendants.[53] These safety measures were ostensibly for the purpose of preventing both injury and escape.

In hospitals where moral treatment predominated, the attendants were trained to be thoughtful and discreet and were advised to treat patients in a candid manner, never using deception or ruse in their interactions. Moreover, the attendants had to be kind and respectful of the insane person, offering encouragement, and tempering firmness with a mild and gentle manner. Since a lack of self-respect and self-esteem was considered to be characteristic of many insane persons, attendants were encouraged to nurture self-respect while at the same time helping patients adhere to rules. Patients needed to establish a predictable and structured routine. They were instructed how to keep promises and honor their word. When patients stepped out of line, it was considered legitimate to remove certain privileges, and in extreme cases to use temporary restraints.[54]

Despite these idyllic descriptions of the attendant-patient interaction and the nature of moral treatment, superintendents of insane asylums were quite aware of the growing concern that these institutions perpetuated a restrictive and cruel form of treatment. Consequently, many practitioners urged physicians and responsible citizens to counter the charges that asylums were like prisons. One superintendent wrote that insane persons were essentially "liars by nature" and that they had a "tendency to have a hostile attitude toward the institution that had helped them in their recovery."[55] Efforts were made to discredit the untrue first-person accounts of persons who had been hospitalized. Like their modern-day counterparts, the first superintendents of asylums were anxious about the bad press they might receive if first-person accounts of abusive treatment became widespread.

Physicians were encouraged not to challenge a community that requested the release of a particular inmate. If the community felt strongly, the superintendent was encouraged to acquiesce to their wishes while at the same time trying to demonstrate the wrongness of the community's position.[56] Superintendents were not, however, to battle public opinion to keep incarcerated any patient who managed to muster public feeling on her or his behalf.

Firsthand Accounts

1840–1865

*I*n their accounts, the women who wrote during this first period referred repeatedly to the persecution they experienced within their families when they attempted to exercise religious freedom. Some who became vocal in their beliefs clearly violated what was thought to be "acceptable" behavior for a woman, and they attributed their involuntary incarceration to having strayed too far outside the sphere relegated to them.

Once in the asylum, these women focused their concerns on the unjust circumstances that led to their being hospitalized in the first place and to the deplorable treatment that they received at the hands of hospital attendants. Despite the fact that the professional literature is filled with accounts of the latest medical treatments, these six women focused very little on those treatments in their accounts.

The women whose accounts are presented are as follows: Elizabeth T. Stone, a patient at the McLean Asylum (Charlestown, Massachusetts) from November 25, 1840, to April 16, 1842; Catherine Beecher, who spent about two months per year between 1843 and the 1850s at the Wesselhoeft Water Cure (Brattleboro, Vermont); Phebe B. Davis, a patient at the New York Lunatic Asylum at Utica between November 7, 1850, and February 3, 1853; Elizabeth Parsons Ware Packard, who between June 18, 1860, and June 18, 1863, and Sophie Olsen, who between August 6, 1862, and an unknown date in 1864, and Tirzah F. Shedd, who between July 7 and mid-October 1865 were patients at the Illinois State Hospital for the Insane (Jacksonville, Illinois).

Elizabeth T. Stone

(1840–1842)

A Sketch of My Life

I was born in Westford, Mass., June 3d, 1811. My father's name was Samuel Stone; he was a mechanic, poor and intemperate. Ten children of us, seven sons, and three daughters; two brothers younger than myself. I was disowned by my father as being his lawful child; I was often ordered away from the house in vile reproach by my father, and my brothers and sisters, from the oldest to the youngest, delighted to tantalize me about it, and my mother would never rebuke them for doing so, but when she would find me crying alone by myself, she would scold me and hold me up in ridicule to them, and call me a weak-minded child for crying, which brought me into fear before them; never daring to say a word for myself.

When I was a very little girl, I would go away alone, and weep and pray to God to take me away from them and let me live among strangers, that would be kind to me. Truly I could

Elizabeth T. Stone, excerpts from A Sketch of the Life of Elizabeth T. Stone, *1842; excerpts from* Remarks by Elizabeth T. Stone, *1843; excerpts from* Exposing the Modern Secret Way of Persecuting Christians, *1859.*

say, that from my mother's womb I was an alien to my mother's children,—a child of sorrow and acquainted with grief. But I kept my troubles all to myself, looking forward to the time when I should go out into the world to earn my living, and be away from their unkind treatment.

At the age of fifteen, I left home with the consent of my parents, to get my living in the Lowell factories. That morning was a bright spot in my life. Before I left the house I went into my chamber, knelt down and prayed to God to keep and guide me through this world, despised as I was by the whole family, that I might not do anything to cause strangers to despise me. I walked to Lowell, ten miles, alone; before this I had never been a mile on the road. I arrived safe, about noon, at Lowell, and got a place to work; and was happy to think I was to be away from the wicked taunts of the family. I always found friends, and was, comparatively, happy; and I never mingled with the family, only enough to avoid the reproach of strangers, for it was just like death to me to go amongst them, for I knew they despised me in their hearts.

From that time forth I never knew what it was to have so much as a skein of thread, but what my hands provided. I sustained an unspotted character, not a person could bring an evil accusation against me. I felt that my parents were poor, and they had troubles, and that it was my duty to help them. Accordingly, I did what I could. My youngest brother I loved with all the tender love of a sister, and I wanted him to have an education, and I worked in the factory to get money to help educate him; and is it possible that a brother, or a human being, could be so hardened or cruel, on account of difference of religion, to put a sister in prison and hire men to try experiments, and to commit rape on a sister, and to delight in her sufferings!

But such is the wickedness of the human heart against the followers of Jesus Christ. That was my brother, James M. Stone.

At the age of twenty-two I placed myself at school in New Hampton, in the year 1834. It was there I found a balm for my wounded heart, a joy for my grief, the one altogether lovely, the chiefest among ten thousand. It was Jesus Christ—the love of God. My heart was changed from the love of pride and vanity to the love of holiness. I was now happy; my earthly sorrows seemed to be nothing to what my happiness was. I now commenced a new life, and on my return home I told my parents of it, and brothers and sisters how I had dedicated myself to God and his Gospel, and then the vilest hatred of the family was brought down upon me; but I was happy amidst all their cruel treatment, always rejoicing before them in the God of my salvation, for my happiness was not in temporal things, neither could they find aught against me as an evil doer, but working with my own hands in the factory, until my sister Nancy and brother James declared I should not go to meeting any more. Because I had chosen the Christian denomination to worship with, they sent for my brother, Stephen S. Stone, to come and get me, shutting me in a room, not allowing any one to see me, abusing me in the most shameful manner, because I would pray to God. I left the mill on Saturday night, attending my work the same as usual; but my sister would not let me go out of the house from Sunday morning until my brother Stephen came from Boston on Wednesday, and asked me to go to his house and spend Thanksgiving with them, pretending to have a family party. Accordingly I accepted of the invitation in order to get away from the persecutions that had risen up against me in Lowell. But, alas! now was their favorable time to carry out their revenge upon me, and use the inquisition power that is kept hid here in

America under that word insanity—Insane Hospitals. No complaint was brought against me by my overseer or any other one, only touching my religion by my family, who had always treated me with the greatest contempt from my childhood days, and do even at the present day. Could I have had the protection of the laws of our land, they never could have imprisoned and experimented upon me; but money can do anything.

I came to Boston on the 24th of November; everything appeared the same as ever. Little did I think I was to be deprived of my happiness so soon, my liberty, and everything that I held dear and sacred to me. Thanksgiving day, Nov. 25th, 1840, I rose as usual. My brother Stephen's wife was sick with the headache; accordingly, in my usual manner, I took care of her, giving her an emetic. At the dinner table I tended my brother Eben's infant child, so that his wife could do the honors of the table. I had nothing to say more than I ever did, I hardly spoke a word, and they cannot bring an accusation in word or deed against me; but as we arose from the dinner table my brother, Stephen, asked me to go and take a ride with him,—the family having had my ruin secretly planned, which, on perusing these pages, reader, it will tell you how it was done.

Every law of the United States was violated, in secretly depriving me of my liberty, on the 25th day of November, 1840, in the Charlestown McLean Asylum, at Somerville, by Stephen S. Stone and Eben W. Stone. My brother Stephen hired Dr. Wheelock Graves, of Lowell, a perfect stranger, to give a line about me; for I was not sick, nor I never was. Neither does he dare to say there was any disease, only my religion was different from my family, and for that he was hired to give a line to deprive me of my liberty, and to be experimented upon in a prison. By this power every free-born citizen of the United

States can be deprived of their liberty and happiness. The real old rank Spanish Inquisition in a more awful, secret way than the burning stake.

THE ASYLUM

I thought it was no place for me, thinking it was a ladies' boarding place among the popular class, and was not the place for a christian in such a weak state. I went out and asked my brother to take me back with him. He seemed to be so angry with me he could hardly control his feeling. He put his hand upon my shoulder and gave me a push, and said he could not carry me back, but would come and see me the next day; I then returned into the parlor and began to take off my things when a tall, black eyed, masculine looking female came and took me by the arm and asked me if she should wait upon me up stairs. I thanked her and walked up stairs with her, thinking she was going to show me my sleeping room. She waited upon me into a long painted gallery with sleep rooms on both sides, and she left the room. There were a number of ladies sitting around in the gallery. I went to the window to take a view of the prospect, and the iron grate met my eye. I turned to a lady and asked her if she would inform me what those iron grates were at the window for. She made me no reply. I turned to another and asked her, and she made no reply, but rose and went into her room. I asked her pardon, I did not intend any offence, I was a stranger there. I then went to the door to go down into the parlor where I came out; but I found the door locked. Upon that I made the expression "grated windows, and locked door, where am I?"

About dark the bell rung to call the ladies down to tea. A

very modest young lady came out of her room and asked me if she should walk with me down to tea. I thanked her, and I was waited upon down into a large room where there was a large table set with all kinds of refreshments. The company presented a strange appearance, the peculiarity of their dress, and many things did not look right. I wondered how my brother came to place me among such creatures, in my weak state. I drank a cup of tea and left the room, thinking it was no place for me, for I had long since left balls and parties, and scenes of mirthfulness. Miss Barber, the same one that had waited upon me up into the gallery, asked me where I was going. I told her I wished to retire to my room. She waited on me up into the same gallery. I went into one of the rooms and knelt down and asked God to deliver me from that place, and to return me to the people of God. Soon Mary Brigham, the attendant, came into the gallery, I asked her many questions to find out where I was, and what kind of boarders they kept there; but she would make me no reply. I asked her if the hourly went into Boston from there, but she made me no reply: She had the marks of a methodist. I thought if she loved God, if I talked of the love of God, I should draw her towards me. I told her how I loved God, and said many things about sanctification, but she made me no re-ply. I thought this was very strange treatment. I then asked her for something to take. She said the Doctor never gave anything under two days. I told her it was necessary, and that I wanted some valerian tea; but she said I could not have any thing that night, and when the bell rung nine, she said it was the hour for the ladies to retire. I went to my room and asked Miss Brigham if my door fastened; she said yes. I asked her for the key; she said she locked the door and kept the key.

After I had retired she came into my room and took my

clothes out. I asked her what that was for; she said it was the rule of the house, and she locked me in alone. I did not sleep any all night, from the excitement of the day, and wondering what my brother should place me with such characters for. I came to the conclusion that it was a place where females of ill-fame boarded, with physicians to get help in time of trouble. In the morning when Mary Brigham came and unlocked my door, I told her I had not slept any all night.—She said, well, that's nothing. I asked her to let me see the Doctor as soon as possible, for I wished to return in the first hourly. She made me no reply. I rose and went to the upper end of the gallery and asked Miss Brigham to excuse me from going to the table, as my dress was not adjusted, and had not brought my combs and hair brush with me, and asked her to let me have a cup of coffee there. She threw a hair comb into my lap and commended me to come to the table; upon which I adjusted my dress as soon as possible and went to the table. Every thing presented a strange appearance. Great tin lid pots and a wooden waiter and broken dishes. A plate of crackers set on the end of the table where I sat; I went to take one, and one of the ladies spoke and said they were hers, but I might have one; I asked her to excuse me, and took a piece of bread. After breakfast I went to go into my room, as I had not slept any all night, and found my door locked; I went and sat down and asked if there was any christians there, when one lady said she was a baptist, and she knew a Mary Stone in Boston. I told her it was my sister. I asked her to be my friend, and she said she would, and that I might lay down in her room.

After I retired, Mary Brigham came into my room and said she had got some medicine for me. I rose up and took it, thinking it was something to do me good. It was a pill and a little mug of mixture, and Mary Brigham went out and locked the door; but O, alas how little did I know where I was and what I was put into that house for. Such a crime I never read of, and it is covered up under the garb of derangement, and I am the poor sufferer. As soon as I took it I was thrown into most violent pain and distress, beyond the power of language to describe, neither can I give any one an adequate idea. The medicine effected my brain, the back part of my head, hardened or petrified it, and the brain is the seat of the nerves, and any one can conceive of the distress that I must be thrown into all over in my body, every nerve in me drawing and straining convulsively. Sometimes I was almost drawn back double and then forward, rolling in the bed from one side to the other in the greatest agony. When my door was unlocked in the morning I rose. As I come out of my room a young lady asked me what made me weak; so I took her hand and asked her to tell me where I was, and what kind of people I was with. She asked me if I did not know, and I told her no. She then told me that I was in the Insane Asylum. I then knew that I was betrayed into the hands of the wicked to be destroyed. I told her that the medicine that they had given me was killing the spirit of Christ in me; and that I was lost. I began to lose all idea of holiness. But I knew it would be covered up under the garb of derangement.

Let there be a mighty cry made by the public, and search into the iniquity of Charlestown McLean Asylum. I know it is held up by what is called the popular class, but it is a combination of men, a system that is worse than slavery, and any crime can be done there and covered up under the garb of derangement, and no one interfere.

Dear Christian reader, I have put forth this appeal to let the christian world know that this knowledge is known upon the earth, and it is in the hands of the wicked. Why is the public so silent upon the sufferings of a poor girl? If I had been taken by the uncivilized red man of the woods and not half so cruelly treated, the papers would have been full of it. If I had led a low, debasing life, and had been murdered like an Ellen Jewett, the public would have been roused and the papers would have been full of it from east to west, and from north to south; but a more horrid crime has been done. O! THAT A DAGGER had been plunged into my HEART in the midnight hour; it would have been but momentary suffering and then my immortal mind growing and expanding throughout the countless ages of eternity in the knowledge and wisdom of God.

Reader, you may be ready to throw it back upon me, saying it is derangement, I expect it; let me once have heard of such a thing and I don't know but I should have thought it derangement. But, christian reader, it is you and you only that can understand a part of my language, speaking about my spiritual life. All who formerly knew me, who see me now, say that some cruelty has been done to me. My old neighbors that knew me from a child, say that I am so altered they hardly know me. My old New Hampton school mates that I have met with since I was taken out of the Hospital, start back with surprise and say that they can hardly trace a look in me that I once had, and not a trait in my deportment that I once possessed. They say "that countenance that once was lit up with happiness is now marked with deep sorrow; those eyes that once sparkled with joy are now dead sunken with grief, and the language, and the voice are so different that some destruction has come upon you"; and when I tell them what it is, my long imprisonment, sixteen months and twenty days, not allowed to see any one that I ever saw before, only three of my folks during the time, not allowed to write; how my happiness is taken from me, my body racked and tortured, the distressed situation that I am in, they are bathed in tears. "O tell me now, Elizabeth, that you are lost; you was once so happy in the love of God," and the deep loud sob bursts from their full hearts, "Can this be Elizabeth Stone; can this crime be done and this cruelty practiced here in the midst of us and covered up and nothing said about it?"

Is this the state of our country, that the rights of a poor female are trampled upon, and the laws of our country, where there has been so much blood spilt to work out the liberty of every free born son and daughter of America. And because I endeavor to make known to the world this crime, I am threatened with a second imprisonment, by my brother Eben. If it is a crazy story surely it will do no harm, and if it is not, why had it not ought to come out. Let a council of physicians be held upon my body and see if I am a person that can enjoy life. I think that minds that understand the organization of the human body and its functions will say that some outrage has been committed upon me. If I had lost my reason is it right to take the advantage of a crazy person and destroy happiness? Charlestown McLean Asylum is to a weak excited person as a grog-shop is to an intemperate man, of a house of ill-fame, to a licentious person; they can be completely ruined. I hope this will be looked into before another one is destroyed, and that those still remaining in that awful place of imprisonment, weeping their hours away, may be relieved by seeing their friends soon. May God awaken the mind of the public to the sufferings of the helpless.

Catherine Beecher

(1843–1850s)

*A*ll the memories of my youth are those of perfect health, and that physical and mental enjoyment that are its natural attendants. Such was the result on a mind constitutionally a cheerful one, that the greatest trouble to me and to my parents was, that I was too happy and too merry to be able to think long of any thing solemn, or to fear any evil in this world or any other.

But when womanhood came, then I must earn my own livelihood. And so, after a period of preparation that shut me up in the house, I started as a teacher of music and painting, and thus was confined in the house to breathe such air as most young girls are condemned to inspire through all their school-life, generally both by night and day, especially at boarding-schools. In less than two years the weak eyes and cutaneous affections of infancy returned, proving that it was pure air and outdoor exercise that had protected me from them all through my childhood and youth.

Catherine Beecher, excerpts from Letters to the People on Health and Happiness, *1855.*

Next came sorrow—the heaviest and bitterest, and then religion, with its solemn realities, urging new and heavy responsibilities. Then, at the age of twenty-three, the institution was commended that, for ten years, employed every energy. During most of that time, as principal of an institution numbering from one hundred to one hundred and sixty scholars, the larger portion boarding pupils, there was an amount of labor, excitement, responsibility, and care involved, such as kept the brain and nervous system on a constant stretch.

During the latter part of that period, in addition to the cutaneous difficulty, an affection was manifested which then was unintelligible, but which, with present knowledge, is easily explained. It was a singular susceptibility of the nervous system to any slight wound, bruise, or sprain. Such slight accidents would bring on an affection in the injured part, which was a semi-paralysis of the nerves of motion, attended by an extreme sensitiveness of the whole nervous system, while the injured limb remained weak and nearly useless for from two to twelve months.

Finally, after ten years of school-teaching, the nervous fountain gave out entirely. I could neither read, write, or converse, nor even bear to hear conversation. From sheer inability to do any thing else, I was driven to journeying about to visit friends.

During the subsequent years of traveling and visiting, medical men of reputation were consulted in every section. Every function of life was preceding in perfect order; every organ seemed in entire health; what could be the cause of this nervous excitability centering, as it usually did, in one limb? Again the regular practitioners tried their skill. One distinguished physician was confident the disease arose from the stomach; and so, though not a symptom of any trouble came from that quarter, dose after dose was administered for that organ.

Next galvanism was prescribed, but without effect. Next the new school of homeopathy was invoked, and a shower of innocent little pellets were poured into the stomach, all to no purpose.

Not a long time after, a very learned professor urged my visiting a clairvoyant, who had performed wonderful cures, and who, he felt sure, could benefit my weak limb.

Soon after this the Water Cure came to my knowledge, and I spent nearly a year at the most celebrated establishment for this treatment. I was duly questioned, and learning that I once had suffered from a cutaneous difficulty, it was clear to my physician that all my trouble of the nerves arose from "humors in the blood." And so all the water-engines were set in full play to wash them out. In the first place a gradual process was pursued on one then so weak as to be scarcely able to walk with two supports. But after some three or four weeks this was the detail of my treatment:

At four in the morning packed in a wet sheet; kept in it from two to three hours; then up, and in a recking perspiration immersed in the coldest plunge-bath. Then a walk as far as strength would allow, and drink five or six tumblers of the coldest water. At eleven A.M. stand under a douche of the coldest water falling eighteen feet, for ten minutes. Then walk, and drink three or four tumblers of water. At three P.M. sit half an hour in a sitz bath (i.e. sitting bath) of the coldest water. Then walk and drink again. At nine P.M. sit half an hour with the feet in the coldest water, then rub them till warm. Then cover the weak limb and a third of the body in wet bandages, and retire to rest. This same wet bandage to be worn all day, and kept constantly wet.

For three months this method was pursued, the doctor and patient all the time looking for "a crisis" that should bring out the "bad humors." At last, after more than a year of persevering efforts, the theory of "humors in the blood," as the cause of the nervous debility, seemed to be on the wane.

Soon after, another establishment was visited by quite a number of the most intelligent of my fellow-patients, who reported wonderful cures by a man who detected disease by a peculiar magnetic power in the ends of his fingers. As a matter of curiosity I joined them, was examined, and found that the cause of my weak limb was "an accumulation of mucus on the coats of the lower intestines."

Next I resided for six months in a Water Cure where the treatment was still more mild, and yet such results were witnessed as strengthened the conviction that the heroic treatment, as it was called, was not fitted for the excitable and debilitated American constitution. After that I resided at intervals in several other Water Cures, chiefly for the benefit of friends, or for purposes of inspection.

Finally, I was led to reside in an institution where the main reliance was placed on exercise, in connection with a strict obedience to all the laws of health. My interest was awakened in this direction by works published in France and England, which were put into my hands by a distinguished female physician (Miss Elizabeth Blackwell, of New York City), who spent several years in the best medical schools of Europe in acquiring her profession.

Thus, during a period of ten or twelve years, I have resided as a patient or boarder at not less than thirteen different health establishments, while, in my extensive journeys and visits, I have come into the sphere of almost every kind of medical treatment, either by my own experience or by that of my intimate friends. I have also resided at different periods in all the Free States.

LETTER EIGHTEENTH
STATISTICS OF FEMALE HEALTH

During my extensive tours in all portions of the Free States, I was brought into most intimate communion, not only with my widely-diffused circle of relatives, but with very many of my former pupils who had become wives and mothers. From such, I learned the secret domestic history both of those I visited and of many of their intimate friends. And oh! what heartaches were the result of these years of quiet observation of the experience of my sex in domestic life. How many young hearts have re- vealed the fact, that what they had been trained to imagine the highest earthly felicity, was but the beginning of care, disap- pointment, and sorrow, and often led to the extremity of mental and physical suffering. Why was it that I was so often told that "young girls little imagined what was before them when they entered married life"? Why did I so often find those united to the most congenial and most devoted husbands expressing the hope that their daughters would never marry? For years these were my quiet, painful conjectures.

But the more I traveled, and the more I resided in health establishments, the more the conviction was pressed on my at- tention that there was a terrible decay of female health all over the land, and that this evil was bringing with it an incredible extent of individual, domestic, and social suffering, that was in- creasing in a most alarming ration.

Phebe B. Davis

(1850–1853)

*I*t is now twenty-one years since people found out that I was crazy, and all because I could not fall in with every vulgar belief that was fashionable. I never could be led by everything and everybody, simply because they all told me their arguments were right, and at the same time they were all in direct opposition to each other, and I knew that all truths harmonized. I kept track of all the Churches in Syracuse for a number of years, and I found that they all persecuted each other. They all coin their own Deity and their own demons; and each one according to the brain that they have to do it with, "and the man that does best is best." Sectarianism in its different phases has chilled my blood into icicles, and my heart has become ossified, but there is just one corner of it that is able to perform its office.

I think that the most of cases of insanity are curable, if the cause could be removed; but the treatment in Asylums is gener-

Phebe B. Davis, Two Years and Three Months in the New York Lunatic Asylum at Utica, *1855.*

ally addressed to the effect, and the cause still exists—the true cause is not always known. My own nervous system was thrown out of balance by external surroundings, but medicine did not reach my case—neither did a long confinement in the Lunatic Asylum do it, for there were no healing qualities in Dr. Benedict nor Dr. Gray—and Dr. Cook was very young, but rather gentlemanly; and Dr. Porter knew more than the other three, but he left soon after I went there.

Most of Drs. that are employed in lunatic asylums do much more to aggravate the disease than they do to cure it. And after I had been through all the pious mills, and crazy mills, and rational mills, I found myself a living skeleton, without means of support or a home, and my strength was all invested in my will power, and I made that my only starting-point when I left the institution; but I kept rather still, for fear I should get outwitted, and in selling my books I found a few individuals that had humanity enough to be capable of restoring the equilibrium of the nervous system to its proper balance; and just as long as I was under kind influences I was perfectly passive, and kindness had been my only medicine.

A poor person that lives for exalted motives, must expect to live in a world of their own, and my world for a time was in a cell in the Lunatic Asylum, and I arranged the most of my other pamphlet while in that cold, chilly cell; the stench was terrible; and during the time I was locked up in that cell, the Doctor sent me an emetic, and the first food after that was cold corned beef and cold boiled potato, and baker's bread and cold water. I partook of the sacrament, but left the beef and potato until I got well enough to partake of all that I could get there.

I wonder how much money it has cost the City of Syracuse to try to govern me; and they have never put me under the supervision of one yet that could govern themselves; I can do that, and always could when I chose; but there are circumstances where "forbearance ceases to be a virtue"; for human endurance is not made of India-rubber, although my own is rather elastic, for I always meant to convert my misfortunes into success—that is all the ability I happen to possess, which will allow me to provide for myself, for real high souled people are but little appreciated in this world—they are never respected until they have been dead two or three hundred years. It has been said that one of our prominent authors wrote the best work that he ever wrote in his life to defray the expenses of his mother's funeral! And who can wonder that the depth of that full-grown soul was called out on such an occasion as that, and I presume that he coined that soul into truths and gave them form, and by the use of language presented them to the world in that peculiar manner that was not to be resisted.

As for my own small productions, I have never thought them great; neither have I ever thought them very interesting; but I claim they are true, and there is the only merit in my disconnected class of ideas that I offer to the public. But how many great men have written out their lives in prison, because they were made legally responsible for thought; and when I was in the asylum they locked me up when they pleased, but what did I care for that as long as they had no key that would fit my mouth. I knew that I should live through it all, and I told them I should, and that when I got out they would hear from me.

While in the Asylum, when the Doctors thought they had got me in a tight place, laughing was the only outlet to the feelings; but I now feel as the lion did when he was kicked by the jack, for pop-guns and shot-guns, and long tongues have not taken effect to amount to much, or not so much but what I can wear them out, which they cannot me, and I still choose my own position.

A few years since I got rather short of funds, and I told some of the pious people of it, and one Saint told me to go to God. And it was news to me that Deity dealt in the articles that we happened to need the most when we get hungry; and I told them I could not find the way into his cellar nor pantry. They told me to pray, and I did, but not in a fashionable way. I took a sheet of paper and wrote my prayer, and thanked God for past favors, if they were small, and told him just what I had and just what I needed, and took my prayer to a printing office and got it printed, and sold about eight dollars worth, and that made me very comfortably off for the time being. When I do obey my impressions the pious people call me crazy, and I found it necessary to cultivate self reliance, and individualize myself.

When I compare the inferior class of women that Syracuse affords with the great noble wrecks of mind that I saw in the Lunatic Asylum, I feel as though the world was a cypher without them. There was Miss Elizabeth Whitning, who has been there for seventeen or eighteen years, who fitted two or three of her brothers for college previous to her going there. She is the greatest genius that I ever saw. Her talent is lost to the world, she is a life patient, but it takes a rogue to cheat her in a bargain now. She is as bright as steel, and she worshipped in spirit and in truth. She was a particular friend of mine and I was proud of her acquaintance, for I could always learn something from her every day.

I find that active nervous temperaments that are full of thought and intellect want full scope to dispose of their energy, for if not they will become extremely excitable. Such a mind cannot bear a tight place, and that is one great reason why women are much more excitable than men, for their minds are more active; but they must be kept in a nut-shell because they are women. An active temperament generates what I call a surplus of thought because one cannot dispose of ideas as fast as they coin them. Society compels them to make their mouth a sealed book, for you must consult fashion at the expense of your reason.

We often see a wire muzzle on the canine nose when the hydrophobia becomes an epidemic; and for all we claim freedom of speech, our mouths are subjected to monarchial government just as much as the dogs are to the muzzle. There is one old fact that I would like to have die out, which is, that a woman must not speak a loud word because St. Paul said that they must not. What if he did say so, he was only one man in the world, and that was only his opinion; and who cares for the opinion of one love sick old bachelor, after he has been dead for centuries. I have been imprisoned over two years simply because I presumed to claim my individual rights.

When I was in the Asylum I saw a concentration of evils in a condensed form; and when I said anything to the Doctors about the wrongs of the house, they would tell me that was my insanity. I told them that a fact was no less a fact because it was told by a crazy person.

. . . and a patient who will not minister to the self-love of the physicians, must expect to be treated with great severity. For that reason the ladies in the better halls make a real trade to flatter the Doctors to gain favors and get away from there, and then they make sport of it to each other. The Doctors have been flattered so much they are fond of admiration. It is a pity that great men should be susceptible of flattery; for in that place, when there is a real mind, that will flatter no one, then you will see the Doctor's revengeful feelings all out. The patient is treated according to their capricious feelings. They walk through the halls as though they thought themselves far superior to their subjects; but in that place I saw the weak points of what is called great men.

Although Dr. Benedict [superintendent of Lunatic Asylum] feels himself a distinguished personage, there is a fault somewhere, for he cannot bear promotion; and it appears to me that he only takes a surface knowledge of things in the institution, as far as the welfare of the institution is concerned, or else he chooses to have them treated as they are, for the purpose of keeping the house full for his own special benefit. His salary is worth looking at—two thousand dollars a year; besides, a great name makes a man feel himself of some consequence in this world, rather too much so to pay due attention to what crazy folks say. It is one of the disagreeable troubles of the house to listen to their complaints, and for that reason the doctors seldom notice what they say, but listen to the help. It makes them much less trouble to pretend not to believe what the patients say at all; for if they were to acknowledge that they believed the patients, and then treated them as they do, after hearing their different complaints, it would look as though they designed to treat them wrong just as they do; but they get along with it all very smooth without committing themselves.

In the first place, the physicians were all young, as a patient said to me one day. Said she, "We need fathers here, but we have only boys," and it is very true. The patients have their own infirmities to bear, together with the infirmities of the doctors and all the ignoramuses whom they hire in the house. On the whole, I do not wonder at the condition of the incurable patients, neither do I wonder at the cases of idiocy. It is very often the most intellectual who become idiots, and I know that the most violent patients whom I saw there were the best educated women in the house, and of Yankee origin. I can assure you that they were to be dreaded when excited.

There was one very interesting lady who died in one of the water-closets—the hospital closet—as I was told. This closet is one of the most loathsome places imaginable; the stench was terrible. I have forgotten the lady's name; but I should think her about fifty-five years of age, rather tall and thin, and very delicate; her clothes were very nice, both in material and the making. She was rather a troublesome patient, and suicidal, they said. The fact is, that woman had been frightened out of her wits, and then she was literally murdered in that house, for she was worn out by brute-like treatment that I was a witness to; I never saw an old canal-horse that was handled more roughly than that lady was when being harnessed down to the bedstead; the girls did not know that I saw that; but I kept promenading the hall on purpose to see how they treated the case; the door was open; I thought, from what I saw, that she could not live long, and she did not; she was a lady of very delicate sensibilities, and of course her powers of endurance were feeble; presently the lady was missing, and on my asking about her, one of the girls told me that her friends had thought it less expensive to take her home and hire a girl to take care of her there; but one of the patients told me she died in the hospital water-closet. I know what that place was, for I was there several days and nights, and took my meals there.

There was a little Mrs. Merritt in one of the medium halls, who was called upon as a servant in the hospital during my visit to the water-closet. Mrs. Merritt was a natural lady, delicate and modest, but her mind was a perfect wreck, though not violent.

Such patients were used as servants in the bad halls, for they do not realize the degradation; they are called upon to do nearly all the drudgery; the hired attendants receive six dollars per month while the patients do all that part of the labor which the attendants feel above doing. Some of the patients are like children, and will do anything for a little sugar, or something good to eat —such as the attendants have selected for themselves, for there is generally an understanding between the hall and kitchen help; they can talk through the waiters at meal time, and as the kitchen girls are Irish, of course the Irish attendants in the halls fare sumptuously. This is in the bad halls. When I was in the basement, I grew poor on skimmed milk in my tea and coffee. Dr. Benedict said my constitution was frail, but with all his medical skill he did not improve it—neither did he improve my morals, nor make me more polite to the medical board. It is not a wonder to me that there are so many readmissions into the institution; I think it very seldom that permanent cure is effected there.

It was not safe for a patient to report one of the attendants to the doctors, for they would listen to hear what the patients said to the doctors, and then they would watch their opportunities for revenge on the patients. They could not reach the doctors to cause them to suffer, but they would always be mad if the doctors listened to what the patients said, especially if they got a reprimand. The physicians would not more than get out of the halls before the help would say, "Now look out, maam, for next bathing day." That meant holding them under the water just as long as they dared, and more than once, too. The bathing troughs are cast iron, and very heavy, and one would be surprised to see the marks of that iron trough on the limbs of the patients between the foot and knee joint. There was generally the variety of colors and shades, such as usually accompany bruises. On a number of patients whom I saw it was frightful to look at them. At first I did not comprehend it, and I asked them the cause. They told me it was the effect of being pushed against the bathing troughs and the bedsteads. I looked at the bedsteads, and they were about as solid as iron; they were made very heavy, with iron bands around each post, made fast with screws. That was right so far, but the side pieces had sharp corners, and they were not so pleasant to run against in a hurry, just when the attendants saw fit to give them a push. I know they are often rather stubborn when being undressed, but they are crazy, and such treatment does not improve them in the least. I sometimes told them I had been a dressmaker, and I appreciated colors, I thought we might as well laugh as cry.

There is a hall in that house, away off by itself, which they call number twelve, and in which there are six cells. When a patient gets there, I believe it is considered the greatest punishment allowable. But they went one degree further with me; I was sent to the hospital water-closet, and received my meals in bed there. When the hospital was waited on, I covered my food and myself up in bed; that was better than no method of avoiding the stench of the place; but still I had to take my meals in a horrible atmosphere.

The patients who occupy the cells at night are generally very filthy, and the rooms have to be cleaned every morning, and of course that causes them to be damp nearly all day—quite too damp to sit or lie on. I had to lie on the floor and run the risk of the consequences. I was quite too weak to stand up all the time, and my shoes were not much thicker than wafers; but I thought I would keep myself alive if I could. I thought I should live to pepper them off just right yet, and I even arranged some of this work while in those cells, which I retain until this day.

. . . it is a common occurrence, in the bad halls, to drag patients around by the hair, and pull their hair when combing it; to-be-sure, that latter cannot always be avoided, but I have often seen it done on purpose. Margaret Loudon was kind to me, but when she combed the hair of patients in the morning, I did not wish to be present. Margaret was English, but a girl of very superior talent, though not cultivated. I once read of the death of a young lady, in consequence of putting up her hair in a manner different from her usual custom, and she lived but a short time after it. I would advise all who take their friends to the Asylum, to cut their hair very short indeed; it is much better for the patients to have their hair cut off short than to have it pulled out by the roots; if it is only shingled, or cut in the neck, it is more convenient for them to get a quick hold, than when it is put up with a comb; but a great many neglect or refuse to wear a comb, and such must look out for their hair; there is no prevention against the attendants making halters of the hair of patients, except by cutting it close to the head.

. . . I will suggest one idea which perhaps will not be lost to the world. I profess to have had a little experience in the insane institution in Utica, and I think it would be a very benevolent act to build an institution for the few that are not insane; for they are so very few that it would be much less expense to fence in a small portion of old mother earth for a kind of protection for those that are unfortunate enough to inherit common sense.

The great trouble in Lunatic Asylums is, they want to cure them by rule. They have their written rules, and all who cannot be cured by being subjected to their code of laws are pronounced incurable at once; and their rules are enough to make a rational person crazy, for they are almost equal to Fox's Book of Martyrs. But there are few physicians who have a good medical talent. Reading books does not always qualify men for eminent physicians. There is no healing qualities in medicine, it only causes the diseased organs of the system to act, but the life and the healing principle is in the person.

Elizabeth Parsons
Ware Packard

(1860–1863)

*I*t was in a Bible-class in Manteno, Kankakee County, Illinois, that I defended some religious opinions which conflicted with the Creed of the Presbyterian Church in that place, which brought upon me the charge of insanity. It was at the invitation of Deacon Dole, the teacher of that Bible-class, that I consented to become his pupil, and it was at his special request that I brought forward my views to the consideration of the class. . . . I had not the least suspicion of danger or harm arising in any way, either to myself or others, from thus complying with his wishes, and thus uttering some of my honestly cherished opinions. I regarded the principle of religious tolerance as the vital principle on which our government was based, and I in my ignorance supposed this right was protected to all American citizens, even to the wives of clergymen. But, alas! my own sad experience has taught me the danger of believing a lie on so

Elizabeth Parsons Ware Packard, *excerpts from* Marital Power Exemplified, *1866; excerpts from* Modern Persecutions, or Insane Asylums Unveiled, *1874; excerpts from* The Great Drama: or, the Millennial Harbinger, *1878.*

vital a question. The result was, I was legally kidnapped and imprisoned three years simply for uttering these opinions under these circumstances.

[I was kidnapped in the following manner.]—Early on the morning of the 18th of June, 1860, as I arose from my bed, preparing to take my morning bath, I saw my husband approaching my door with two physicians, both members of his church and of our Bible-class,—and a stranger gentleman, sheriff Burgess. Fearing exposure I hastily locked my door, and proceeded with the greatest dispatch to dress myself. But before I had hardly commenced, my husband forced an entrance into my room through the window with an axe! And I, for shelter and protection against an exposure in a state of almost entire nudity, sprang into bed, just in time to receive my unexpected guests. The trio approached my bed, and each doctor felt my pulse, and without asking a single question both pronounced me insane. So it seems that in the estimation of these two M.D.'s, Dr. Merrick and Newkirk, insanity is indicated by the action of the pulse instead of the mind! Of course, my pulse was bounding at the time from excessive fright; and I ask, what lady of refinement and fine and tender sensibilities would not have a quickened pulse by such an untimely, unexpected, unmanly, and even outrageous entrance into her private sleeping room? I say it would be impossible for any woman, unless she was either insane or insensible to her surroundings, not to be agitated under such circumstances. This was the only medical examination I had. This was the only trial of *any kind* that I was allowed to have, to prove the charge of insanity brought against me by my husband. I had no chance of *self defense* whatever. My husband then informed me that the "forms of law" were all complied with, and he therefore requested me to dress myself for a ride to

Jacksonville to enter the Insane Asylum as an inmate. I objected, and protested against being imprisoned without any trial. But to no purpose. My husband insisted upon it that I had no protection in the law, but himself, and that he was doing by me just as the laws of the State allowed him to do. I could not then credit this statement, but now know it to be too sadly true; for the Statute of Illinois expressly states that a man may put his wife into an Insane Asylum without evidence of insanity. This law now stands on the 26th page, section 10, of the Illinois statute book, under the general head of "charities"! The law was passed February 15, 1851.

I told my husband that I should not go voluntarily into the Asylum and leave my six children and my precious babe of eighteen months, without some kind of trial; and that the law of force, brute force, would be the only power that should thus put me there. I then begged of him to handle me gently, if he was determined to force me, as I was easily hurt, and should make no physical resistance. I was soon in the hands of the sheriff, who forced me from my home by ordering two men to carry me to the wagon which took me to the depot. Esquire Labrie, our nearest neighbor, who witnessed this scene, said he was willing to testify before any court under oath, that "Mrs. Packard was literally kidnapped." I was carried to the cars from the depot in the arms of two strong men, whom my husband appointed for this purpose, amid the silent and almost speechless gaze of a large crowd of citizens who had collected for the purpose of rescuing me from the hands of my persecutors. But they were prevented from executing their purpose by the lie Deacon Dole was requested by my husband to tell the excited crowd, viz: that "The Sheriff has legal papers to defend this proceeding," and they well knew that for them to resist the Sheriff, the laws would expose themselves to imprisonment. The Sheriff confessed afterwards to persons who are now willing to testify under oath, that he told them that he did not have a sign of a legal paper with him, simply because the probate court refused to give him any, because, as they affirmed, he had not given them one evidence of insanity in the case. Sheriff Burgess died while I was incarcerated.

When once in the Asylum I was beyond the reach of all human aid, except what could come through my husband, since the law allows no one to take them out, except the one who put them in, or by his consent; and my husband determined never to take me out, until I recanted my new opinions, claiming that I was incurably insane so long as I could not return to my old standpoint of religious belief. Of course, I could not believe at my option, but only as light and evidence was presented to my own mind, and I was too conscientious to act the hypocrite, by professing to believe what I could not believe. I was therefore pronounced "hopelessly insane," and in about six weeks from the date of my imprisonment, my husband made his arrangements to have me, henceforth, legally regarded as hopelessly insane. . . .

. . . it may be merely a foolish pride which prompts the feeling, but I can't help feeling an instinctive aversion to being called insane. There seems to be a kind of disparagement of intellect attending this idea, which seems to stain the purity and darken the lustre of the reputation forever after. . . .

Before I entered an insane asylum and learned its hidden life from the standpoint of a patient, I had not supposed that the inmates were outlaws, in the sense that the law did not protect them in any of their inalienable rights. I had ignorantly supposed that their right to "life, liberty, and the pursuit of happiness," was recognized and respected as human beings.

But now I have learned it is not the case; but on the contrary, the law and society have so regulated this principle, that the insane are permitted to be treated and regarded as having no rights that any one is bound to respect—not, not even so much as the slaves are, for they have the rights of their master's selfish interests to shield their own rights.

But the rights of the insane are not even shielded by the principle of selfishness. What does the keeper of this class care for the rights of the menials beneath him?

Nothing. His salary is secured by law, whether there be few or many under the roof which shelters him. Unlike slave-holder, he can torment and abuse unto death, and his interests are not impaired by this wreck of human faculties and human life.

Indeed this wreck is oftentimes made a necessity to the Superintendent, to prevent the exposure of his criminal acts.

And since there is no law to shield the insane person, he is, by law, subject to an absolute despotism. Thus the despot is protected in his despotism, no matter how severe and rigorous he may become.

Now since the object of government should be to protect the rights of its citizens, it seems to me that the insane have rights which the government ought to respect, acknowledge, and protect. . . .

I cannot believe that there is any class of convicts or criminals in our land, who are not treated with more humanity—with more decency—with less of utter contempt and abuse, than you treat your insane patients here. Most criminals have some sort of a trial before they are punished; but here, all that is required, is the misrepresentation of an angry attendant, who thus secures to her helpless victim the punishment, which her own conduct justly merits upon herself. . . .

Is there any spot in this great universe where human anguish is equal to what is experienced in Lunatic Asylums!

Are we not experiencing the sum of human wretchedness? . . .

Insane Asylums are the "Inquisitions" of the American government. . . .

Whoever can leave an insane asylum without a feeling of moral degradation, and a self loathing, debased feeling of himself, as a human being, must have attained to the highest plane of divine influences. His human nature must have been sublimated into the divine. . . .

I lay closely imprisoned three years, being never allowed to step my foot on the ground after the first four months. At the expiration of three years, my oldest son, Theophilus, became of age, when he immediately availed himself of his manhood, by a legal compromise with his father and the trustees, wherein he volunteered to hold himself wholly responsible for my support for life, if his father would only consent to take me out of my prison. This proposition was accepted by Mr. Packard, with this proviso: that if ever I returned to my own home and children he should put me in again for life. . . .

Elizabeth Packard's Liberation

The Trustees now ordered Mr. Packard to take me away, as no one else could legally remove me. I protested against being put into his hands without some protection, knowing, as I did, that he intended to incarcerate me for life in Northampton Asylum, if he ever removed me from this. But, like as I entered the Asylum against my will, and in spite of my protest, so I was put out of it into the absolute power of my persecutor again, against my will, and in spite of my protest to the contrary.

I was accordingly removed to Granville, Putnam County, Illinois, and placed in the family of Mr. David Field, who married my adopted sister, where my son paid my board for about four months. During this time, Granville community became acquainted with me and the facts in the case, and after holding a meeting of the citizens on the subject the result was, that Sheriff Leaper was appointed to communicate to me their decision, which was, that I go home to my children taking their voluntary pledge as my protection; that, should Mr. Packard again attempt to imprison me without a trial, that they would use their influence to get him imprisoned in a penitentiary, where they thought the laws of this Commonwealth would place him. They presented me thirty dollars also to defray the expenses of my journey home to Manteno. I returned to my husband and little ones, only to be again treated as a lunatic. He cut me off from communication with this community, and my other friends, by intercepting my mail; made me a close prisoner in my own house; refused me interviews with friends who called to see me, so that he might meet with no interference in carrying out the plan he had devised to get me incarcerated again for life. This plan was providentially disclosed to me, by some letters he accidentally left in my room one night, wherein I saw that I was to be entered, in a few days, into Northampton Insane Asylum for life; as one of these letters from Doctor Prince, Superintendent of that Asylum, assured me of this fact.

When I had read these letters over three or four times, to make it sure I had not mistaken their import; and even took copies of some of them, I determined upon the following expedient as my last and only resort, as a self defensive act.

There was a stranger man who passed my window daily to get water from our pump. One day as he passed I beckoned to him to take a note which I had pushed down through where the windows come together, (my windows were firmly nailed down and screwed together, so that I could not open them,) directed to Mrs. A. C. Haslett, the most efficient friend I knew of in Manteno, wherein I informed her of my imminent danger, and begged of her if it was possible in any way to rescue me to do so, forthwith, for in a few days I should be beyond the reach of human help. She communicated these facts to the citizens, when mob law was suggested as the only available means of rescue which lay in their power to use, as no law existed which defended a wife from a husband's power, and no man dared to take the responsibility of protecting me against my husband. And one hint was communicated to me clandestinely that if I would only break through my window, a company was formed who would defend me when once outside my house. This rather unlady like mode of self defense I did not like to resort to, knowing as I did, if I should not finally succeed in this attempt, my persecutors would gain advantage over me, in that I had once injured property, as a reason why I should be locked up. As yet, none of my persecutors had not the shadow of capital to make out the charge of insanity upon outside, of my opinions; for my conduct and deportment had uniformly been kind, lady-like and Christian; and even to this date, January, 1866, I challenge any individual to prove me guilty of one unreasonable or insane act.

Mrs. Packard's Bills

Bill No. 1

No person shall be regarded or treated as an Insane person, or a Monomaniac, simply for the expression of opinions, no matter how absurd these opinions may appear to others.

Reasons

1st. This law is needed for the personal safety of Reformers. We are living in a Progressive Age. Everything is in a state of transmutation, as our laws now are, the Reformer, The Pioneer, the Originator of any new idea is liable to be treated as a monomaniac, with imprisonment.

2nd. It is a crime against human progress to allow Reformers to be treated as Monomaniacs; for, who will dare to be true to the inspirations of the divinity within them, if the Pioneers of truth are thus liable to lose their personal liberty for life by so doing?

3rd. It is Treason against the principles of our Government to treat opinions as Insanity, and to imprison for it, as our present laws allow.

4th. There always are those in every age who are opposed to every thing new, and if allowed, will persecute Reformers with the stigma of Insanity. This has been the fate of all Reformers, from the days of Christ—the Great Reformer—until the present age.

5th. Our Government, of all others, ought especially to guard, by legislation, the vital principle on which it is based, namely: individuality, which guarantees an individual right of opinion to all persons.

Therefore, gentlemen, protect your thinkers! by a law, against the charge of Monomania, and posterity shall bless our government, as a model government, and Massachusetts as the Pioneer State, in thus protecting individuality as the vital principle on which the highest development of humanity rests.

Bill No. 2

No person shall be imprisoned, and treated as an insane person, except for irregularities of conduct, such as indicate that the individual is so lost to reason, as to render him an unaccountable moral agent.

Reasons

Multitudes are now imprisoned, without the least evidence that reason is dethroned, as indicated by this test. And I am a representative of this class of prisoners; for, when Dr. McFarland was driven to give his reasons for regarding me as insane, on this basis, the only reason which he could name, after closely inspecting my conduct for three years, was, that I once "fell down stairs"!

I do insist upon it, gentlemen, that no person should be imprisoned without a just cause; for personal liberty is the most blessed boon of our existence, and ought therefore to be reasonably guarded as an inalienable right. But it is not reasonably protected under our present legislation, while it allows the simple opinion of two doctors to imprison a person for life, without proof in the conduct of the accused, that he is an unaccountable moral agent. We do not hang a person on the simple opinion that he is a murderer, but proof is required from the accused's own actions, that he is guilty of the charge which forfeits his life. So the charge which forfeits our personal liberty ought to be proved from the individual's own conduct, before imprisonment.

So long as insanity is treated as a crime, instead of a misfortune, as our present system practically does so treat it, the protection of our individual liberty imperatively demands such an enactment. Many contend that every person is insane on some point. On this ground, all persons are liable to be legally imprisoned, under our present system: for intelligent physicians are everywhere to be found, who will not scruple to give a certificate that an individual is a Monomaniac on that point where he differs from him in opinion! This Monomania in many instances is not Insanity, but individuality, which is the highest natural development of a human being.

Gentlemen, I know, and have felt, the horrors—the untold soul agonies—attendant on such a persecution. Therefore, as Philanthropists, I beg of you to guard your own liberties, and those of your countrymen, by recommending the adoption of these two Bills as an imperative necessity.

Sophie Olsen

(1862–1864)

*A*ugust 6th was the fatal day in which the formidable doors of that institution, the world calls an "Asylum," were locked upon me, and I found myself indeed a prisoner. Finding it inevitable, I submitted with cheerfulness. This submission however was given under a very mistaken idea of the gloom impending over me.

THE FIFTH WARD

"Hail horrors! Hail infernal world!"

If the inhabitants of the Twentieth century should ever have the real condition of this terrible prison described as it now exists, and be informed of the purpose to which it is applied, they will not only see the perfect propriety of my quotation at the head

Elizabeth Parsons Ware Packard, *excerpts from* Modern Persecutions, or Insane Asylums Unveiled, *vol. I, 1873; excerpts from* Mrs. Olsen's Narrative of Her One Year at Jacksonville Insane Asylum, *1868.*

of this chapter, but will regard this prison with the same feelings as we now do the Spanish Inquisition and its abettors and apologists.

As, under the guidance of the ill-fated Dr. Tenny, I descended the three long flights of stairs leading to this charnel house of human woe, I felt a dizzy heart-sickness which almost deprived me of the power of articulation. Was it a prescience of those "coming events" which "cast their shadows before," that affected me thus? I could not tell, but was only conscious of a faintness and weakness which nearly deprived me of the power of locomotion. I asked Dr. Tenny to give me a formal introduction to the attendant, having never seen her. He complied, and though her countenance had an expression of stern repulsiveness, I determined, if there was any goodness in her, to find it out. I would, by the patience and assiduous kindness of my own deportment, awaken and develop all of goodness and humanity that might possibly be found smouldering beneath the icy surface of her heart.

Perceiving that she was Irish, I remarked "Oh, you are an Irish lady; I love the Irish dearly; many of them have shown me much kindness. I know your people are kindhearted. Well, you may be sure that I shall give you no trouble. I always obey the rules, and try to help my attendants; indeed, Miss Bonner, I think you must have much work to do here, with so many to take care of, and perhaps I may be able to assist you some in your labor."

I thus attempted to conciliate, and enlist her kind feelings. But slander and hatred had taken fearfully that start of me. She replied, as I had said I should give her no trouble, "Indeed you'd better not make me any trouble, it won't be well fur ye if ye do."

I confess I was "taken back a few miles"!

She continued, "yee's no better'n the rest of em; yee'r all jist alike here, un ye needn't ixpict iny better treatment un the rest of um git. Now ye jist set down (pointing to a hard stationary bench) un mind yer business. Yer the wust un the cracyest of em all in the hull Institution; yees a nuisance."

After this most amiable delivery, she stopped to take breath, and fearing she might again start on a fresh "heat," I immediately obeyed her, by sitting down in silence on the bench she had assigned me. I began to doubt my power over the insane. Here indeed I saw "the insane" without mistake, but I then thought, and never afterwards changed my opinion, that Lizzy Bonner was more insane than any one in her care! I did not fear them, with all their fury; but I confess I did fear her, with her much wilder fury! I had always some expedient by which I could easily disarm her very wildest maniacs, but I never could disarm or tame their far more ferocious keeper?

Beside me, sitting, or rather crouching on the same bench, were a few silent and very filthy women, with their one garment indecently torn, and a puddle of unfragrant water on the floor under their feet. Some, in more remote parts of the hall, were screaming fearfully, at which I did not wonder. If I had been a screamer, or at all nervous, I should doubtless have swelled the concert, so full was this Pandemonium of every imaginable horror!

The faces of many were frightfully blackened by blows, received, partly from each other in their internecine conflicts, but mostly, I subsequently discovered by their attendants! One very fat old woman who could not speak in English, was sitting on the floor with a perfectly idiotic expression upon her face. One pale girl sat weeping bitterly, and shivering upon a bench with very thin clothing. Several were silent and appeared to take no notice of anything. These were melancholics in nearly the last stages of despair. One, in quite the last stage, as I inferred, was tied to her hard bench with her arms and chest tightly confined by a straight jacket, and attempting to commit suicide by fiercely beating her head back against the wall. The sight of this poor young female, in her frantic attempts to rush from an obvious hell into the untried scenes of an undiscovered future, was too appalling for me to gaze upon. I turned away my eyes with a sick horror, but still heard her pounding her bruised head.

No one here was working, for all capable of being made to work, were at this time engaged in some of the numerous toiling departments of the establishment. Some were lying on the floor, exhibiting the most indescribably indecent appearances.

The windows were all open; I was shivering with cold, being at this time, in the incipient stages of fever and ague. This disease was probably acquired by inhaling the "mephitic exhalations" of the Eighth ward. I drew my woolen shawl closely about my person, covering my head and eyes, from these terrific sights and sounds, and sat in dumb amazement. Is this, I silently ejaculated, the destiny to which I am doomed for an indefinite period? Oh, the insufferable anguish of those moments of horror! Language cannot portray it; it is utterly powerless. Every faculty of mind was intensified to the utmost, in those few moments of dumb tearless agony. It seemed as if my palsied heart must cease its beating.

In this prison was exacted the most immediate and uncompromising obedience to rules and requirements which a slave holder would have blushed to inflict upon his human chattels. Our own preferences were never consulted. "You must do this because I want ye to," was all the reason given.

Does the public think this a good way for lost sanity to be regained? Alas, what has the public hitherto known about it? There is absolutely no escape from obedience here, no matter what is required. I have many times, seen even tardy or reluctant obedience punished with fearful severity; I have seen the attendant strike and unmercifully beat on the head, her patient's with a bunch of heavy keys, which she carried fastened by a cord around her waist: leaving their faces blackened and scarred for weeks. I have seen her twist their arms and cross them behind the back, tie them in that position, and then beat the victim till the other patients would cry out, begging her to desist. I have seen her punish them by pouring cold water into their bosoms, a pailful at a time, leaving it to dry without changing their wet clothing, the remainder of the day, several hours; I have seen her strike them prostrate to the floor, with great violence, then beat and kick them.

I have seen her do all this too, without any proof that they had been guilty of what she had accused them. And even when others had accused them, she was always more ready to believe the accuser than anything the accused could say in self-defense.

At last one of our number, a very intelligent married lady, made the following proposition, namely: That we should make a general onslaught or campaign against the State's property, and in various ways, destroy all we possibly could without discovery. Thus we should make apparent to our persecutor, that this most desperate movement was but the natural and legitimate result of his own extreme severity to his victims—that it was the complete desperation of our circumstances which evolved this "military necessity."

Let those who may blame us for acting upon this, remember that we were fighting for our lives. Compelled as we were to inhale the poisonous gases from so many diseased bodies while sleeping so near each other, and the still deadlier exhalations arising from typhoid and other fevers, ulcerated lungs, and fetid sores, all confined in one hall; we felt, that between the above influences, and the sudden blows and violence which all the time menaced us, by the fierce maniacs and their fiercer keeper, that our lives were most essentially imperilled.

The Resurrection

It is time to conduct my readers out of this horrible ward, and I am sure they think so too. My health now became extremely enfeebled; I could not sleep except when utterly prostrate from long wakefulness, nature could hold out no longer. It was my practice to stuff cotton into my ears to deaden the sounds of the terrible shrieks which came from all directions. As a last resort, in my persistent endeavors to counteract these influences, and thus protect my sanity, I used to rise in the night, from my recumbent position, and sit up with these large wads of cotton bound tightly about my ears, at the same time vigorously pressing my head and face downwards to divert the blood from the cerebral veins.

Day after day, three times each day, did the great "Asylum" bell summon us to take our meals for the protraction of wretched existences. Such a crowded table! More than seventy women in all degrees of sanity and of insanity, of virtue and of vice, and of every gradation between these extremes,—promiscuously huddled,—jammed, literally crammed together at these tables! All wanted to have "their say," except a few silent ones, who rarely spoke at all. I was, on these occasions generally silent, in order to better observe the practical application of "our accomplished Superintendent's" method of applying the "Physiology of Dietetics" to the restoration of diseased intellects!

We were often commanded to "hurry! hurry up! I want to clear the table, then take your biscuit to your room and finish it there." Sometimes I have seen half a dozen or more at a time running with a half-munched hot biscuit in hand to their bedrooms, while the attendant was behind, impatiently swinging her keys ready to lock them up.

At every opportunity, we banded together in little secret societies, in earnest, agonizing consultation. One proposed that all who were reliable should combine together, and when the attendants were out of sight, and the Superintendent in the hall, we should unite upon an agreed signal in an attack upon himself. We were to form around him; then one of the strongest in our number was to confine his mouth by her hand, to keep him from calling for aid; others, on each side, were to secure his limbs, and then we were to demand our liberty at the peril of his life. Several of the bolder wished at once to act upon this programme; others objected, so we decided to adjourn for further consideration. At our next meeting the infeasibility of this plan was eloquently presented by one of the speakers, and the final fate of this bill was to be unanimously voted down. We know if so bold a scheme should fail of practical success, we should be subjected to the most fearful tortures as punishment.

WIVES AND HUSBANDS

Returning from a walk one day with others, I observed, on coming up this long flight of stairs, a scene which gave my feelings a severe shock. The attendant evidently did not wish us to see this, for she kept hurrying us along to our hall, but the circumstances were such we could not help it. A husband who that morning had made a brief visit to his wife, was then taking leave of her. She failed to recognize the propriety of being left, and wished to return to her home with her husband. She entreated him, with tears that ceased not flowing, to let her go home and see her children. "Oh husband dear, do let me go home; I don't want to stay here any longer, it don't do me any good. I must go, O I must live at home with you and my children. Dear, dear husband, do not leave me here!" The husband hesitated, looked at her streaming tears, then at the door; he lingered; there was an evident struggle in his mind. Perhaps he thought of his courtship life, of all her youthful charms ere her toiling fidelity to him had faded the early beauty from that now pale cheek and tear-dimmed eye. Perhaps he remembered love's promises, his marriage vow of everlasting protection and union of home and interests. Perhaps he thought of God's injunction "they twain shall be one." Perhaps—ah! I know not what cogitations were in his mind. The agitated wife perceiving his indecision, seizing the advantage, took his arm within her own, and embracing him, exclaimed again, in tones of agony, "O husband, I must, I must go home with you, do not, do not leave me here!"

Several of the officials of the Asylum were standing near, the husband had evidently been receiving instruction from them instead of his own conscience; then with one violent effort, he disengaged himself from the trembling grasp of the pleading wife, left her and walked hastily down the stairs. In her anguish she sank down powerless upon the floor, and was dragged by two men, still gazing after her husband's receding form, to all the horrors of locks, keys, and imprisonments!

We all returned to our hall in sadness and silence, the attendant soon left. When we found ourselves unwatched, one said, "O, how could that man have the heart to leave her, when she so begged to go with him?" Another replied, that "he had been befooled by the Doctor who had told him it would not be safe to take her home." Said a third, "what a fool a man must be, to let another man judge between himself and his wife! he ought to have known himself whether she should have gone home. If he wanted to go and attend to his affairs, he ought to have considered that she had the same right, for his home duties and her own were the same." Another spoke with apparent disgust, in her turn, to the last speaker. "Do you think such husbands possess the faculty of consideration! I don't agree with you, it appears to me that all their own consideration, all their faculty of independent thinking has become weakened if not destroyed when they give up to the stupid prejudice that another man can better guide a woman than her own husband!" Said another voice, "now they will call this poor woman noisy and excited, say it hurts her to have her friends visit her, because she can not help crying and grieving about his leaving her; then they will put her down into a lower ward, where of course she will grow worse, and may become incurable. Yes, this is the way they do here; I wish the public knew it."

"My God!" echoed yet another hitherto silent voice, "it makes me shudder to think how many splendid minds are made incurable lunatics, or worried into a sickness which ends in death, by just these barbarous means!"

My Departure

My brothers began to think vigorously on the subject of my leaving the "Asylum." They saw that my husband had confided me entirely to the disposition of Dr. McFarland, and they had serious misgivings about the propriety of letting me remain longer in such hands. So they concerted together as to what plan could now be adopted for my liberation.

They were not satisfied with the way I was being managed, and now took the business into their own hands. By what authority they acquired the power to release me I never cared to inquire. Lawyers were consulted, letters without number written, and plans discussed. More than six months passed in these tiresome negotiations and delays before they were able to shape a way by which my deliverance could be effected. If they had known that all this time, my health was going to ruin, that I was literally dying by inches, they would not thus have protracted my lingering misery. But such was their confidence in Dr. Mc-Farland, and in his most fallacious reports, they presumed all was going on right, only my long detention gave them uneasiness. I longed beyond all expression to have some rest. O, I was so weary, weary; I longed for some Asylum from "Lunatic Asylums"!

My limits will not permit me to relate the scene of parting with my sisters in bonds. It was such as to confirm my affection and devotion to them and to all who bear the dreadful name of Lunatic, forever. I leave you, my sad suffering sisters, in your "bonds and imprisonments," but most deeply unworthy should I prove myself of the sacred boon of liberty, if I fail to remember you in bonds as still bound with you.

Tirzah F. Shedd

(1865)

*I*t is for the benefit of those now in Jacksonville Insane Asylum that I give the following testimony to the public, hoping it may stimulate the people to provide some remedy for existing evils.

This is to certify, that I, Mrs. T. F. Shedd, was incarcerated in this Asylum on the 7th of July, 1865. I was imprisoned there fourteen weeks. My baby was five months and a half old, when I was taken from her, and my two other little girls, and forced entirely against my will and protest, into this prison-house, for an indefinite length of time, on the charge of monomania or spiritualism, brought against me by my husband.

True I had a mock jury trial at Geneva court-house, as the statute law of 1865 requires, still I felt that justice could not be done me before such a tribunal of prejudice as existed against me on the ground of my spiritualism. And so it proved. My case

Elizabeth Parsons Ware Packard, excerpts from Modern Persecutions, or Married Woman's Liabilities, *vol. II, 1874.*

was not fairly tried before an impartial tribunal, and therefore, I was condemned as insane on the subject of spiritualism.

This decision therefore placed my personal liberty entirely in the hands of my husband who was fully determined to use this legal power to subject my views to his will and wishes. I, of course, resisted this claim, and assured him I should never yield my right to my personal liberty to him or any other power; for so long as he could bring nothing against me but what I regarded as my religion, I claimed the protection of my personal liberty under the flag of religious toleration.

Notwithstanding all my arguments, my entreaties, my prayers, my protests and my vigorous resistance, by fighting single-handed and alone my six strong men captors, for forty-five minutes, I was finally taken from my sick bed, bruised and sore from this brutal assault, and carried in my undress to the cars, with the handcuffs dangling at my side, leaving my little girls screaming in agony at this unnatural bereavement of their tender, loving mother. And yet this is a land of religious freedom! It may be a land of freedom for the men, but I am sure it is not for the married women!

And although entirely sane, the heartless Dr. McFarland did receive me, when my last hope of liberty died within me, and I found myself entirely in the power of a man, whom I had sad reasons to fear was not worthy of the unbounded trust and confidence he was then receiving from the people.

I have no confidence in that man's honesty. His policy is stronger than his principles; and I told him this opinion too, in my letter to him in these words:

"You took my husband by the hand and when alone said to him, 'Mr. Shedd, this woman, meaning me, is not crazy, nor ever has been. Excited she may have been from various causes, but temporary derangement is not possible with such an organization, although I shall pronounce her hopelessly insane, because she will not say she has changed her mind!' "

Is not this decision that I am insane, the dictation of his selfish policy, instead of his honest conviction? It seems to me that he is willing to believe his own judgement to shield himself and my persecutors from harm. And the written advice he gave my husband, strengthens this conviction, viz.

"Mr. Shedd, you must not tyrannize over her, but flatter her with presents, and let her have her own way as much as you can."

Why is this? Is he not afraid I shall become exasperated toward this party including himself, and expose them in consequence? It seems so to me, for he says it is impossible for me to become insane, and this advice did not seem to be needed for my protection or good.

I think Dr. McFarland is not fit for his place, and as I view it, the safest course for him to pursue now is to resign; and I advised him to do so in my letter, viz.:

"All that I now ask is that you give up that position which you confessed to me you were sick of five years ago, and release those women you hold there as prisoners, under the will of cruel husbands, and others who call themselves friends."

There were a great many spiritualists there, whom he called insane like myself, for this reason alone, seeming to fear them as witnesses against him, unless they carried his diploma of "hopeless insanity" upon them. He has been obliged to liberate many such of late, by the enforcement of the law for the "Protection of Personal Liberty," and he was very careful too to send this class of "hopelessly insane"(?) prisoners before the time appointed by the Legislature for their jury trial, so that by this policy they were denied the opportunity of a jury trial, in vindication of their sanity. And had the jury's decision contradicted the Doctor's opinion, as it did in Mrs. Packard's case, he might have had more reason to fear their influence.

One day after I had cut and made me a neat and becoming white dress, the Doctor seeing me in it remarked:

"I don't see how a man could put a lady like you from her home."

At another time, he remarked:

"If you were my wife, I should want you at home." Would he want an insane wife at the head of his family?

I enjoyed many privileges there which others did not, and I might have used these liberties to escape; but I chose rather to remain until all my prison keepers had had a fair opportunity to see that I was not insane. I also wished to look into the secret workings of this prison, but in order to do this I knew I must first secure their entire confidence, and any attempt to escape I knew would at once circumscribe my limits of observation. By the course I have pursued the Doctor has had a fair opportunity for arriving at the candid conviction he expressed to my husband of my sanity, viz:

"Mrs. Shedd is not crazy nor can she be with her organization."

The confidence my keepers had in my sanity was expressed in various ways. Once was by their allowing me to have my own pen-knife and scissors during all my incarceration, which act is strictly forbidden by the by-laws; and, of course, it would be necessary to keep these articles from insane people.

I know the State has a heavy wine bill to pay yearly, charged for the "good of the patients"; but judging from both of the Doctors' appearance at times, I should think they made free use of it themselves, and I am sure they and their guests use far more of it than the patients do.

The prisoners are kept uniformly on the plainest and coarsest kind of fare, far better suited to a class of working men, than sick women. Even butter is not always furnished, and when it is, it is often so very poor that it is not fit to eat, and I have known meat sent to the wards so very foul that the attendants would not put it upon the table, and the boarders would have nothing left them to eat but molasses and bread.

Only once a week are we allowed any kind of sauce or relish of any kind to eat with our butterless bread. It is true the prisoners have the privilege of looking through the iron grates of their prison windows at the twenty-five nice fat cows, "headed by the buffalo" on their way to and from their rich pasture; but it would afford us far more solid satisfaction to have been allowed to use some of their new milk and sweet butter, for our health and comfort.

It does seem that with all the money the State expends on this Institution that its boarders ought to be decently fed. But they are not.

Great injustice is done the prisoners in respect to their clothing, by losing much of it, which the Doctor accounts for on the false plea, oftentimes, that "the patients tear their own clothes." Some of the prisoners do tear their own clothes, but most of their losses in clothing, are the result of wrong conduct on the part of the employees.

I once saw Miss Conkling held under the water, until almost dead, and I feared she would never get her breath again.

I saw Mrs. Comb held by the hair of her head under a streaming faucet, and handfuls of hair were pulled from her head, by their rough handling, simply because she would not eat when she was not hungry.

I have seen the attendants strike the hands of the patients with their keys, so as to leave black and blue spots for days.

I have seen them pinch their ears and arms and shoulders and shake them, when they felt that they could not eat; and were thus forced to eat when their stomachs were so rejecting it as to be retching at the time.

There is one married woman there who has been imprisoned seven times by her husband, and yet she is intelligent and entirely sane.

When will married women be safe from her husband's power?

And yet, she must assert her own rights, for the government does not protect her rights, as it does her husband's, and then run the risk of being called insane for so doing! I do not think the men who make the laws for us, would be willing to exchange places with us.

This house seems to me to be more a place of punishment, than a place of cure. I have often heard the patients say:

"This is a wholesale slaughter-house!"

And there is more truth than the people ought to allow in this remark. They bury the dead in the night, and with no more religious ceremony than the brute has. We can hear the dead cart go round the house in the night to bury those prisoners who have been killed by abuse; and their next door room-mates would not know, sometimes for months, what had become of them, because they were told they had gone home, when they had gone to their silent graves!

I have heard of one case where the patient had been dead one year, before the doctor informed the friends of the death of their relative!

The prisoners are not allowed to write to their friends what kind of treatment they are receiving, and an attempt to do so clandestinely, is punished as an offense. The punishment for this offense is, they must have their term of imprisonment lengthened for it. I once knew the Doctor to threaten to keep one prisoner longer even for aiding another in getting a letter to her friends.

The indefinite time for which they are imprisoned renders this prison all the more dismal. If the prisoner could but know for how long a time he must suffer this incarceration, it would be a wonderful relief. Then the Superintendent could not perpetuate it at his own option, as he now can and does.

These prisoners are much more at the mercy of their keepers than the penitentiary convicts. As it is now conducted I should choose the place of the convict in the penitentiary, rather than the place of a patient in Jacksonville Insane Asylum. And yet there is not one in a hundred probably, of the patients who is treated as well as I was during the fourteen weeks I was imprisoned there.

The above statement, I stand responsible for as the truth as it was when I was there; and I now challenge the people of Illinois to bring forward proof, if it can be found to refute it. Indeed I court and invite the most rigid investigation, knowing that the result will only be a confirmation of this statement.

PERIOD II

1 8 6 6 – 1 8 9 0

Women's Lives

*T*he True Woman continued to be an idealized image of womanhood into the closing decades of the nineteenth century. This image began to be challenged, however, by an alternative and competing presence: the New Woman. The New Woman was an educated, intellectual young woman who valued self-fulfillment and service to her community. She engaged in activities that took her outside the boundaries of her family and her home. The image of the New Woman depicted a young woman who sought an independent lifestyle and it became an appealing model for writers, professionals, and reformers.[1]

Paradoxically, young women drawn to the image of the New Woman were often the daughters of women whose lives had been shaped by the image of the True Woman.[2] Those mothers nurtured their daughters, imbued them with family values, but also encouraged them to want more than a life at home for themselves. A family's middle-class or upper-class affluence freed a young woman to consider broader alternatives for herself. While New Women wanted to be economically independent and free of traditional roles, they continued to espouse the domestic female agenda followed by their mothers. In contrast to their mothers, however, they chose to take their nurturing maternal mission to arenas outside the traditional family home.

New Women felt comfortable expressing anger at the injustice of male dominance and at the arbitrariness of male privilege; yet they affirmed their femaleness.[3] In no way did the New Women in the closing decades of the nineteenth century want to be men; they wanted to be women with greater options and more power. It is not surprising that while the True Woman was seen as a bulwark of traditional family values and the established order, the New Woman was believed to be a direct challenge to the way things had been.

Perhaps the one event that symbolized the emergence of the New Woman into society was the founding of women's colleges in the 1870s and 1880s. While it is true that these colleges offered opportunities for only a few women, they represented the movement of women into the larger society.[4] By and large, the first generation of college women remained single or married late; they were actively choosing an independent, educated life over the more traditional choices made by their mothers. Such choices did not go unnoticed, however, by educators and by critics of women's education, causing the proponents of women's colleges to issue reassurances. The president of Smith College, for example, assured her colleagues that education for women would not make women less feminine; instead, it would render women better able to serve their families, since education would only enhance a woman's ability to perform her domestic tasks.[5]

In particular, the medical establishment was concerned about the debilitating impact that intellectual activity might have on the fragile mind and delicate sensibilities of girls. Educators needed to be mindful that their programs for women be wholesome, healthful, and structured, emphasizing physical activity as much as intellectual pursuits. Such balanced programs would guarantee that women would not be ruined by their movement into an intellectual and more traditionally masculine arena. Nonetheless, concerns that mental strain was causing not only insanity but also infertility persisted.[6]

The New Woman, whether she was college-educated herself or merely inspired by the expanded possibilities of her educated sisters, moved her attention beyond the sphere of the home in several ways. Women's clubs proliferated during the period after the Civil War. These organizations, often founded by a group of cousins and sisters who met together in each other's homes to discuss literature, civic concerns, and philosophical issues, were akin to early consciousness-raising groups.[7] Clubs afforded women the experience of coming together, sharing their knowledge and insight with one another, challenging themselves as leaders, and valuing each other for intellectual and creative pursuits outside of the home. While these clubs were seen as an adjunct to the primary task of raising families and running homes, these clubs gave a woman an identity as an independent and intellectual person, an identity that went beyond the role of wife and mother.[8]

The average woman who joined a club was in her thirties or forties and was often coming to the end of her active mothering years. For her, club involvement was one relatively safe way of expanding her interests beyond the home. While she did not see herself as being as daring and avant-garde as the young women who were attending women's colleges, the club woman was acknowledging that she had an intellectual as well as a domestic side. By the beginning of the twentieth century women's involvement in these clubs was so widespread that the General Federation of Women's Clubs could claim 150,000 affiliates representing over one million women.[9]

More daring than the club movement was the reform movement, which took New Women beyond the confines of the home. The reform-minded New Women of the 1880s declared their intention to bring a mothering, female consciousness into the political and social world beyond the family. These women believed that a woman's work should not be confined to her home, but rather that women needed to extend the harmony and nurturance of a female sensibility to all worldly endeavors.[10] The life of the human race, not just the life of the family, became the concern of New Women.[11]

Since both men and women acknowledged that women were the morally superior gender, women had a legitimate argument for applying their particular talents to the welfare and needs of disenfranchised or morally lax groups. Battered wives, prostitutes, criminals, and insane persons all became the symbolic children and families of the New Women.

Not coincidentally, these active reformers successfully achieved their own goal of having independent and fulfilling lives while at the same time expanding the domestic agenda far beyond the confines of the home. The settlement houses in which educated single women lived among the poor families and struggling women they were trying to help became a liberating alternative community for daughters who did not want to become True Women like their mothers.[12]

The desire of women to act independently, the expansion of the domestic agenda into the larger community, and women's anger at male prerogative and dominance all coalesced in the movement that spawned the Women's Christian Temperance Union. Ostensibly, the purpose of the Temperance Union was to redeem men from the evils of alcohol. The early leaders of the movement argued that since women were the primary victims of male alcoholism and the resulting irresponsible behavior, women should lead the fight for temperance. Drunken men beat their wives and children, spent the family money, failed to work or provide for the family's needs, and left women lonely and isolated by going off to drink with their friends.[13] Advocates of temperance believed that women had the prerogative to protect their homes by demanding that men change their irresponsible ways.

Frances Willard, the outspoken president of the Temperance Union, maintained that societal forces were out of control and needed to be reined in by women, who were morally superior to men and who could apply their virtuous intent to taming male behavior. It was not her intention, however, that women cease to be women. Her statement "Womanliness first, afterwards what you will" captured her politically astute sense that the temperance movement would fare better if its proponents maintained certain traditionally feminine behaviors.[14]

While the movement began with temperance as a focus, it quickly expanded to include a much broader feminist agenda. The Temperance Union eventually called for suffrage for women, although it initially supported a more limited home protection ballot in which women were granted suffrage so that they could participate in decisions about liquor stores and taverns. The expanded agenda of the Temperance Union went on to call for prison reform, free kindergartens, employment centers for young women, foster care homes for orphaned children, and training schools for girls.[15] The movement became one that championed human rights and societal reform in a much broader and more general way, and advocated for a political agenda that explicitly addressed the needs and concerns of women.

By championing what was called the "white life," WCTU members challenged men to live a life of social purity and to make their responsibilities to family and homelife their most important priorities.[16] Men who subscribed to the "white life" could be expected to be more nurturing, more sympathetic, less greedy, less competitive, and more involved in family life; that is, they would be more like True Women.

While the Women's Christian Temperance Union served to further the cause of temperance and to espouse a higher moral order within the community, it was also a way in which women could express their anger, frustration, and upset at the men in their lives and at the constricted roles that society prescribed for women.[17] The reform movement allowed women to take their personal unhappiness and dissatisfaction and turn it into a political and social cause.

While many women turned their attention to the social and political reform agenda, a number of activists continued to focus their attention primarily on the issue of suffrage. In 1869 the suffrage effort splintered into two separate organizations. The American Woman Suffrage Association, with Lucy Stone at the helm, advocated the single issue of obtaining the vote for women. The National Woman Suffrage Association, headed by Susan B. Anthony and Elizabeth Cady Stanton, argued for a broader agenda. The newsletter published by the National Association, for example, was called *Revolution* and became a forum for feminist theory. Principally, the *Revolution* advocated economic independence and higher education for women. Its motto—"Men, their rights and nothing more, women their rights and nothing less"—clearly stated the National's broad intent and wide-ranging mission.[18]

In 1878 the Susan B. Anthony amendment was introduced into Congress declaring that the right to vote not be denied to any citizen on account of sex.[19] By 1890 the two suffrage groups had united once again, forming the National American Woman Suffrage Association, under the leadership of Carrie Chapman Catt. At this time, the single agenda of obtaining the vote was the focus of the organization.[20]

As a result of the heightened visibility of the New Woman, who took her reformist agenda beyond the home and directly challenged male behavior and impropriety, the 1870s and 1880s were witness to the first evidence of a backlash against women. During this period, that bastion of male authority the American Medical Association successfully lobbied to criminalize abortion.[21] In 1873 Congress passed the Comstock laws making discussions of conception and contraception illegal.[22] Psychiatrist Richard Krafft-Ebing coined the phrase "the mannish lesbian" to denote a woman who was really a man trapped in a female body; lesbianism was labeled as deviant.[23] These attacks on female sexuality and female friendship were partly in response to the female camaraderie that was central to both the women's club movement and the more activist reform movement.

As part of the backlash, the closing decades of the nineteenth century saw an idealization, not of the True Woman or the New Woman, but of the weak woman, the neurasthenic, debilitated, and frail woman who was unable to perform any of her household tasks.[24] Idle, gentle, frail, and somewhat irrational, the weak woman became a romantic ideal. Although she was trivialized and often dismissed, the frail woman was also pampered. However, unlike the New Woman, the frail woman posed no threat to male power or to the established order; she was not as caretaking and nurturing as the True Woman, but she was definitely not independent and challenging like the New Woman.

THE PSYCHIATRIC ESTABLISHMENT

With 45,000 known insane persons being treated in institutions throughout the country in 1870, the profession of psychiatry became increasingly established.[25] Not only did psychiatry attain respectability and power but the treatment of persons with mental disorders became increasingly medicalized and scientific. Consequently, physicians began to insist that scientific nomenclature, known primarily to physicians, be used when referring to people with psychiatric problems.[26]

The debate over the moral and medical causes of insanity abated during this period as insanity was increasingly regarded as a disease of the brain regardless of its cause.[27] During this period, however, perhaps more than at any other time, specialized treatments were developed for treating women patients whose illnesses were considered to be connected to their gynecological functioning.

In general, the causes of insanity were divided into what were called predisposing and exciting causes. Predisposing causes were factors such as heredity, birth trauma, pregnancy, and alcoholism, and they heightened the likelihood that a given individual would experience a mental breakdown. Exciting causes were akin to acute precipitants and were further subdivided into physical and moral types. Physical exciting causes included fever, medical illness, poison, organic infections of the brain, and deformity of the cranium. Moral exciting causes represented the psychosocial end of the spectrum and included such factors as interpersonal and familial troubles, disappointments, poverty and destitution, bad treatment, and excessive intellectual work.[28] In general, practitioners held to the belief that life was becoming more complicated and stressful and that the demands of city life were contributory factors in the greater incidence of mental disease.[29]

In the spirit of scientific inquiry, researchers began to make the distinction between symptoms and causes in understanding psychiatric illness. Previously, when presented with a religious delusion, the practitioner would be inclined to list religion as the cause of the illness. More scientifically minded practitioners began to argue that the religious delusion was merely a symptom, not a cause, and that symptoms might take the form of religious, persecutory, or romantic delusions. Causality, they argued, was of a different order and was often multifactorial, with several different events contributing to the ultimate breakdown of an individual's mind.[30]

While the medical literature in general toward the end of the nineteenth century became increasingly scientific, the discussions of mental illness in women remained decidedly unscientific. In the writings of some practitioners we can see what looks like a backlash against those women who chose to leave the limited sphere of the home. Failing to fulfill the roles of wife and mother and following occupations and professions for which they "are not suited," for example, were listed as a cause of insanity in women. These researchers assumed that unfeminine activities caused uterine derangement, which in turn caused mental illness.[31]

Throughout this period, the belief persisted that uterine disease was a direct cause of insanity. This belief remained widespread despite the lack of confirmatory scientific evidence.[32] Statements such as the following were not uncommon in the established psychiatric literature: "Not only the uterus and ovaries, but also the bladder, rectum, vagina, clitoris, labia, perineum, and the now so fashionable fallopian tubes all join in producing local or reflex neuroses."[33] While occasional articles challenged these unfounded hypotheses, they continued to attract large numbers of adherents.

During the late nineteenth century, references began to be made to the association of emotional problems with menstruation. A number of reports appeared in which women described emotional upset prior to or during the time of their menstrual period.[34] Another particularly female problem involved persistent delusions about being attacked by one's husband with knives, guns, and fists.[35] While these reports were believed to be evidence of delusional thinking, they may have been the first record of the psychological sequelae of the battered wife syndrome.

In addition to these gender-specific causes of mental illnesses, two specific syndromes were identified during this period, which seemed to affect a disproportionate number of women: neurasthenia and hysteria. Neurasthenia—a general state of malaise, depression, impaired intellect, and irritability, accompanied by neuralgia and muscle weakness—was thought to be caused by excessive mental labor, anxiety, or deficient nutrition.[36] The neurasthenic woman was the medical equivalent of the weak or frail woman, who at that time was idealized as a counterpoint to the aggressive and independent woman who had made her debut in the closing decades of the nineteenth century.

Hysteria was recognized as a particularly female malady during this time period as well. Anything that weakened a woman was believed to be capable of bringing about a hysterical attack.[37] Descriptions of the particular features of hysteria barely mask the contempt and derision of the medical establishment:

> The patient, when the hysterical feelings come upon her, does not feel disposed to make the slightest effort to resist them, and yields to her emotions, whatever they may be. She will laugh or cry on the slightest provocation, and is very nervous and excitable. She cares nothing for her duties and seemingly takes pleasure in exaggerating all her slight discomforts and annoyances, and by her suspicious, exacting and unreasonable behavior, makes life generally uncomfortable to those about her. She indignantly resents all attempts and efforts for her comfort and cure, and discards all advice from her best friends, but will eagerly listen to the counsel of the many friends who come in to pity, sympathize and condole with her. She will say that for her to do certain things is absolutely impossible, but under the stimulus of strong desires or wishes will, if unobserved, do precisely the things declared to be impossible.[38]

The author of this "scientific" description demonstrates scorn and derision for the hysterical woman, who is seen as a willful bad girl unwilling to accept her duties and responsibilities.

From a more feminist perspective, Charlotte Perkins Gilman declared the affluent and idle matron to be an evolutionary anomaly. Gilman likened the idle woman to a platypus, a creature with no purpose. It came, then, as no surprise that such a woman felt distraught and unable to manage her life. For

Gilman the "cure" for such difficulties lay in choosing the path of an independent life.[39] However, for practitioners during this time, the cure lay in returning a woman to her traditional role.

In general, treatment for mental illness during this period was an amalgam of different experimental approaches. Women received a set of gender-neutral treatments and at the same time were subject to a range of specialized treatments that specifically focused on their reproductive organs or that were designed to modify certain undesirable behaviors.

Many of the standard treatments were designed to calm an excitable psyche. Cold baths were used to calm nervous irritability, warm baths to ease mania, massage therapy to induce general relaxation, and electricity to reverse acute dementia.[40] Chemical restraints in the form of sedatives became the prevailing method for subduing patients, although excessive use of these drugs caused some practitioners to warn against the use of sedatives as chemical straitjackets.[41] Restraint continued to be an adjunct to treatment, although the use of mechanical restraints and physical seclusion generally declined during the last part of the nineteenth century.[42]

In the 1880s, inspired by reform efforts in other arenas, there was a move toward more individualized treatment. Hospitals began to provide patients with opportunities for employment and vocational activity while they were undergoing their cures.[43]

In addition to these generic treatments, which applied to both men and women, the 1880s and 1890s saw the evolution of a number of treatments expressly intended for women. Based on the unfounded assumptions that psychiatric illness resulted from gynecological disease, these treatments were directed at women's reproductive organs. The removal of ovaries, for example, was performed to calm women whose symptoms seemed especially acute during their menstrual periods.[44] When ovaries were not removed, other practitioners opted to treat ovarian dysfunction by encouraging women to gain weight. These physicians believed that "the fat laden, over hanging wall of the abdomen" would keep the ovaries from slipping and causing discomfort.[45]

Other women were subject to electrical charges applied to the uterus. In nonvirgins, the "double uterine exciter," which applied an electrical current to the uterus, was employed for periods lasting up to a maximum of ten minutes.[46] Other women were treated by hot water injections into the vagina, a method once again designed to calm the deranged uterine system.[47] For women whose insanity was believed to be linked to excessive masturbation, a procedure of clitoral cauterization was recommended.[48]

Some practitioners realized that these treatments bordered on the sadistic and that they were all based on the unproven speculation that genital dysfunction led to insanity. One practitioner even warned that if women did to male genitals what was being done to theirs, men had better look out, suggesting to his colleagues that someday "turnabout might be fair play."[49]

In addition to these physical treatments, women who suffered from psychological problems were treated with a form of paternalistic behavior modification. The chief proponent of what was called the rest cure was S. Weir Mitchell, who recommended that women who were suffering from emotional exhaustion take to their beds for six weeks to two months.[50] These women were forbidden from sewing, reading, writing, and, often for the first month, from even sitting up. Patients were fed by a nurse and consigned to use a bedpan. They lay in a dim or darkened room and were instructed to be as still as possible. S. Weir Mitchell maintained that women who followed his regimen would be fattened up, like turkeys being taken to market.[51]

During his medical career, Dr. Mitchell influenced the treatment of many women. He was an authoritarian practitioner whose methods demanded that the physician have his way.[52] He based his interventions on the assumption that a woman was enjoying her illness. Consequently, being ill should be made sufficiently aversive so that the woman would readily return to her chores and responsibilities as wife and mother. In the process she would learn that it was her male physician, not she herself, who was in charge of making decisions and who would determine how she should live her life.

During this time, some practitioners argued for the introduction of female physicians, but not so that derogatory and sexist practices cease. Two arguments were put forward by those who favored women physicians. First, since women patients were thought to be so sensitive and easily embarrassed, they might be less ashamed of revealing their delusions to another woman.[53] Second, the incidence of sexual fantasies and delusions about male doctors might decrease if women physicians were engaged.[54]

During the latter part of the nineteenth century, asylums continued to be the primary locus of treatment for people with serious mental illnesses. The Association of Medical Superintendents of American Institutions for the Insane declared at its twenty-fifth meeting in 1871 that there was a need for the institutional treatment of the vast majority of insane persons. At this meeting, they argued against the separation of acute and chronic patients in distinct facilities, saying that all individuals deserved the most enlightened care.[55]

It was also during this period that asylum care came to be

seen as the duty and responsibility of the state. In a sexist analogy, one writer likened the state's duty to care for the weak and insane to the responsibility to care for women: "Just as the weakness of woman secures to her that chivalrous protection in society which her own frail arms could not obtain for her," so, too, should the society be engaged in caring for infirm and insane individuals.[56]

Asylums consisted of substantial buildings; they were funded by public money; they received government supervision; and they provided acute and long-term care and treatment for all who needed to be there. Ideally, the medical treatment was administered by reputable doctors who were mandated to protect the legal rights of the individuals detained at the asylum, granting them the utmost of personal liberty.[57] The actual physical facilities of asylums improved during this period, with an emphasis on better heating, ventilation, air, and light.[58]

In an attempt to provide better overall care, practitioners also called for special training for attendants. Training programs were developed so that attendants might receive clinical instruction as well as lectures on relevant topics.[59] Criteria were established for the discharge of patients from the asylum; patients were considered ready to leave and return to their homes and communities when they were not depressed or elated, when they were free of moral perversion, when they were free from irritability and restlessness, and when they felt kindly toward friends and the asylum itself.[60] Asylum officials felt that a cure had been effected when a self-centered individual who lacked an appreciation of the consequences of his or her behavior had become a person who realized that he or she was part of a community and needed to be responsible for personal actions.[61]

During this time period, several alternatives were proposed to asylum care. While the prevailing wisdom continued to advocate that individuals needed to be treated outside of their own homes, a number of alternatives to traditional asylums were suggested. Some practitioners proposed mini-asylums that would function as colonies of the main hospital; these would be primarily for long-stay chronic patients who needed lifelong care.[62] In these smaller facilities, individuals would enjoy a more homey atmosphere and would receive attention that was still suitable but less costly. The suggestion was raised that psychiatric patients, rather than being treated in asylums specifically for the care of patients with mental disease, be treated on wards in general hospitals.[63] Such an innovation would utilize the resources of existing hospital facilities and reduce the cost of building entire asylum complexes.

Adult foster care placements were suggested as alternatives to expensive asylum care. In a system of foster care placements, chronic patients would go to live in the homes of stable and established families, families other than their own, who would provide room, board, and minimal supervision. Some practitioners expressed concern that patients living in these homes would be subject to abusive treatment because of the lax supervision.[64]

The adult foster care movement became a women's issue for several reasons. Not only were many of the recipients of care women but most of the providers of care also were women. Taking in boarders was traditionally a way whereby women could legitimately earn extra money while remaining within their domestic role. The care of mentally ill women in the homes of other women who were both poorly supervised and poorly paid for their services suggests a women's issue that was not addressed during this period.

In keeping with the reform spirit that swept the country

during the 1880s and 1890s, asylum care facilities were subject to new scrutiny. The National Association for the Protection of the Insane and the Prevention of Insanity was formed in 1880 to encourage clinical oversight of asylums.[65] It proposed public education about insanity and encouraged the early treatment of mental disorders by teaching people how to recognize some of the initial warning signs. The association further proposed to influence legislation in favor of persons with mental illnesses and to allay the public distrust of the insane. Some of the specific asylum practices that were targeted for reform were overcrowding, the use of restraints, the use of damaging narcotics and other drugs, inadequate recordkeeping, and the curtailment of a patient's rights once he or she entered the asylum.[66] The medical community itself called for smaller, less crowded hospitals, better attendants, and better supervision. In an attempt to calm public anxieties about abusive treatment, physicians supported a move to involve public officials in the oversight of large mental hospitals.[67]

Legal reform altered the laws governing the commitment and retention of individuals in hospitals. The two physicians who signed commitment forms were now mandated to appear before a judge, who would be the final arbiter and who would issue the warrant to commit an individual.[68] In many states, a board was created to act as a Commission of Lunacy, set up to investigate questions raised by any person committed to an asylum.[69] A number of the women who wrote about the injustices they experienced while hospitalized were active in advocating for some of the asylum reforms that took place during this period.

Firsthand Accounts

1866–1890

*T*he spirit of reform that was felt in the country in general during this period made its way into the eight accounts presented here. Several of these women had specific recommendations for how asylum commitment and asylum treatment might be reformed. However, they felt that it was both their right and their duty to let the tax-paying public know of the disgraceful conditions within the asylums for the mentally ill. When they were not indicting the legal system for failing to protect individual rights, they were citing specific instances of cruelty and inhumanity on the part of treatment and care providers.

The women whose accounts are presented are as follows: Adriana P. Brinckle, hospitalized at the State Hospital for the Insane at Harrisburg, Pennsylvania, for the twenty-eight years between July 13, 1857, and summer 1885; Adeline T. P. Lunt, who spent an unknown period of time at a facility in New England she refers to as the "———— Insane Retreat"; Ada Metcalf, who had two relatively brief admissions to the Southern Ohio Lunatic Asylum (Dayton), one for five months in 1869 and the second for four months in 1873; Lydia A. Smith, first admitted to a private institution, Brigham Hall in Canandaigua, New York, on August 18, 1865, and then transferred, in March 1867, to a public facility, the Kalamazoo Asylum (Kalamazoo, Michigan), where she remained until February 1871; Anna Agnew, a patient at the Central Indiana Hospital for Insane (Indianapolis) between 1878 and 1885; Lemira Clarissa Pennell, a patient at the Maine Insane Hospital at Augusta for ten weeks in April 1880; Clarissa Caldwell Lathrop, who was admitted to the New York State Lunatic Asylum at Utica on October 19, 1880, and discharged on December 8, 1882; and Charlotte Perkins Gilman, who spent six weeks in the spring of 1887 undergoing Dr. S. Weir Mitchell's rest cure at his private facility.

Adriana P. Brinckle

(1857–1885)

I don't think any woman in America is better qualified than I
to supply the material for a good sermon on insane asylums—
for I was locked up in one for twenty-eight years.

During those years I never lost my reason—it is a wonder I
did not—and so what I say may be relied upon as being truthful.
The authority for my statement that I am not insane is the
Committee on Lunacy of the Board of Public Charities of
Pennsylvania, through whose influence, in the summer of 1885,
my unjust imprisonment came to an end.

My story is simple, I was put in the asylum for two reasons:
the first was that I was extravagant and too fond of dress. What
a lot of asylums there would be if all people whose natures were
like mine had to be locked up! The other reason was that my
family wanted me relieved of the disgrace of being publicly accused of obtaining goods under false representations, by resort-

Adriana P. Brinckle, excerpts from "Life Among the Insane," North American Review, *1887.*

ing to the insanity defense, which, nowadays, seems reserved for the use of defendants in murder or arson cases.

But to begin. I was born in 1825, and am, therefore, now sixty years old. My father was William Draper Brinckle, a physician, who lived in Girard Row, Philadelphia. My mother died while I was young.

On July 13, 1857, I was placed in the State Hospital for the Insane at Harrisburg, Penn., on the commitment of two physicians, one my father, the other a stranger to me. An excuse, perhaps, for the difficulty in which I became involved was that I had no own mother to guide me. My father, occupied with his professional duties, was of course much away from home, so that I grew up, wandering at my own pleasure. Yet my education was by no means neglected; for I received a thorough training in the ordinary English branches, became quite familiar with the French language, and acquired a thorough knowledge of music.

I was naturally of a gay temperament and inclined to extravagance, and I knew that I had my father, and an uncle who resided in our family, to help me out of possible financial straits. My father's property was invested in the mercantile business of the uncle to whom I have referred. In the year in which I was placed in the asylum there was a general panic in mercantile circles, and my father and uncle were unable to pay my debts.

The particular difficulty in which I became involved was that of buying furniture on part credit, for a parlor which I had rented in the house of two old ladies, distant relatives of my father's family. Their house was small and I had no room for a piano. Having been musically educated it was a great deprivation to me to have no piano; I therefore moved to a larger house in the same neighborhood, securing furnished parlors.

Having no use for the furniture which I had purchased for the smaller house, I sold it. This proceeding came to the knowledge of the dealer from whom it had been purchased, and he prosecuted me. Before the time came for my appearance in court I was placed in the asylum. My father was advised to take this course by the late Judge George W. Woodward, then of the Supreme Court of Pennsylvania. The examination of both physicians was very brief. My father asked me a few simple questions and then took his departure. The late Dr. George McClellan, the other examiner, inquired how I was in bodily health. I complained merely of a slight headache, having no idea that the visit was made with an alleged view of determining my mental condition. He also asked me if I was able to take a journey and where I would like to go. I replied that I was quite able and willing, and would like to go to Long Branch, remembering that my health generally had been much improved on a former occasion at that place. My father subsequently informed me of the purpose of the examination and of the determination to send me to an asylum, explaining to me that he did not think I was insane, but that it was all that could be done under the circumstances.

I remember very distinctly that on the way to Harrisburg I did not relish the idea of being classed with lunatics, but Judge Woodward, who accompanied me, represented that it was better than being imprisoned in a jail, and that insanity was after all the bluntest horn of the dilemma, because it preserved family honor. So, on that eventful day, I was led into the presence of Dr. John Curwen, at that time the superintendent of the institution (now in charge of the State Hospital at Warren, Pa.), and Mrs. Cole, its matron. To these people Judge Woodward, in my presence, spoke of my extravagant tendencies; what he said when my back was turned I do not know. He wished me good-bye rather sorrowfully, and I think when he left it was with a little remorse at what he had done.

Everything in the institution was strange to me. I felt that I, as sane a person as any of the attendants, or any one else for that matter, was in the asylum under false pretenses. I make the hint of the distinction between the state of mind of the nurses of the insane, and the state of mind of members of the general community, because my observation convinced me that the nurses at the Harrisburg Hospital, for some reason or other, were not all rational beings. Perhaps it was the contact with mad women. Perhaps the fact that some were promoted to be nurses, first having been patients, made this seem to me true.

They put me in the best ward at first. I found life insupportably dull. The only things that made existence tolerable were music, which I loved passionately, and fancy work, which I liked less because of its monotony. It was a change, however, from the sameness of idling. . . .

In June, 1858, my father came to see me for the first time, and complimented me on my rosy cheeks and generally healthy look. That was all very well, but I wanted to get out, and I told him so. He promised me that if I would wait until the troubles caused by my debts had blown over he would have me released. Then he went away. I never saw him again, and he died four years later. He wrote to me, however, and his letters gave me the impression that my release would be a more difficult matter than I had anticipated. The man who can be said to have managed my detention was Judge Woodward, whose visits to me were frequent.

WARD LIFE

Untrained nurses in a hospital for the insane know no more about treating insane people than I know about prescribing for a case of fever. The secret of proper conduct toward the insane is management. It requires tact. The ex-laundry-woman or factory girl who becomes a nurse cannot understand such a problem as the mind, and when the patient is refractory she can only meet it with brutality. That is wrong. Those who are deprived of reason cannot understand violence, nor has it any good effect on them. They can only turn their poor puzzled eyes in apologetic rebuke to those who assault them, and wonder what it all means. I have seen a patient who had been struck look in surprise at the nurse who struck her, and ask, "Why do you do that? What have I done?" Many patients cannot be made to comprehend that what they do is not right, and violence to them is worse than useless. We may just as well thrash a cripple for limping, or vent our malice upon a blind man because he cannot see.

The only way in which patients can get on the right side of sane nurses is by doing their work for them. They are often expected to help to sweep and clean up. Of course to coerce the insane to do this is criminal. They should be regarded as human beings whose misfortunes entitle them to sympathy and pity, and not as scape-goats and laughing-stocks because of their uselessness to society.

I saw a harmless patient who was sitting listlessly on a heating register attacked and beaten because she would not work. One nurse knocked her down and then called another with homicidal mania to join and they pounded the unfortunate creature until she was black and blue. Her brother and husband happened to call and see her that very night, and to them some untrue story of the cause of her bruises was given. They were not satisfied, however, and they removed her.

One of the patients in a ward adjoining mine was one morning found hanging with her head wedged between the transom and the door-frame. She was quite dead. How she had ever got in that position was a mystery. Probably one of her associates helped her up with a chair and then removed it. One of the inmates suggested to a weak-minded companion in an adjoining ward to tie a handkerchief around her (the companion's) neck and to pull it tight. The poor demented creature did as she was told, and it was not until she became very black in the face and was evidently suffocating, that her tempter became alarmed and called for help. In doing so she calmly remarked to the nurse: "I have a suspicion that Mrs. So-and-so is trying to kill herself. . . ."

I do not think the nurses behaved with propriety in removing the remains of dead patients. They made a frolic of the occasion. The poor, half-witted wards of the State remarked upon the disrespect with which the clay of their dead comrades was treated. It was in much the same manner that patients were removed from one ward to another.

In the fall of 1884 a notice, which the new law required, was posted up in our ward, telling us that if we had any grievances, we could write freely about them to the Committee on Lunacy of the Board of Public Charities. Before I had time to avail myself of that opportunity of getting a hearing, I was taken very ill and was too weak to do anything for some time. When I recovered I found that the patients had torn up and otherwise destroyed the printed law the committee had had posted up; and I did not remember the name of any gentleman upon it. Fortunately Miss Annie Drinker, a convalescent, recollected the name of the medical member of the committee, and wrote to him on September 27, 1884. We waited for weeks, expecting a reply or a visit, but none came. It appears that the latter miscarried. We did nothing until December 31st, 1884, when we wrote again. The letter reached the committee, and my appeal for liberty was at once looked into. On March 16th, 1885, I sent a letter to Dr. A. J. Ourt, secretary of the committee, and shortly afterwards I was visited by him, Dr. Morton, and Mr. Philip C. Garrett, chairman of the committee. Soon after this the committee fully investigated my case and ordered my immediate release, and I was allowed to go free. As my means were limited (my board had been always paid out of funds left to me), and as I hardly knew what to do, I went to the Convalescents' Retreat, Glenn Mill, Pennsylvania, where I now am.

I do not think my story can create in the mind of the reader any but the one impression—that I am a wronged woman, and that there has been something amiss in the system of dealing with those alleged to be insane.

No one, it appears, is now responsible for my incarceration. My counsel informs me that an action will not lie against the State or the hospital authorities, as my commitment was made in due form of law. Apart from this, all those who procured my incarceration have long since died. My release came about solely under the operation of the new lunacy law of Pennsylvania, and the zealous efforts of the gentlemen whose duty it is to carry the law (of May, 1883), into effect.

Before the law was passed, appeals from inmates of an insane asylum generally fell upon dull and unheeding ears. The only method of release legally provided was an application to a court of law. In the absence of outside friends this was practically impossible.

The law requires the Committee on Lunacy to personally

examine the complaint of every asylum inmate, and since the investment of its power and authority, others, who, like myself, seemed doomed to a living death, have been freed from their bonds, and have been once more established in the society from which they were so cruelly removed. At their knock, the door of every asylum, public or private, within the broad confines of this State, must open. At their command the shackles on every lunatic must be loosed, and the blackness of the dark cell has been made to give place to light and air. Handcuffs, straight-jackets, balls and chains, iron rings, and all other such relics of barbarism, are things of the past in Pennsylvania.

To the gentlemen of this committee I am, under a gracious Providence, forever indebted that, after more than a quarter of a century, and at the age of sixty years, I am once more free. Even for this much I thank Him in whose unfailing love, in the darkest hours of my trial, I never lost faith.

Adeline T. P. Lunt

(Date Unknown)

*A*nd what is the actual legalized condition of the patient in an insane asylum? In some measure the patient's mental and physical state directs his treatment, but normally and aggregately this is his latitude. Here are certain grounds bounded by high fences and locked gateways. Within them are large buildings, with barred windows and snapping doors. Inside these buildings, long rooms or galleries, opening on each side into bedrooms, are the homes of the patients. Here they are locked in. Here, behind the bars of these iron-framed windows, they may look with envy and longing upon the outer world. Inside of this is their world. The outside is only a vestige of the past, which they are to banish from life, from thought, from memory if they can. Here, after some fashion, they work, read, sleep, think, and live—not, it may be, for a period of disease, during a certain mania, or fit of melancholia, but for months and years of a rational existence. Here, behind these mortared walls and iron

Mrs. George Lunt, excerpts from Behind Bars, *1871.*

bars, men of thought, of culture, of social calibre, of business capacity, are doomed to live. Here, women of intelligence, of spirit, of refinement, with homes, with families, and possessing the power to comfort, cherish, and adorn these, are left to stagnate. They are not patients; they are members of this household. Brought here once for treatment, now they have become the subjects of a life-treatment; they are resident boarders, so called. Rather, they are prisoners. How many sane persons placed under circumstances like these could live on composedly and unconcernedly? How many would not be made wild with the thought of the narrowed situation? Imagine yourself reading behind these "story limits."

It is very generally believed by a mistaken society who think of the insane, and even by those individuals who have been personally connected with some of these sufferers, that an asylum confines only the violent, dangerous, or utterly imbecile, and that few persons of a state described above are normally detained there beyond the absolutely necessary term from convalescence to health. This is a remarkably wide-spread error. The convalescent galleries, so called, differ very little, outwardly regarded, from a ladies' boarding-house in any part of the world; that is to say, as far as the patients give the impression. And a close, careful study and intimacy with these patients affords no stronger development of irregularity, eccentricity, or idiosyncrasy, either in language, deportment, or manner, than might be met with in any society of women thrown together, endeavoring to make the most of life under the most adverse and opposing circumstances.

To-night, if not to-day, that lady will be bound, chest, arms, hands, will be compressed, tied into a sleeved corset, as it seems, only it is rough, like tow-cloth; and she will be told to go to sleep. This new garment, this unusual style of habiliment, this of itself is sufficient to "murder sleep." She does not sleep, and must pay the penalty. She is watched if she turns, if she struggles to get free, if she strives to rise, if she weeps. She is reported upon, and morning comes with its accusing record written in a "Watch Book" for the physician's eye, of "no sleep"; and through grief, wakefulness, waiting, watching, homesickness, bewilderment, and the poor woman is made more frantic with torture and opposition to nature. She is locked into this building. Yesterday at home, with the world to choose from, cherished, indulged, tended, with love, with liberty—to-day she is ordered, tortured, harassed, locked up, tied down; to-night perhaps worse befalls, and to make all safe and sure, she is tied to a bed!

Blest independence of social government, that systems do not allow! Let any man presume to maintain his own inherent eccentricity, idiosyncrasy, or whatever may stamp his personality, let him indulge in his own whim of opinion or habit of life by his form of speech or expression, within the tabooed domains of an asylum, and unless this be on a footing with the codes of uniformity there prescribed, unless it reach the wanted standard of this or that line of government, he may as well begin to study the art of doffing his true character, of suppressing and merging himself into the imaginary man or woman of system's carving, into the image of the figure-head that is chiselled in wood and serves as a model for all; which says, "Until you cut yourself to my pattern, abandon hope; until you learn to give eye for eye, to pay off system in its own coin, you have no more chance of escaping from those walls, than if habeas corpus or personal liberty bills had never existed." Much of the conduct that passes current as insanity in the asylum the world would never discover as such, or deem it any way so very remarkable or extraordinary. Association and habit, the fact of condensing life into a methodical course, or discipline, have the effect of constraining and narrowing the minds of those who govern these systems; and the fact that a man has once been insane, brief or temporary as the fit may have been, is sufficient to cast doubt or suspicion in the minds of some upon him forever.

The very same opinions that might be expressed in any polite society in the world, measured by narrow judgement,—and in fact they are always on the alert to catch a ray of disease,—are again (in the asylum) openly denounced as "crazy talk." Too often are patients interrupted in an innocent original expression of thought by this rebuke: "Come, come; don't talk so; that's crazy." This is heard repeatedly, not from the attendants, from whom we could not expect any particular nicety of judgement, but from those who pretend to govern with discretion the minds of the patients. A practice like this is evil and foolish. It not only prevents the patient from expressing himself, which is essential to his real progress, but it discourages and disparages him with regard to his condition, and blights any hope that he may entertain of being considered again a rational being. Free scope for the development of his conversational faculties and expressions of opinion are as necessary and vital to his well-being as the air which nourishes him, and to cramp the very thought as well as person is treatment which can hardly of itself be called rational. Here, indeed, men may fear those who would not kill the body only, but both body and soul. For as we are not machines, but human souls, and as one soul differeth from another in capacity, it is impossible to measure one man's conduct or line of life by that of another, as it is equally impossible to bring all men up to one line or rule of thought.

This moral confinement allows not one iota of individual

scope or latitude, but would hew men and women down to the similitude of sticks and stones. Thus it would seem to the eye of the world at large, that what is called technically well by the asylum codes is at the same time, in the light of a broader vision, simply a passive state of being; all impulses or natural emotions are made prostrate to a law of obedience, and the ultimate consequences dependent on this obedience.

There are patients who, possessed with but one idea,—that of getting home,—have perspicacity enough, finally, to see through this gauze of moral restraint, and immediately they strive, like school-girls, for the reward of merit. This requires but a piece of acting; they are assured that silence is safe, that to suppress a natural characteristic flow of spirits or talk is an important step for them, that to sit in lady-like attire, pretty straight in a chair, with a book or work before them, "inveterate in virtue," smoothed down with a moral flat-iron, results in being patted panegyrically on the head by the head itself, and pronounced by that important functionary, "better." Patients experiment on the faculty in this way, after exhausting themselves in every other trick to escape; finally they renounce their own characters, and acting on this plan, they have walked out of the asylum with a diploma of good conduct and with "well" printed on their persons. It need not be necessary to say that these patients were more agreeable and companionable when acting themselves, than after their submission. Whoever is strong enough to condense his nature after this fashion may reach the goal, but by what a gigantic effort!

THERE are but few persons in an asylum whose sense of honor is quite strong enough to preclude them from exerting, by every device within their intelligent faculties, the means of an escape. Of course, while there, they are possessed with but one idea, and in one sense they are indeed monomaniacs, or rather home-maniacs. Nor do they discern the nicety of the phrase getting well above that of getting home. They have just one thought, and one general topic of conversation—home. This is the guiding star, the beacon ahead, the goal for which they exist. They dwell upon all its reminiscences, and commemorate its delightfulness. When will it be reached? How will it be reached? Then what wonder is that they should be always on the alert to catch the nearest way to their ambition, or to plan and practice, if possible, any decent means to attain their object! . . . There are romantic legends of escapes written on every asylum wall; the patients keep these alive, and they are handed down from generation to generation with marvelous piquancy. How the physicians hate these records! It is a positive wickedness to allude to them. . . . it would be incessantly proved that the asylum was supported by a class who need not be there. There are two thirds or more on an average of such patients in asylums. To be sure, the end does come, and they are sent home; but why were they detained a year or more beyond what necessity demanded? A month, a week, a day, even, is imprisonment, tyranny, oppression inflicted by the system, and torture and anguish for the patient. It is a safeguard of the system, say the physicians, in defense of their inordinate detention of patients, a prevention of ills they know not of, which blossom in their imagination, and grow and ripen with tyrannic determination under their management, until they become established conclusions.

When they talk prophetically of certain risks and dangers to be avoided in the speedy cure, and the freedom of life again, they do not hint or allude to another risk which is not altogether to be lost sight of in their system—the danger of a falling into apathy of the patient, growing out of a too protracted detention. But there is such a state, and in many cases patients are seen who but a while ago were all sanguine and ready to leap at the first chance of getting away; but when the time really and honorably came to them, when doors, and gates, and bars were unfastened, and the physician said go, and friends bade them welcome, who positively sank back, and had almost said, as the breath of air might be deemed to the suffocating man—it is too late. Are the physicians careful enough in guarding against this other extreme? No. Their sole idea seems to be to fix the patient to a routine of life identical with the asylum itself, and bound up by its regulations, which must be adopted at the first step for every patient alike, without individuality, a regular course of deprivations, denials, disappointments, until the patient himself is fairly vanquished and lost sight of in the system. They do not regard these apathetic states as having anything to do with their treatment, or as a possible result of certain dismally prolonged months of asylum life. On the contrary, it is an instrument of defence and self-flattery, which they can use to confirm their pet theories, by asserting that such a one likes it so well that he is positively reluctant to leave, and would rather stay than go. Let no one believe that any person, except a demented one, would choose the life of an asylum (if it may be called life) in preference to any other, unless it be that something in the system has fostered, and finally brought them to a sort of despair of any other, and they have fallen into that apathy and heart-sickness which hope deferred proverbially creates.

It cannot be denied that, universally, asylums have fallen into a rut of apathy with regard to the discipline, and it is evident that it is so from the fact, that of late so much inquiry and research have been made into their condition and the causes of the detention of patients. Professedly they are for the cure of insanity; literally they are for encouraging, and in some cases, it almost seems making insanity. Thus, for instance, in the dictionary of this opinion it might be defined as follows:—

INSANE ASYLUM. A place where insanity is made.

Indeed, this definition of it has sometimes struck the writer with peculiar application, upon witnessing the terrible downward career of many of the patients.

Ada Metcalf

(1869 and 1873)

*H*istory informs us that it is less than two hundred years
since many sick, suffering, bedridden, and perhaps eccentric,
though innocent, souls, were not only rudely imprisoned, but
many, like the vilest criminals, were actually hung "by the neck
until they were dead." And why? The physicians, in a little out
of the way village in Massachusetts, unable to account for certain maladies or disorders that a few would-be notorious young
girls of the place presumed to be affected with, pronounced
them bewitched. And the doctor—the individual who has succeeded fairly or unfairly, as the case may be, in getting an M.D.
attached to his name, though but a stupid, witless donkey,—if
he asserts anything, in some communities, the profoundest sage
may reason in vain to confute it; so this people, not yet two
hundred years ago, in the wildest excitement over the doctors
assertions, clamored loudly for the death of the witches; and as

Ada Metcalf, excerpts from Lunatic Asylums: and How I Became an Inmate of One, *1876.*

the suffering, bedridden beings were the less able to defend or protect themselves they were the more readily victimized.

The doctors asserted the existence of witches; and the people, with frenzied excitement, soon hunted and dragged forth the weak and defenceless, the law arraigned, tried, and convicted them; then pronounced the death penalty, and enforced it. And presumptuous ignorance never opened its eyes to look into this indiscriminate rashness, until its folly began to involve the more honored, the more moneyed and more learned among its victims. Even individuals high in power began to fear for their safety. Then the owls opened their eyes and hooted to check the current of opinion; and soon the tidal wave of shameful ignorance and superstition began to ebb and abate; but only to abate, for yet the same wave breaks forth through other channels.

For I know what I am saying when I state that to-day, with this page of history before us, there are many sick, suffering invalids, gloomy and depressed from physical ailments only, who are dragged from good homes and kind friends into Lunatic Asylums—good institutions for officer and employees, but purgatories for patients—some to be tortured to madness, and resulting to others in a fearful curtailing of their lives.

Many of these cruelly tortured victims die; many, in an almost dying state, are dragged through long and incommodious journeys, to breathe their last breath soon after reaching their home, and the sad story of their wrongs is buried with them. And, there being so few left to tell the tale of cruel injustice so blindly imposed, the dire work goes on.

The witches are still hung; and the people, unknowingly are aiding and abetting the deed!

PART II—INSIDE THE ASYLUM

The patients of that hall (hall No. 10) were less noisy, and conducted themselves somewhat better at the table than those in
"No. 2" and so far it was less disagreeable to me. But sleeping
in a room with six or seven lunatics was intolerable. I have
awakened in the night and found the atmosphere in our room
so rife with stench, that it was distressingly sickening and suffocating to me. I discovered the cause to be, two or more tin
vessels, without lid or cover, filled half full, or to the brim, with
every conceivable filth, for us to inhale. And I have staggeringly
walked to a window, and for long, weary hours, pressed my face
close between the iron bars to catch a few breaths of the pure
air that God has bountifully scattered throughout the length
and breadth of the land—free to all—but which I was dragged
from, and deprived of, through ignorance, bigotry, indifference,
and a spirit of tyranny and oppression that grows rank in the
hearts of those under whose dominion the helpless and unfortunate are kept subject.

I asked the doctor for essence of peppermint, which I kept
under my pillow every night, to aid me to endure the vitiated
atmosphere. Often during those lone hours I thought of my
comfortable room at home, filled with pure, refreshing air, going to waste, as it seemed, because no one was there to breathe
it—and also of the many wronged human souls by whom I was
surrounded—and the cause that brought them there—until the
cry, "How long? Oh Lord! How long?" would escape me in
silent prayer.

And another reason for my being stronger, aside from the
cool weather, will not be amiss to tell here. It was simply an
occasional bath. For during the three months I was in "No. 2

hall," I was never bathed! I was unable to do it myself, and the number of times that I asked the attendants to assist me was not even replied to or noticed in any way. But after my removal into "No. 10," I hired one of the patients in it—Mattie Morris—to help me wash myself decently, which she did on several occasions. And I recompensed her with dark calico wrapper, and several other little things, which she appeared delighted to get —as the State furnished her scanty wardrobe.

The attendant—"Mary," we called her—generally took a survey of the apartments near the time of his [the doctor's] daily round, to see if the beds, etc., in each room were in due order. So on that morning when on her inspecting tour, she halted at the door of my chamber, and seeing me still lying in bed, indifferently remarked: "Why, I forgot you!" then carelessly passed on.

While I felt the lack of a little decent attention was partly, at least, the cause of my being compelled to keep my bed, yet I made no complaint of neglect, as such complaints from patients, too often there, tend only to add insult to injury! But I asked for a seidlitz powder to be sent to me, and a sleeping draught of chloral, on that evening—hoping a night's sleep would restore me sufficiently to get away from that detestable place—which requests were complied with.

My attendant—or, more properly speaking, my non-attendant—was present at my bedside during the doctor's call on me. I think she felt a prick of guilt, which made her fear I might expose her neglect. And she wished to be ready to contradict me, as attendants almost universally do—or, in other words, attendants in lunatic asylums invariably lie!

Now I began looking up my wardrobe. I found the greater part of my clothing, which was due more to the oversight I had ever kept over it, than from any proper care the employees bestowed on patients clothes. But a number of pieces were missing, that I could not account for—stolen, though, no doubt—as it is an easy matter to practice theft there; though sometimes when the nice, comfortable clothing of an insane patient is missing it is not stolen—"Oh, no! only taken for the benefit of some one else!" for what need have crazy people with decent apparel? and how can they find out what becomes of it?—for should they during their better moments chance to inquire for some well-remembered, but missing article, how soon they are told, if replied to at all: "Oh! you have torn it up!" or "You have destroyed it!"

But this answer too often fails to satisfy the mind of the patient. Yet why need an insane prisoner contend with, or refute, his "vigilance committee," who know they are masters of their situations? So robbery stalks boldly through asylum halls!

Are the superintendents and physicians who profess to practice the art of healing inside of those buildings—Fools?—or "Villains"?

To illustrate my meaning, or rather, to give my reason for proposing this question, which has been forced from me, by bitter experimental knowledge and observation, I will simply state, that any one, who is cognizant, day after day, week after week, and month after month, to the piteous pleading of human souls—for home, friends, and liberty—For pure air, pure water, pure food—For a voice of kindness—For a look of sympathy, or an expression of love—For everything that tends to cheer, and sustain—until they sink low, and still lower, into the abysmal depths of hopeless despair, and yet believe "it is best," to thus keep them imprisoned! and "for their good!"—*is a "fool."*

But otherwise, any one having cognizance of all this misery, daily seeing souls that are thus being wrecked by this unnatural —and therefore most unbearable—mode of torture—and yet retains them—still keeps them riveted fast-through indifference to their woes—or, through some interested politic—until the shackles that fettered them are loosened and broken, only by the power of death—*is a "villain."*

CONCLUSION

Let me ask the public a few questions. For what purpose were Lunatic Asylums built? What mean those strong, iron-barred windows, those solid, massive, spring-bolted doors, that slam and jar upon the ear with sad and heavy oppressiveness? What mean those bunches of keys, so often heard jingling through those buildings; or seen dangling from the belts of coarse vis-aged women, and stout, daring-faced girls; or carried in the hands of ponderous, broad-shouldered men, of rough physique, and great, stalwart boys, who unlock and bar those massive doors to pass in or out certain individuals or parties who may claim the privilege, liberty, or gratification of an idle curiosity, thus to come and go at their own option?

Does not the very name of the building, Lunatic Asylum, with its peculiarly significant structure, and its mode of admittance, indicate it to be a place for the confinement of the insane? Again let me ask, are not those buildings erected, and all their expenditures met by the people? And are they not therefore State property?

Now, let me come right home, and ask Ohio, what was the original motive or design that founded these institutions in her midst? And what is the present motive or design she has in sustaining them? Was it not a benevolent object that prompted and forwarded their erection, for the purpose, not only of se-curing the safety of the public against lunatics, but, also to pro-vide for these unfortunate beings a comfortable refuge or home, for an indefinite time, where they should receive such care and attention, from persons paid by the State for their services, as will be most conducive to their restoration and well-being?

Now, I will ask the public a few more questions: Is the ob-ject or design of these asylums being effected? How many of the people who aid in supporting these institutions know anything of their real character? How many, in their own quiet homes, think, or care, that these poor, helpless sufferers are being sub-jected to the most shameless impositions? . . .

I still cannot yield this subject of Insane Asylums without a few more words, in order to show more plainly the necessity of a change in the now-existing laws of my native state, in regard to the mode of admittance of persons, as patients, into them.

Now the law of admittance of persons into asylums, as it stands on the statute books of Ohio to-day, grants liberty to any physician who may be termed "respectable,"—and one may pass for "respectable" and yet be knave or fool—to file an affi-davit in the office of the Probate judge, or before the magnate, in the resident county of the parties, to the effect that a certain individual is insane. And by this act that person can be deprived of his or her personal liberty!

And the hosts of patients, that are being injuriously dragged into asylums—by this one-doctor's opinion—is costing the State a vast deal more money than the simple expense of granting to every one a jury trial before admittance could; while, so many who are now not only being deprived of their liberty, but their life, by the present mode of admittance, would most undoubtedly be saved—both liberty and life—by the decision of an intelligent body of jurors.

In regard to the position before the public of one who has once been an inmate—as a patient, as they are called, but far more truthfully, as a slave—in one of those "Inquisitorial Prisons." It is a truth that can be clearly asserted and proven, that the ills of life are made tenfold more difficult to meet for one who bears the asylum stamp—than before that curse was fixed upon them!

In conclusion I will add, that I am not solicitous for any new code of law for the admittance of persons as patients into the Ohio Insane Hospital, in the hope of any benefit that I may directly derive from it—for I am fully content in regard to the matter of my ever being a patient in one of them again—for, even should I become a maniac—which is very improbable, since I have been in the crucible and furnace in which they are manufactured by scores, at asylums, and yet escaped that doom! —my friends, I am confident, would not forsake me, in my present condition of health, or ever suffer me to enter a place so detestable to me—as a lunatic asylum. But it is for you and your fathers and mothers—your husbands and wives—your brothers and sisters—your children and friends—that I desire not only a new code of laws, for their admittance as patients into these hospitals, but also laws for their benefit and protection when inside.

Lydia A. Smith

(1865–1871)

THE HOSPITAL

The asylum is situated about a mile—perhaps a little more than a mile—from the principal business part of Kalamazoo. You approach the asylum building from the west Schoolcraft Road. The buildings stand on a high elevation, and as you arrive within sight of the towers and domes, which flash and sparkle in the sunlight, you are reminded of some ancient tower. The grounds about the asylum, until within a few years, presented a dreary and forbidding aspect. Now you are greeted with more display and show of modern improvements. The grounds have been put under a better state of cultivation, and additional building has been done at great expense to the state. The asylum building, which is occupied by the lady patients now, can be approached by the front walk, or by a more circuitous route, taking the side path a little north of the building. Suppose we take this path and follow it up until we come to the coal car, thence down to the water works back of the asylum

Lydia A. Smith, excerpts from Behind the Scenes; or, Life in an Insane Asylum, *1878.*

building; then we will take a more circuitous route still, until we come to the barn and cattle stalls. Judging from the appearance of the barn, the cattle and swine, you would conclude the patients fared pretty well. We stop and visit the gentlemen's wards, which are kept in good order as a general thing. Some of them are furnished nicely,—with games and amusements of various kinds. Everything we see so far looks quite pleasant and attractive. We leave the gentlemen's asylum and continue the beaten path until we approach the old asylum building again. We enter at the front door, and if we have our admission ticket we are ushered into the reception-room, there to hear a glowing account of what is being done by the master mind of E. H. Vandusen [superintendent]. Then you are shown through the kitchen department, laundry, etc.; then back through the chapel and down again and through No. 10 hall, the pride and glory of the institution. You are now ready to go away, highly pleased. You have seen the great asylum of notoriety. But have you seen all you came to see? Have you been in any of the sideshows? Well, they "don't amount to much." But come, let us go together a little further behind the scenes, behind the bolted doors and barred windows, back to the dens of misery. Oh, no, you don't want to go. Very well, then, we will wait here behind the screen, and see how this thing is managed. If we stay long enough we may be able to see through the flimsy guise which covers the slimy serpent.

On the patient's arrival at the asylum they are first put into a bath. This is necessary and perfectly right, if done in a proper way. In a most inhuman manner I was plunged into a bath, the water of which was not quite boiling hot, and held down by a strong grip on my throat, until I felt a strange sensation, and everything began to turn black. Just at this time I heard a per-

son say to the unnatural brute who was acting as attendant:
"Oh, my! Let her up quick; she is black in the face." (The
person who made this remark, I afterwards learned was the matron of the institution.) When I became conscious I found myself being jerked from one side to the other, with my hands
confined in the stocks, or "muff," as it is termed at the asylum,
and a stout leather belt attached to an iron buckle, was around
me. This belt is sufficiently long to fasten at the back, so as to
let the patient walk, but closely confined; or to fasten to a seat,
or bench, thus keeping the patient in a sitting position, which is
very tiresome, especially when one is obliged to remain in that
position any length of time. At this particular time I was not
fastened in a seat, but was taken (or rather jerked) into a small
division off from the main hall, and thrown into a "crib." This
is a square box, on which is a cover, made to close and lock, and
has huge posts, separated so as to leave a small space between
for ventilation. The strap attached to the "muff" was fastened
to the "crib" in such a manner as to tighten around my waist,
and across the pit of my stomach, with such a pressure that it
actually seemed to me that I could not breathe. My feet were
fastened to the foot of the "crib" so tight, and remained there
so long, that when they did unfasten them they were swollen so
that it was impossible for me to stand upon them. A short time
after I was placed in this "delightful" position, this same inhuman monster [the attendant] came to me with a cup in one hand
and a wedge in the other. This wedge was five or six inches
long, one inch thick at one end, and tapered down to an eighth
of an inch in thickness, and was used to force the mouth open,
so that medicine, etc., could be poured down the throat of the
patient. I soon felt the weight of the attendant on me, with one
knee pressing directly on my stomach, and one hand, like the
grip of a tiger, on my head. The wedge was then forced into

one side of my mouth, crowding out a tooth in its progress—a tooth which had been filled not long before—causing the most excruciating pain. I cannot tell why, unless it was convulsions, caused by the great pressure on my stomach, but my teeth were set, my lips seemed glued together, and I could not have opened my mouth, even had I known what they wanted me to do. Crash! Crash! went another of my teeth, and another, until five were either knocked out or broken off. I lay in a pool of blood that night. Not content with knocking my teeth out and forcing the medicine down me, which I would have willingly taken had I known what they wanted me to do, the attendant, after giving me the medicine, which was all that was required of her, clinched my throat, while her teeth grated together with rage for the trouble I had given her. The grip on my throat was not a gentle touch by any means, neither were the raps which came thick and fast on both sides of my head and face, meant for tokens of love. The cover of the "crib" was then shut down with a slam, and this unnatural specimen of humanity flouted herself out of the narrow space, locked the door, and I was left alone in this awful condition.

This was my first experience in an insane asylum. I will give you some idea, my patient reader, a "faint idea," how the drugs are forced down a patient. One attendant clinches the patient's hair, jerking her suddenly backward on the floor; another plants her knees directly on the pit of the patient's stomach, while another sits on their knees, holding them down; and the fourth one pries the mouth open with the wedge; and, with the assistance of the attendant who has hold of the patient's hair, succeeds in getting the contents of the cup down the patient's throat by pinching their nose and choking them, nearly strangling them. . . .

It is a very fashionable and easy thing now to make a person out to be insane. If a man tires of his wife, and is befooled after some other woman, it is not a very difficult matter to get her in an institution of this kind. Belladonna and chloroform will give her the appearance of being crazy enough, and after the asylum doors have closed upon her, adieu to the beautiful world and all home associations. I ask you, my dear friends, you who are a wife and mother, what would be your feelings were you torn from your children, your home, and all that you hold dear on earth, and thrust into an institution of this kind, and what would your appearance be? Did you ever stop to think? You might plead and beg; it would all be taken for insanity. Yes, all you could say and all you could do would only be some symptom of the fatal disease. If you were quiet and passive, even submissive, you would be reported as a hopeless case; but if you would rave and storm, as almost any one would, you would be put in the close room. Perhaps you do not know what that is; well, it is called the cell at the asylum, and if you should once get in there it would be very doubtful if you ever came out alive. When a person is put in a cell they at the asylum know what it means. And when once there you need never hope for anything better.

Anna Agnew

(1878–1885)

I presume I am one in whom the insane temperament predominates in a marked degree since, in a retrospective view of my life almost to infancy, I can recall many peculiarities of character not usual in children—aspirations and longings, repeated attempts at accomplishing things beyond childish attainment, with their consequent failures. And I can recall days of gloom—when too young yet to have even heard of the traditional "silver lined clouds"—the memory of which, even now, makes me shudder, that a child should be so hopeless, even for one moment!

I think I was born with a suicidal tendency; and in every trouble of my life, real or fancied, this was my predominant impulse—the hope by this means of escaping from an impatiently borne life. And I do not remember the time, when opportunity suggested the trial—such as standing upon an eleva-

Anna Agnew, excerpts from From Under the Cloud or, Personal Reminiscences of Insanity, *1886.*

tion, or being upon water of sufficient depth, that I had not to exercise the utmost strength of will to control the impulse to then and there cross the invisible line, and be free from the tormenting, persistent feeling of pursuit and unrest. To escape, if possible, from the terrible shadowy something constantly haunting me, whose influence made itself felt in my happiest moments, giving character even to my dreams, and whose climax was insanity! I often wonder, now, if my life might not have been different—surely it would have been brighter—had there been some one to whom I could have unbosomed myself; to whom I could have talked freely of these shadows that so oppressed me. I was proud, willful, and not always an obedient child. But to my father never intentionally disobedient or disrespectful. And from him I inherited my most pronounced traits of character.

I wonder of whom I got my pride. And I wonder greatly of what I was proud. In imagination I can see my father's troubled face, and hear his anxious voice, as he said once to me, when I—then a young girl—was giving utterance of some grievance in an emphatic manner: "Mark my word, my daughter! Your pride will be brought low, before you die."

On the night of November nineteenth—seventy-six—I sat sewing upon a garment for one of my children, until quite late, but put it away not quite done! And I never finished it! (Something had come over me!) I wakened the following Sunday morning, bathed in a cold, clammy perspiration (with an inexpressibly horrible sensation, as though falling—falling into some dreadful place of darkness! I had not the strength to speak, or move! And a cold, shadowy something seemed settling down upon me—indescribable, but altogether horrible!).

When fully awake, I recognized my condition! For the second time within the year I was completely helpless from "nervous prostration"! And, startling as a flash of lightning in a clear sky, came the revelation, this "something!" that had been with me all my life! walking by my side! invisible, but felt even in my happiest moments! haunting me, and threatening to overwhelm me at some unexpected, happy moment, had come! and it was insanity!

And then it was, as has so heartlessly been said of me, "I deliberately folded my hands, and announced my intention of being sick." My hands were folded! my work taken out of them! But it was not I who did it! They were busy, helping hands before! A power stronger than mine made them helpless! They were horribly folded—and for six miserable years only busied themselves in fruitless attempts to end my wretched existence. All life, all beauty, all brightness was gone from me! And yet I could not die! Oh! ye whose hearts are tender, pity me!

Unfortunately, for all concerned, I was not taken to the asylum for a period of several years after the time when common sense, if not common humanity, should have decided that such was the proper place for me. I sincerely believe that the miserable record of those years, the impressions made and received by me, when my case was so cruelly, or ignorantly, which? misunderstood outside of the asylum, made seven years inside of its walls a necessity, for which I must hold my immediate family, in a measure, responsible, granting at the same time, they intended kindness to me in keeping me home. But I was neither treated as an insane, nor yet wholly responsible woman. Often, not with the consideration shown a willful child. At times charged with being a hypocrite. Of feigning insanity to evade the responsibilities of my home duties. Of acting the fool. Of simply having the devil in me.

I had been an inmate of the asylum about nine months, and was standing one morning, as I frequently did, at the window, wishing, oh, so anxiously, for a newspaper. Just at this moment our supervisoress touched my arm and said, "Come with me, Mrs. Agnew," and walking down the hall to my room, opened the door, and there stood my husband. I think, for a moment or so, I never was so happy. It was his first visit to me. And only a moment ago I was feeling so utterly wretched and alone. But my husband had come, and he did care something for me after all. After I had entered the room, and closed the door, he stood looking at me, but not speaking a word until I said, "For heaven's sake, don't stand there staring at me in such a manner as that; sit down and say something to me; ask me something, or I shall scream through sheer nervousness." So he took the chair I offered him, drew it closely up to mine, and gazing into my eyes, said: "Were you insane when you were married?" Not one single, little word of kindness or gesture of tenderness, not the shadow of a greeting; simply this cruel, calculating question. Evidently, he had even then formed the determination that I should never leave that asylum alive. I did not then think this, however, and answered, more assuredly, "I was not insane when we were married." I have changed my opinion since then, materially, and willingly admit I was insane, and my most pronounced symptom was that I married him. After a time I said, "Have you nothing to say to me? Can't you tell me something of my children?" "Your children!" he replied. "Why, I hadn't an idea you cared to hear from them. You don't certainly presume to profess to love them?" Oh, it was inhuman, to so torture a poor, helpless woman; yet I doubt if in his egotism he realized my suffering. He asked if I wished to see my children, and I said, "No, I did not dare to see them," and this, I presume, was additional proof of his charitable(?) soul, of my hatred of my children, and he said, "Very well I will never bring those children to see you until you ask me to." After obtaining permission from the physician in charge, he took me out walking, and while there, my outraged feelings got the better of my pride, and I charged him with having lost all regard or affection for me, and he answered, "Oh, no, Anna, you are quite mistaken; I love you just as well as I ever did"; and then followed rapid questions, to which he demanded answers that proved the nature of his regard for me, past and present, and from that moment my faith in his purity was a thing of the past. Another "delusion" gotten clear of.

One subject I feel it is my duty, for the sake of like sufferers, to speak freely of, even at the risk of offending sensitive, fastidious readers. I must enter my most emphatic protest against patients being compelled to eat, and particularly of being held and forcibly made to swallow food. Certainly if I could make the human physician understand that even now I am made deathly sick at the mere recollection of my horribly disgusting "delusions" regarding the nature of the food I was compelled to swallow for weeks together, they would, without a single exception, strike that clause from their "ward rules." Think of it for a moment: at times I would feel fearfully hungry, but the moment I was seated at the table, every single article would become alive, creeping, squirming vermin of all disgusting characters was in the food put upon my plate; and when, as was natural, I could not put those vile things into my mouth, an attendant would hold my hands behind me, and another pour liquids down my throat, choking me so I must swallow or strangle human filth. Raw eggs, without a suspicion of salt, pepper or any thing else to make them in the least palatable, were freely choked into my rebellious stomach; and the reality of my dreadful "delusion" would not be more disgusting to me now than it was then. But I was helpless, and so are thousands of other poor women. Under that man's reign I have seen those heartless girls fill a quart cup with a mixture of all the vegetables on the table, then salt and pepper and mustard by the spoonful, and after filling up the cup with vinegar, stir up the nasty mess, and feed it by tablespoonsful to some miserable wretch, crowding it down the unwilling throat—at the same time taunting and giggling over the misery—all this to teach them to "eat decently, like other folks." I pity the lowest wretch that ever fell into their clutches.

In a letter from my sister, in which she asks: "What do you mean by night medicine?" "Have you ever been a victim of opiates?" I did not know until a year later that my husband, in a letter to my sister, charged me with being also an "opium eater," a drug I never even so much as tasted, to my knowledge, and I answered her thus: "Night medicine" is a preparation of chloral, and it was given me the first night I spent in this place, and has been continued every night since, excepting as occasionally it would occur to Dr. Walker that probably I might be deriving some comfort from its use, and he would discontinue its use for a time. At such periods I was wild and wretched in the extreme! Not that it served its purpose with me—that of producing sleep! It simply kept me from continuous thought, and kept me in bed too, since its effect upon me was to make me drunk—so that I would fall helpless upon the floor, unable, without the assistance of the "night watch," to get up again. But deprived of it, all night long I would walk the floor wringing my hands, with my familiar spirit ever by my side, with its horrible accusations repeated.

My husband visited me for the last time Dec. 17, 1883, at which time I was confined to my bed, as was the case and had been periodically for several years, during which periods I suffered intensely, relief only being afforded by morphine administered by my physician. But at this stage of my convalescence I was able to relieve the monotony somewhat by reading, and had at the time on my bed a book in biology, in which I told him I was deeply interested. He looked at it and said, "What sort of thing is it?" And I answered: "You will understand that better after you read it." "Oh," he answered, "I have no time to read for the cultivation of my intellect. My 'time' is employed solely in getting bread and butter for 'my children.'" He had persistently claimed an exclusive ownership in our children, and I told him he should certainly take out a "patent on that right" as something a little out of the ordinary. He spent a portion of the afternoon with me, and during the time I insisted that he should read a number of letters written me by my sister, in which she urged me to keep up good heart and I would soon be able to go home to my family. He said, "You seem from these replies to have written very freely to your sister." And as he was leaving he said: "I reckon you won't write to me!" One month later, after having had special treatment and close attention from Dr. Sarah Stockton, and finding myself greatly improved, I wrote him quite a lengthy letter, wrote just as kindly as I felt. Told him how much better I was, and how encouraged I felt at the prospect of getting well. I asked him to send me a good pair of glasses and some postage stamps. Within three days his answer came! A scrap of blank paper, inclosing twenty-eight cents in postage stamps, in a sealed envelope directed to me! I immediately returned him a note for the same amount of stamps, "payable to him or his order one day after date!" and within a month was out of his debt! And the battle had opened between us!

After my complete recovery, during the year in which I was in a measure the "guest of the State of Indiana," I was allowed free access to several fine medical libraries, also had permission to read valuable authorities on points of especial interest to me.

Through the thoughtfulness of Dr. Thomas, arrangements were made for my employment in the sewing room, the trustee agreeing to pay me a small sum monthly, dating from March 5, 1884, and continuing until my discharge, April 21, 1885. It was a great relief from the monotony of ward life, and the money, too, was very acceptably received, and though I was only expected to spend a part of the day serving, I gave my whole time exclusively to my work; I had been a pensioner—upon the bounty of the State—for so many years, that I felt it my duty to make all the return in my power.

I remember with amusement the perfect storm of indignation that was aroused among the attendants when soon after Dr. Fletcher's appointment as superintendent, he abolished "mechanical restraints" of all descriptions. This action of the superintendent, together with the fact of his making a bonfire of the restraints in the presence of the majority of patients, and accompanied by religious services, singing, prayer, etc., was at the time commented upon in all the Western newspapers, very few commending the wholesale sacrifice, many considering (while they did not directly approve of the system of "restraints,") that the manner of getting clear of the objectionable articles, might have been managed with less of the sensational phase.

But the attendants, what a blow at their dignity! What a

curtailment of long established fearfully abused power! How they did sputter. Only think of it. Not allowed to "twist arms," can't even "camisole," Why don't you think, the carpenter came in to-day and took out the very last one of our "restraint chairs." How ever we are to manage the set in our ward, the Lord only knows. And don't you forget it, every single one of the "nasty things" knew before two days that we did not dare restrain them any more. Oh, its just too bad. I believe it is generally conceded that the change was a beneficial one, both to patients and conscientious attendants. The wards are sweeter—as to atmosphere—and pleasanter to the sight. Since the majority of "restraints" are suggestive of possible outrages in the hands of irresponsible people, I have frequently heard such remarks as the following from the attendants: "Who is the best judge of the propriety of restraining a patient, the physician who only sees the person for a few moments each day, when of course the patient knows enough to be quiet, or 'us attendants'?" "Knows enough to be quiet!"—knows enough always to feel that in a kind and considerate physician they have a "friend at court," and it is well indeed not to give this authority into the hands of persons who do not know enough to be trusted; to remember that these persons, so unfortunate as to be obliged to stay there, are human.

Men, all over this beautiful land of ours, it is your mother, wife, daughter, and sister who are being thus outraged. In every asylum in the land some such scenes are daily enacted, and it will be so, must be, until state laws are so amended as to make such abuses impossible. The willing hands and sympathetic hearts of our noble band of superintendents and their corps of assistant physicians must be encouraged and strengthened by furnishing them experienced nurses, in place of present thoughtless, heartless girls. The establishment of suitable "training schools" will necessarily require time, but, in the meantime, there are hundreds of worthy needy women, widowed mothers, who, having themselves suffered sorrow, have pitying hearts toward their afflicted sisters. Such should speedily replace the others, most of whom consider they are doing the different states honor, since they condescend to accept their money by simply gracing the wards of these asylums for the insane.

Reforms are being instituted all over the land in hospital treatment, and the humane heads of these institutions need only the hearty cooperation of the law-makers to make these hospitals asylums indeed to the unfortunate victims of fate and heritage. Let the public make this a personal matter, since there is scarcely a family exempt from this fearfully increasing malady. The bolt may strike some beloved member of your immediate family circle today, my friend, with whom I am talking; and lightning strikes twice or thrice, sometimes, in the same household.

Lemira Clarissa Pennell

(1880)

SUGGESTED REFORMS

*F*irst.—That every doctor after being called to examine a person for insanity shall immediately notify the proper authorities of such application, stating who is the applicant, and what is the ground for charging insanity.

Second.—That all persons confined in an asylum, public or private, for the purpose of being treated for mental disease, shall be allowed to sleep as many hours as they wish, never to be required to prepare for, and eat breakfast by, gaslight, nor at any time to be aroused from needed slumber to take meals or medicine.

Third.—That the excessive habit of using opium, tobacco, or intoxicating liquors, shall disqualify any man for Superintendent, or a subordinate position in any hospital.

Fourth.—That any person charged with insanity, and examined as the law directs, not being found insane, may forth-

Lemira Clarissa Pennell, excerpts from This Red Book Is Partly a Reprint of What Was Published in 1883, and Later, *1886.*

with choose three persons as a Committee, who shall at once rigidly examine the party who made the allegation of insanity, and determine what amount of compensation, if any, is due the injured person. The expense of the Committee shall be paid by the party examined, who shall testify under oath.

Mr. Chairman and Gentlemen:

As the subject of this hearing is one liable at any moment to become a personal matter to any member of this Committee, and my own personal grievance is in their hands for consideration, I believe the class I am most desirous to serve can be best assisted by personal relations of real facts—designed to illustrate the existing causes for what is so popularly treated of, as the increase of insanity.

First.—When I first met Dr. Jelly, or rather at the second interview, he said, "At least fifty times a year I am called on to examine people for insanity who are no more insane than myself." I said, "Do you give those persons any certificate showing that you do not find them of unsound mind?" "Certainly not; that is not my business. Besides, some other doctor may very likely differ from me." Everybody knows that is so, and that plenty of doctors can be found who will certify that they have examined a person they have never seen. The doctors who certified in my case proclaimed their own infamy by asking "remuneration for expenses incurred in the Pennell suit, on the ground that they refused to certify until the mayor promised them that if any litigation grew out of it the city should pay the bills." Ostensibly the City paid three hundred and eighty-five dollars, but really the church paid it. Now, is it not a fearful thing that human lives are thus signed away? And it is a well-known fact that this is common. Many a doctor admits this, and says, "Why, only a few weeks or days since I was asked to certify that a person was insane. I said: No, thank you." Now there is no way in the world to injure a person like charging them with insanity. Now, then, if doctors were required to register who asks them to certify, with or without an examination, and what is the ground for charging insanity, it would not be so likely that "scores of people would go to Dr. Jelly, and ask him to commit Mrs. L. C. Pennell to an insane hospital," as he says they have done, but will not tell who they are. A doctor first told me of this, and that Dr. Jelly thought I would become insane; I saw Dr. Jelly, and learned from himself that this was true. The power of an official person is immense.

Second.—That all persons confined in any asylum shall be allowed needed sleep, would seem at first glance not expedient to legislate on. But when it is remembered that all persons who live to report the horrors of insane hospitals dwell on the remembrance of this feature of treatment with the same accuracy, that the entrance of the doctor into the bed-chamber of an insane woman at half-past five or six A.M., is as much an outrage as if she were sane; that to arouse them from needed sleep by unbuttoning night-gowns, stripping down the sheets, and hauling them out of bed at unseemly hours, is not always the work of attendants, and if the Supt. is not responsible, who should be? An insane hospital is not a very good place to sleep in any time, for reasons which need not be recounted here and now; insomnia is almost sure to be one of the characteristics of insanity, and insane people are no more sure of sleeping at the proper time than sane people are, and if after a restless, sleepless night they fall into the sleep of exhaustion just before the early summons to "hurry up, and be quick about it, too," the enforcement of the rules of the institution is the surest way in the world to prevent recovery. And the brutal methods of enforcing such rules call loudly for a law which will secure to insane people the right to a chance for mental preservation.

Third.—That excessive use of opium or intoxicating liquors by Superintendents or subordinates in insane hospitals is such a crime as calls for legislative prohibition, no one for an instant doubts who has looked with open eyes, will fail to see. More than a year ago, a doctor in charge of a Charitable Institution in this City, said, "I've got an item for you, Mrs. Pennell; a man was discharged from our place for getting drunk again and again; he went right to Danvers, and engaged as attendant." Not long after, I read in a paper that "a patient had been killed by jumping from a window at Danvers, and nobody to blame, as usual." Total abstinence from all which stupefies the senses is of the greatest importance in the managers of the insane, whose varying moods demand the most careful care; and as a large share of insanity is due to the effects of tobacco, and the patient must be restrained in its use, it is very inconsistent for those in charge to indulge themselves in the loathsome, filthy habits which have wrecked the health and reason of the madmen.

I have talked of this feature of the bill with hundreds of people, many of them doctors, some of whom use tobacco moderately, that is smoke occasionally, and fully endorse the need of the entire absence of the poison. And opium would not be used by homeopathists or eclectics, so that it would not be hard to find those who could fill these places, and having ambition to report a favorable change in the condition of patients, less need would remain for room for incurables, chronics. Nine months among the insane, which did not improve, but only made me more dangerous, and what I have learned since, has shown me what official eyes do not choose to see.

Fourth.—The need of immediate protection, with provision for paying the Committee chosen to serve in behalf of those charged falsely with insanity, seems too obvious to require a great deal said in the support of this fourth clause of the bill. Let it be legal for arbitration to determine what amount of injury Frank Sanborn can do by such letters as he has written about me, and such statements as he has made to the Judiciary Committee that he did instruct Dr. Jelly to incarcerate me under the Emergency Law, that I was of unsound mind, so not responsible, &c., and the complication in my case would soon be shorn of its formidable proportions, and many another who has been robbed of all that was most precious to them would be free to enjoy their constitutional right to life, liberty, and the pursuit of happiness, with whatever they had been deprived of restored to them. When for any reason a person is wanted put out of the way, insane hospitals stand with outstretched arms ready to embrace them. Brute force, as has been used in my case, but too often is substituted for the preliminaries supposed to precede commitments; once inside that hell of torment, association with a class which visitors frequently faint away without advancing among, strikes terror to the ordinary mortal which could easily be attributed to insanity. The cost and responsibility of getting one out is immense, then there is no redress for the wrong, no penalty for the wrong-doer. I could fill quires of paper with such cases I have been asked to look into in this Commonwealth.

Clarissa Caldwell Lathrop

(1880–1882)

W e drove off, and after a pleasant ride of about a mile, I saw before us a beautiful lawn dotted with shrubbery which was shut in by a high iron gate. A carriage drive and walk led to a large stone building which stretched across the entire width of the grounds. The entrance to this building was approached through massive Corinthian columns.

We could not read the invisible inscription over the entrance, written in the heart's blood of the unfortunate inmates, "Who enters here must leave all hope behind." Had I done so, I would have shrunk back in terror from the fate that awaited me, and a thrill of horror would have drawn from me a piteous cry for mercy that might have moved the stony heart of the unfeeling young doctor. Silent and grim, no sign was given to its human prey as I innocently entered that living tomb that fatal day,—the nineteenth of October, 1880. Little had I thought two weeks before when I had attended to my daily

Clarissa Caldwell Lathrop, excerpts from A Secret Institution, *1890.*

school duties as usual, that I would be brought here to die! Little did I dream that the most precious boon known to man was to be taken from me; that here I should beg in vain for liberty! Here were no noble, humane hearts to regard my appeals!

By this time we had reached the centre of this long hall and some steps. We went up these steps which led into a bare room furnished with a few wooden benches and chairs, which I afterwards learned was a reception room for the patients to receive their friends in. Through this room we passed into another hall, which to my terror I discovered was full of people whom at the first glance I inferred were dangerous lunatics. Then for the first time I realized I was on the ward of an insane asylum. Terror-stricken, I imagined each person was ready to attack me or do me some personal violence. I shrunk back and hesitated about going further.

Then we came to the back wards. Here a scene met my horrified gaze which I was totally unprepared for! On the floor, on straw mattresses, lay poor, sick, or insane women, chained or strapped by the wrists to the floor, huddled together like sheep. As I gazed on some of these delicate women, sleeping on the floor probably for the first time in their life until they came to this place, and thought of the almost empty ward I had just left with its comfortable beds, and recalled the fact that many patients who were perfectly sane and who might as well be on the first ward were kept on the back wards as a matter of discipline, and who were constantly associated with raving maniacs,—the utter heartlessness of this treatment filled me with indignation and sympathy. I pondered in silence on the fate which compelled these poor women, (many undoubtedly the former inmates of comfortable homes,) to sleep on these hard boards when there was one empty bed in the entire building unoccupied.

Her Incarceration

Had I lived in a lonely country place, the change would not have been so great, and perhaps not as trying. Now this isolation in itself seemed unbearable. How I longed to go out in the free, fresh air! As I looked at the beautiful lawn through the cruel iron bars which shut me out from the world, the blinding tears would come into my longing eyes, only to be repressed by anxious fear. I had seen enough to learn that it was not best to allow any one to see me weep, lest it might be said in addition to their former absurd statements, that I was a victim of Melancholia. I consequently studied a calm appearance, and said little of my repressed feeling to any one.

I had been in the habit of remaining in my room the greater part of the time, avoiding the sight of visitors and patients. Towards evening I would retire to the veranda, a small enclosure at the end of the hall which was shut in with glass windows, barred across with iron bars, where I walked to and fro for exercise, and if possible to exhaust myself, to secure sleep, and also in order to retain and increase my strength. Mine had been an active, busy life, filled with the daily occupations which had been my strength and comfort for years, and this confinement was torture in the extreme. I felt as if I could dash myself against the cruel iron bars and cry aloud for liberty. As I paced to and fro impatiently, I was reminded of the little bear I had watched with sympathy in Central Park as he walked back and forth in his little cage.

The affidavit of two physicians! What did that mean? I inquired of the patients and attendants, and then learned that the certificates of two physicians as to the insanity of the patient was necessary to insure imprisonment in an asylum. Soon after, as I did not receive any response to my letter to Dr. Grey I asked to see Dr. Brush, and questioned him as to the prospect of my release.

"Why must I stay here?" I asked.

"Because you think you were poisoned," he replied.

"But," I said, "I do not know whether I was or not. I have always been open to proof and conviction."

"You claim you were placed here by conspiracy," he said, and then turned away and left me.

I had never made use of that word, in fact had not thought of it exactly in that light, but the fitness of his words struck me as too appropriate. I could not deny his statement. Besides, I was too much overcome by the futility of my appeals.

During the second summer of my sojourn in the asylum, a poor widow was incarcerated there who was perfectly sane. She was entered, I think, on the same ward I was on, the first ward. She was a poor washerwoman, and had supported a family of seven children by her daily labor. A doctor who resided in the same village desired her to wash for his family when he had company. She had refused to do so, as she had prior engagements. He told her she would be sorry, and one night on her return from work she found a man awaiting her who said he was sent from the poor master, and that she was to get ready and go with him to an insane asylum.

During the last year of my imprisonment, two events occurred of a public and sensational nature. The first was that great national calamity, when all alike, north and south, political friends and enemies, were shocked by the assassination of our noble President, Gen. Garfield. The news spread rapidly on the ward, and we were allowed the daily papers to read the particulars of the tragedy, and the details attendant upon his death. Later the accounts of the investigation as to the sanity of Guiteau, which I selected from the old papers sent to the asylum from the newspaper offices, especially the expert testimony given in that famous trial, was read by me with unceasing interest, particularly that of Dr. Grey, the supposed wonderful insanity expert, who was called upon to testify in this celebrated case. With what bitterness I read his carefully expressed opinions of the sanity of the prisoner, and his definitions of insanity, and how I hated and despised him more and more as I read the elaborate and detailed reports! I felt, however, that this trial was a great source of education to me, situated as I was and having the objects of study before me daily, in fact brought into constant contact with them.

I thought with exasperation: "Dr. Grey can go to Washington to see a man like Guiteau, and can testify to his belief in the sanity of an unfortunate man who commits a murder without any particular provocation, a man evidently of impaired perceptions, because he receives a large sum from the Government for so doing; but a helpless patient who was kidnapped and trapped into his asylum, because she made repeated efforts to protect her own life and that of her family from any possible danger, he calls insane. He confines her indefinitely in his own institution which he never visits, and where he knows nothing whatever of what takes place within its walls, unless he visits it in the night, when we are unconscious of his presence.

I had been in the asylum about a year and a half when

the second incident occurred. One noon we had just finished our dinner. We were sitting at the table, awaiting the signal which was always given for departure, when Miss Morris said:

"Ladies, I wish to tell you that Dr. Grey was shot last night. We do not know whether the wound is dangerous or not."

There were no remarks made as we were not allowed to converse at meals, and the impression was doubtless diverse. I felt no sympathy for this man, believing it a just retribution, and could not refrain from saying to a patient who was in sympathy with me:

"The wonder is, not that he is shot now, but that he was not shot long before!"

"Ah," I thought; "if the fathers and brothers of many of the unfortunate women who are confined in this building only knew the truth they would come in a body and tear this doctor and his assistants to pieces, and pull down the walls of this building over their heads!" Why had Dr. Grey been spared so long? was my query.

GENERAL ABUSES

I wish to call attention to two important facts, both of which are the greatest protection to asylum abuses. The most powerful evil is the first which I shall call your attention to, and is what has been denominated "the one man power" of asylum superintendent, whose fiat is final as to the sanity or insanity of his unfortunate patient. Even if zealous and conscientious in his work, it is impossible that he should have a personal knowledge and interest in each individual committed to his charge, when so many hundred are herded together in one enormous building; and if unscrupulous, and careless or indifferent to all but pecuniary advantages, as was Dr. Grey, he knows he is accountable to no one for his abuse or neglect of duty, his conscious supremacy having a tendency to create indifference on his part, even in regard to revelations by the public press.

The principle studied by asylum superintendents is to create the idea that there is some very mysterious and skillful method of treatment required for the insane; whereas, if the facts were known and the truth brought to light, there is little real so-called "special treatment" given save simple food, methodical rules of living, uniform hours for meals, regular hours for rising and retiring, (6 to half past 6 o'clock on the "disturbed" wards, 8 o'clock on the second ward, and 9 o'clock on the first or convalescent ward) and restraint or sequestration when a patient is violent. Of course where insanity proceeds from disease, remedies must be applied which are used in any ordinary medical hospital for the same difficulty, the removal of the cause leading to a natural restoration to sanity. In an acute form of typhoid fever when the patient is called delirious, the disease is understood and the cause located and no one calls such a patient insane, because it is known that on the disappearance of the fever the mind will resume its former vigor; so it is with insanity, which the most prominent alienists attribute to disease alone. The disease may have been induced by a variety of causes, which at first baffles his skill to determine, not having had constant opportunity to study his patient, but a conscientious and able physician, who has this privilege, would soon be able to determine the cause of the difficulty, and could then direct his healing powers to effect the restoration of a healthful condition, of a sound mind in a sound body.

CONCLUSION

To you, my friends, I reveal my heart and history, as I send forth this book as a plea for your sympathy and interest in the welfare of the insane, and as a means to this end, for ordinary hospital rules and treatment in place of the existing One Man Power over SECRET INSTITUTIONS. I have been obliged to lay aside this book for weeks and months at a time, as the memories of the horrors I was cognizant of crowded upon me and sickened me. It is a faint production of life in an asylum, which Dr. Grey himself once compared to a miniature city, with the same conflicting natures, tastes, temperaments and characteristics which mark our daily lives. An insane person's nature is not transformed by a temporary aberration,—his identity, his tastes, his aspirations may be diverted by sickness from their natural channel. Oh, that he might receive the tender, fostering care, the medical skill his condition demands! And when reason dawns once more on the clouded brain,—oh, that the afflicted one might have all the aids our civilization demands, and which an enlightened age can command, to ensure and retain his sanity! Then the time will not be far distant when our institutions for the insane can not be vast prisons and dens of iniquity to enrich venal asylum superintendents and to shield and foster crimes which can be so readily concealed and denied, and where sane people can be deprived ruthlessly of "liberty and the pursuit of happiness" by an unfeeling jailer, who fears no punishment because so securely entrenched in an institution which is supported at the expense of the State, from which he draws a revenue sufficiently large to enable him to crush his victim when she seeks to make known her sufferings and to obtain that vindication which her wrongs demand from a just and sympathetic public.

Charlotte Perkins Gilman

(1887)

COURTSHIP

There was the pleasure of association with a noble soul, with one who read and studied and cared for real things, of sharing high thought and purpose, of sympathy in many common deprivations and endurances. There was the natural force of sex-attraction between two lonely young people, the influence of propinquity.

Then, on my part, periods of bitter revulsion, of desperate efforts to regain the dispassionate poise, the balanced judgment I was used to. My mind was not fully clear as to whether I should or should not marry. On the one hand I knew it was normal and right in general, and held that a woman should be able to have marriage and motherhood, and do her work in the world also. On the other, I felt strongly that for me it was not right, that the nature of the life before me forbade it, that I ought to forego the more intimate personal happiness for complete devotion to my work.

A lover more tender, a husband more devoted, woman could not ask. He helped in the housework more and more as my strength began to fail, for something was going wrong from the first. The steady cheerfulness, the strong, tireless spirit sank away. A sort of gray fog drifted across my mind, a cloud that grew and darkened.

"Feel sick and remain so all day." "Walter stays home and does everything for me." "Walter gets breakfast." October 10th: "I have coffee in bed mornings while Walter briskly makes fires and gets breakfast." "O dear! That I should come to this!" By October 13th the diary stops altogether, until January 1, 1885. "My journal has been long neglected by reason of ill-health. This day has not been a successful one as I was sicker than for some weeks. Walter also was not very well, and stayed at home, principally on my account. He has worked for me and for us both, waited on me in every tenderest way, played to me, read to me, done all for me as he always does. God be thanked for my husband."

February 16th: "A well-nigh sleepless night. Hot, cold, hot, restless, nervous, hysterical. Walter is love and patience personified, gets up over and over, gets me warm winter green bromide, hot foot-bath, more bromide—all to no purpose."

Then, with impressive inscription: "March 23rd, 1885. This day, at about five minutes to nine in the morning, was born my child, Katharine."

> *Brief ecstasy. Long pain.*
> *Then years of joy again.*

Motherhood means giving. . . .
We had attributed all my increasing weakness and depres-

sion to pregnancy, and looked forward to prompt recovery now. All was normal and ordinary enough, but I was already plunged into an extreme of nervous exhaustion which no one observed or understood in the least. Of all angelic babies that darling was the best, a heavenly baby. My nurse, Maria Pease of Boston, was a joy while she lasted, and remained a lifelong friend. But after her month was up and I was left alone with the child I broke so fast that we sent for my mother, who had been visiting Thomas in Utah, and that baby-worshiping grandmother came to take care of the darling, I being incapable of doing that—or anything else, a mental wreck.

Presently we moved to a better house, on Humboldt Avenue near by, and a German servant girl of unparalleled virtues was installed. Here was a charming home; a loving and devoted husband; an exquisite baby, healthy, intelligent and good; a highly competent mother to run things; a wholly satisfactory servant—and I lay all day on the lounge and cried.

THE BREAKDOWN

In those days a new disease had dawned on the medical horizon. It was called "nervous prostration." No one knew much about it, and there were many who openly scoffed, saying it was only a new name for laziness. To be recognizably ill one must be confined to one's bed and preferably in pain.

That a heretofore markedly vigorous young woman, with every comfort about her, should collapse in this lamentable manner was inexplicable. "You should use your will," said earnest friends. I had used it, hard and long, perhaps too hard too long; at any rate it wouldn't work now.

"Force some happiness into your life," said one sympathizer. "Take an agreeable book to bed with you, occupy your mind with pleasant things." She did not realize that I was unable to read, and that my mind was exclusively occupied with unpleasant things. This disorder involved a growing melancholia, and that, as those know who have tasted it, consists of every painful mental sensation, shame, fear, remorse, a blind oppressive confusion, utter weakness, a steady brainache that fills the conscious mind with crowding images of distress.

The misery is doubtless as physical as a toothache, but a brain, of its own nature, gropes for reasons for its misery. Feeling the sensation fear, the mind suggests every possible calamity; the sensation shame—remorse—and one remembers every mistake and misdeeds of a lifetime, and grovels to the earth in abasement.

"If you would get up and do something you would feel better," said my mother. I rose drearily, and essayed to brush up the floor a little, with a dustpan and small whiskbroom, but soon dropped those implements exhausted, and wept again in helpless shame.

I, ceaselessly industrious, could do no work of any kind. I was so weak that the knife and fork sank from my hands—too tired to eat. I could not read nor write nor paint nor sew nor talk nor listen to talking, nor anything. I lay on that lounge and wept all day. The tears ran down into my ears on either side. I went to bed crying, woke in the night crying, sat on the edge of the bed in the morning and cried—from sheer continuous pain. Not physical, the doctors examined me and found nothing the matter.

The only physical pain I ever knew, besides dentistry and one sore finger, was having a baby, and I would rather have a baby every week than suffer as I suffered in my mind. A constant dragging weariness miles below zero. Absolute incapacity. Absolute misery. To the spirit it was as if one were an armless, legless, eyeless, voiceless cripple. Prominent among the tumbling suggestions of a suffering brain was the thought, "You did it yourself! You did it yourself! You had health and strength and hope and glorious work before you—and you threw it all away. You were called to serve humanity, and you cannot serve yourself. No good as a wife, no good as a mother, no good at anything. And you did it yourself!" . . .

The baby? I nursed her for five months. I would hold her close—that lovely child!—and instead of love and happiness, feel only pain. The tears ran down on my breast—Nothing was more utterly bitter than this, that even motherhood brought no joy.

The doctor said I must wean her, and go away, for a change. So she was duly weaned and throve finely on Mellins' Food, drinking eagerly from the cup—no bottle needed. With mother there and the excellent maid I was free to go.

Those always kind friends, the Channings, had gone to Pasadena to live, and invited me to spend the winter with them. Feeble and hopeless I set forth, armed with tonics and sedatives, to cross the continent. From the moment the wheels began to turn, the train to move, I felt better.

Leaving California in March, in the warm rush of its rich spring, I found snow in Denver, and from then on hardly saw the sun for a fortnight. I reached home with a heavy bronchial cold, which hung on long, the dark fog rose again in my mind, the miserable weakness—within a month I was as low as before leaving. . . .

This was a worse horror than before, for now I saw the stark fact—that I was well while away and sick while at home—a heartening prospect! Soon ensued the same utter prostration, the unbearable inner misery, the ceaseless tears. A new tonic had been invented, Essence of Oats, which was given me, and did some good for a time. I pulled up enough to do a little painting that fall, but soon slipped down again and stayed down. An old friend of my mother's dear Mrs. Diman, was so grieved at this condition that she gave me a hundred dollars and urged me to go away somewhere and get cured.

At that time the greatest nerve specialist in the country was Dr. S. W. Mitchell of Philadelphia. Through the kindness of a friend of Mr. Stetson's living in that city, I went to him and took "the rest cure"; went with the utmost confidence, prefacing the visit with a long letter giving "the history of the case" in a way a modern psychologist would have appreciated. Dr. Mitchell only thought it proved self-conceit. He had a prejudice against the Beechers. "I've had two women of your blood here already," he told me scornfully. This eminent physician was well versed in two kinds of nervous prostration; that of the business man exhausted from too much work, and the society woman exhausted from too much play. The kind I had was evidently beyond him. But he did reassure me on one point—there was no dementia, he said, only hysteria.

I was put to bed and kept there. I was fed, bathed, rubbed, and responded with the vigorous body of twenty-six. As far as he could see there was nothing the matter with me, so after a month of this agreeable treatment he sent me home, with this prescription:

"Live as domestic a life as possible. Have your child with you all the time." (Be it remarked that if I did but dress the baby it left me shaking and crying—certainly far from a healthy companionship for her, to say nothing of the effect on me.) "Lie down an hour after each meal. Have but two hours' intellectual life a day. And never touch pen, brush or pencil as long as you live."

I went home, followed those directions rigidly for months, and came perilously near to losing my mind. The mental agony grew so unbearable that I would sit blankly moving my head from side to side—to get out from under the pain. Not physical pain, not the least "headache" even, just mental torment, and so heavy in its nightmare gloom that it seemed real enough to dodge.

I made a rag baby, hung it on a doorknob and played with it. I would crawl into remote closets and under beds—to hide from the grinding pressure of that profound distress. . . .

Finally, in the fall of '87, in a moment of clear vision, we agreed to separate, to get a divorce. There was no quarrel, no blame for either one, never an unkind word between us, unbroken mutual affection—but it seemed plain that if I went crazy it would do my husband no good, and be a deadly injury to my child.

What this meant to the young artist, the devoted husband, the loving father, was so bitter a grief and loss that nothing would have justified breaking the marriage save this worse loss which threatened. It was not a choice between going and staying, but between going, sane, and staying, insane. If I had been of the slightest use to him or to the child, I would have "stuck it," as the English say. But this progressive weakening of the mind made a horror unnecessary to face; better for that dear child to have separated parents than a lunatic mother.

We had been married four years and more. This miserable condition of mind, this darkness, feebleness and gloom, had begun in those difficult years of courtship, had grown rapidly worse after marriage, and was now threatening utter loss; whereas I had repeated proof that the moment I left home I began to recover. It seemed right to give up a mistaken marriage.

1891–1920

WOMEN'S LIVES

*T*he turn of the century ushered in the second generation of New Women. These women were more independent, more rebellious, and more self-involved than the New Women who preceded them.[1] By and large, these New Women remained college-educated, reform-minded, and desirous of an independent life.[2] However, the New Women of the twentieth century distinguished themselves from their predecessors in one important way: they were the first generation of women who were openly sexual and who saw themselves not just as mothers and nurturers but also as sexual beings.[3]

The acknowledgment of sexuality as an essential component of a woman's nature engendered several very different responses. In 1898 Charlotte Perkins Gilman published her famous work *Women and Economics* in which she maintained that women used their sexuality in order to win the support and the protection of men.[4] Gilman wrote that rather than being liberated by her sexuality, a woman's reliance on sexual attractiveness was just one more way in which she allowed herself to be stereotyped and thus used by men.

Despite her opposition to sexual gamesmanship, Gilman was at least willing to acknowledge the existence of female sexuality. On the other hand, the proponents of "virtuous womanhood," Sheila Rothman's term for the asexual reformers who applied their mothering skills to the woes of the community, continued to deny the reality of female sexuality. They maintained that a woman's activities needed to be consistent with her moral superiority, her virtue, and her maternal nature.[5] The values of "virtuous womanhood" were echoed by then President Theodore Roosevelt, who declared that when a woman shirked her duty as wife and mother, she earned the contempt of her country.[6] The country's ambivalence about female sexuality was also mirrored in the nascent film industry, which continued to depict women as pure, shy, and submissive. Mary Pickford and Lillian Gish, two starlets of the early twentieth century, frequently portrayed heroines who were sexually naïve and virginal.[7]

Despite the prominence of New Women, the beginning acceptance of female sexuality, and the birth of the term "feminism," the image of woman as Mother remained very powerful during the early decades of the twentieth century. The twentieth century was declared the century of the child. Even women like independent and nontraditional Jane Addams referred to the power of the "family claim," which demanded that a woman devote herself to her husband and children if she was married, or to her family and relatives if she was not.[8]

Two new images that emerged at the turn of the century spoke to the attempt to combine the more worldly focus of the New Woman with the traditional images of Wife and Mother. The "scientific homemaker" was a woman involved in applying the principles of home economics to running her home and her family more efficiently.[9] The "educated mother" was the woman who applied the special skills and training that she learned at college to the difficult task of being a mother.[10] Both scientific homemaking and educated motherhood attempted to give women a way in which they might apply their new learning without drastically altering their traditional roles.

In the twentieth century, the settlement house movement was nurtured by career-minded women who sought an arena in which they could apply their mothering skills. Settlement houses, which grew in number to four hundred nationally by the year 1910, were community centers designed to address the concerns of poor women.[11] Settlement houses also provided a social support system for the middle-class women who lived and worked there. The reform-minded women who staffed the settlement houses were committed to urban and social welfare, and formed the committed core of the new profession of social work.

At the turn of the century, the study clubs, which had nurtured female bonding and sociability, switched their agenda from educating their members to addressing more pressing social concerns.[12] Issues of municipal housekeeping now preoccupied these middle-aged women.

The settlement house and social motherhood movements dovetailed with the progressivism that swept the country in the first decade of the twentieth century. The progressive position was that government should turn its attention to improving social conditions. Home and urban life had deteriorated as a result of industrialization and increased population. There was a great need for the society in general and women in particular to focus on ameliorating societal ills and problems.

Hull House in Chicago led the way in outlining the reformist agenda. Many of the women who graduated from the Hull

House program were at the forefront of the progressive movement.[13] Florence Kelley founded the National Consumers' League in 1899 with the intent of influencing national policies that affected consumers. Mother Jones, in 1903, was active in drafting legislation designed to limit child labor. In 1906 the Pure Food and Drug Act was passed in large measure because of the lobbying efforts of the General Federation of Women's Clubs. The Mann Act, in 1910, prohibited the transportation of women across state lines for the purposes of prostitution, and in 1912 the Children's Bureau was created to monitor the needs and concerns of children. All of these national efforts took place because of the energy of reform-minded women, who felt justified in expanding their maternal mission into the social and political arenas.[14]

In most cases women advocated for the rights and concerns of those less fortunate. The Heterodoxy Club, founded in New York City in 1912, advocated directly for a feminist agenda. Led by Marie Jenny Howe, this avant-garde collective of women was committed to the economic independence and sexual liberation of women in general. The club took the position that women had the same rights as men and challenged traditional roles and societal expectations directly.[15]

At the beginning of the twentieth century, no issue occupied the concerns and consciousness of women more than the issue of suffrage. For years women had been attempting to gain the vote. At the turn of the century, however, with the ascendancy of Carrie Chapman Catt to the leadership of the National American Woman Suffrage Association, the women's rights advocates finally developed a "winning plan" for obtaining the vote. Their strategy combined lobbying efforts in Washington with fieldwork in the states to make voting rights for women a reality. By 1918 two million women belonged to the National American Woman Suffrage Association, making it the largest voluntary organization in the country.[16]

The suffragettes at the turn of the century used three arguments to put forth the case for women's suffrage. First, they argued that the country was in disarray and that a "cleanup" effort would benefit from the domestic housekeeping skills of women. Since women were skilled at cleaning up messes in general, they would "sweep the scoundrels" from office and thus improve living conditions for all. Suffragettes also argued that women needed to protect their homes from the ever-increasing dangers of urban society, and that they could best accomplish this mission by being voting members of society. Finally, in a less lofty voice, the suffragettes appealed to xenophobic concerns. As increased numbers of immigrants had come into the country, the suffragettes argued that the only way to keep power in the hands of the Anglo-Saxon majority was to give the vote to women, thereby doubling the number of white Anglo-Saxons in the voting constituency.[17]

In 1893 Colorado became the first state to grant suffrage to women.[18] By 1912 the Bull Moose Party, under the leadership of the once chauvinistic Teddy Roosevelt, included suffrage in its platform.[19] By 1913 the Congressional Union was formed as a splinter group from the National American Woman Suffrage Association to lobby congressional leaders for the passage of the suffrage amendment.[20] On August 26, 1920, Tennessee became the thirty-sixth state to ratify the amendment granting women the right to vote.[21]

While it is certainly the case that suffrage empowered women, it is also the case that women received suffrage because they were already powerful. The reform agenda that became reality in the first two decades of the twentieth century was largely fueled by the concerns of women. Had women not been successful in advocating for these social reforms and changes, they might not have been granted the vote when they were.[22]

During the period from 1890 to 1920 women entered the labor force in record numbers. By 1900 women were employed in all but 9 of the 369 U.S. industries.[23] Twenty-five percent of women over the age of fourteen were employed in the labor force.[24] The modal female worker, however, was a young unmarried woman whose job was a temporary hiatus on her road to marriage and family.[25]

Despite media portrayals of "career women," most workingwomen labored for their own and their family's economic survival. When married women worked, they worked because their families were poor. The myth that married women worked for "pin money" was just that, a myth.[26] Women worked because their incomes were a necessary part of their families' support.

When they worked in industry, women generally were confined to the pool of unskilled labor. In offices women worked as typists; in stores as salesclerks; and in schools as teachers. They frequently took the dead-end jobs that men did not want.[27] At work a woman often experienced some sexual harassment, less pay for doing equal work, a glass ceiling beyond which her advancement was impossible, and a segregated work environment in which she associated only with other women.[28]

Although the period from 1910 to 1920 was the high point of union organization of workingwomen, most women remained outside of the union ranks and in low-paying jobs. Because of their often transitory status in the workforce and because they worked primarily in unskilled or domestic service jobs, women were difficult to unionize. Men were reluctant to include women in the labor movement, believing that women would replace male workers.[29]

Even more than unionization, protective legislation, which sought to ensure safe working conditions for women and children, greatly affected the lives of workingwomen. The reform spirit of the times generalized to the workforce, and reformers were concerned about making a safer, more humane work environment for women. In the landmark case of *Muller vs. Oregon* in 1908, the argument was made that women's work hours should be shortened because long hours damaged a woman's reproductive capacities.[30] While this protectionist legislation made work safer and more humane for women and for children, it had other less desirable consequences. By defining women as weaker and more vulnerable workers than men, protective claims undermined the arguments of women's rights advocates who wanted men and women to be treated equally. Protective legislation also had the paradoxic effect of making women more expensive employees who needed special working conditions.[31] These special provisions gave small businesses an excuse for not hiring women.

Two organizations founded at the beginning of the twentieth century, one public and the other private, also influenced the lives of workingwomen. In 1905 the Women's Trade Union League was organized to educate and train young women workers.[32] Its mission was to improve the demeanor and working skills of young immigrant women so that they might have more mobility in the labor market. The league's focus was more on improving the conditions for individual women than on labor activism or the unionization of women. The league did attempt to join the agenda of working-class women with that of middle-class reformers by offering financial and moral support to workingwomen who wanted to organize their coworkers.

Also during this period, the Women's Bureau was established within the Department of Labor. The bureau's mission was to protect the concerns of female workers and to educate the public about women's economic role.[33]

No single event had more impact on how women worked than did World War I. Jobs that had been previously closed to women became available as men went off to war. Women fulfilled their patriotic duty by going to work. Previous concerns about the ability of women to perform certain jobs evaporated as the country's need for female labor increased.

Women have always been the unwitting beneficiaries of major social or political upheaval. The Civil War, the westward migration, and both world wars all redefined what was acceptable behavior for women. When emergency circumstances necessitate that women step out of role and perform traditionally male jobs and functions, the society gives permission, even encouragement, for this reversal. When peace and stability return, however, women are usually forced to return to more traditional pursuits.

The Psychiatric Establishment

By the turn of the century there were 328 institutions for the insane nationwide.[34] These institutions cared for almost 200,000 individuals, according to the 1904 census report.[35] There was thus one mentally ill and institutionalized person for every 530 people in the population.[36] The demographics of the institutionalized population also changed due to the influx of immigrants.[37]

With the increasing number of cases, it became apparent that a more systematic approach to indexing cases was necessary. The psychiatric nomenclature changed dramatically in the first decades of the twentieth century, and the indexing of psychiatric cases came close to resembling the diagnostic and statistical manual used by modern-day physicians. Psychoses were divided into traumatic, toxic, organic, and undifferentiated types; depression, hysteria, and the psychoneuroses were identified as well; and dementia praecox, or schizophrenia, was subdivided into paranoid, catatonic, hebephrenic, and simple types.[38]

During this time, an effort was also made to standardize the process of psychiatric assessment, to include the routine history and physical examinations that are now an accepted part of all psychiatric evaluations.[39] It was proposed that every patient have a neurologic, physical, and mental status examination and that an assessment of family and personal history be routinely done.[40] The standardization of assessment and diagnosis resulted in an increase in the amount of recordkeeping and paperwork required of physicians. As a result, the individual folder system for maintaining records was instituted at this time, replacing the single, continuous record book that had been the mainstay of many institutions.[41]

By the early 1890s, the theoretical premise of psychophysical parallelism underlay much of the research into the causes of mental illness. This theory maintained that for every mental state, there was a "correlated physical concomitant" believed to have caused the psychiatric dysfunction.[42] The ascendancy of psychophysical parallelism as a theory led researchers to look into chemical imbalances, metabolic processes, and brain changes, as well as histological and neurohistological variability in the search for causes of psychiatric illness.[43]

Despite the focus on physical bases for mental disturbances, many practitioners continued to believe that certain excesses of modern life contributed to some psychiatric conditions. Neurasthenia in particular was believed to derive from overwork, anxiety, and worry resulting from the stresses of modern life.[44] Also during this time, Freudian theories about the cause of psychiatric illness began to make appearances in the United States. The early formulations that identified infantile sexual trauma as the cause of psychiatric dysfunction was replaced by ideas focusing on psychosexual development. Within this theory, neurosis was related to a fixation of the personality at a prior stage of psychosocial development.[45]

In addition to these generic causes for mental illness, a host of causes specific to women was put forth by twentieth-century practitioners. These "gender-specific" causes can be divided into three separate types: those causes related to the female body, those concerning female sexuality, and those pertaining to the female role and lifestyle.

Menstruation and pregnancy were correlated with psychiatric distress. Menstruation was often cited as affecting mental integrity, causing one writer to suggest that "imbeciles" who committed a criminal act while they were menstruating should not be held responsible.[46] The specific syndrome of puerperal or postpartum insanity also received much attention during this period. Puerperal insanity was believed to commence two to six weeks after a woman gave birth and was characterized by a loss of sleep, general restlessness, irritability, distrustfulness, disorientation, and confusion. In addition to these psychiatric symptoms, the puerperal woman was said to be antagonistic to her husband.[47] Even when childbirth did not result in this specific psychiatric syndrome, pregnant women were seen as being irresponsible, and their particular longings or cravings were thought to derive from "obsessions and a generally weak-willed character."[48]

It may have occurred to the reader that some of the syndromes mentioned here resemble the diagnoses of premenstrual syndrome and postpartum depression used by modern-day practitioners. What is significant about these early formulations, however, is that they served not only to further the understanding of a woman's physiology but also to keep women in their "proper" place.

Beyond menstruation and pregnancy, female sexuality itself was targeted as a cause of nervous distress in women. In particular, the sexual practice of interrupted coitus used to prevent conception was believed to cause nervousness and irritability in both men and women.[49] Women were especially susceptible to this kind of distress because the fear of getting pregnant complicated their sexual activity. During this time period, a specific type of oversexed female neurotic was identified. The "erotopath" focused her sexual preoccupation on her doctor, lawyer, priest, or some other prominent man in her life. The fixated erotopath was seen as being an "annoying menace" to the men on whom her desires focused.[50]

Several authors cited aspects of the female role and the female lifestyle as causing psychiatric distress. In particular, the isolated and solitary life of the rural wife was seen as being especially problematic.[51] One researcher coined the phrase "the neurosis of the housewife" to describe what he called an occupational neurosis particular to women and due to the monotony, discontent, poverty, loss of beauty, and difficulties in childbearing that housewives tended to suffer.[52] In the *Alienist and Neurologist*, a leading journal of the time, a 1911 humorous epitaph described the demise of a woman presumably afflicted by the neurosis of the housewife:

HER EPITAPH

He said he loved her!
Then he let her toil,
Fry, bake and stew, stew, bake and broil,
Mop, scrub and iron, wash and rake and hoe
Sweep leaves in Fall in Winter shovel snow,
Bare seven children, sew and darn and mend,
Care for his parents and to the neighborhood lend
Whatever minutes she could find betimes.—

Then when she died he wrote two-coupled rhymes
And on her gravestone had them neatly cut:
I have them here! They sound alright, but, but,
Beloved by me the woman 'neath this moss,
She was my helpmate, and I mourn her loss![53]

In some of the seemingly scientific discussion about the specific causes of insanity in women are hints of misogynous trends, evidence of a backlash against women who had strayed too far from their home environment and their prescribed roles. Some writers specifically attacked the New Women and the feminists of the day for violating natural laws by tampering with their God-given roles as mothers.[54] One writer asserted that excessive masturbation in *intellectual* women was a main cause of divorce in later life.[55]

At the turn of the century, most individuals with diagnosed mental illness continued to receive their treatment at institutions. Because of the increased numbers of insane persons, however, there were repeated cries in the professional literature about the need for new and different kinds of hospitals and about the problems of overcrowding within existing institutions. Several authors suggested a three-part system whereby cities would be served by different hospital formats depending on population density. Smaller cities of from 10,000 to 20,000 persons, for example, might be best served by having psychiatric patients on psychopathic wards in general hospitals.[56] These psychiatry wards would be available to provide temporary care for patients who were not yet deemed ready or in need of commitment to more long-stay institutions. While some of these patients treated in general hospitals would eventually go on to receive institutional care, others might receive all the care they needed and be suitable for discharge. The inclusion of psychiatric wards in general hospitals would also provide an opportunity to teach psychiatry to general practitioners.[57]

In midsize cities, those ranging from 20,000 to 50,000 residents, separate psychopathic hospitals might be built near general hospitals.[58] These psychiatric facilities would be located right in town, with convenient access to every quarter of the city.[59]

For large cities there was the state hospital or public institution. During this period, a number of plans for judicious construction of these hospitals were put forth. By and large, the pavilion plan seemed to be the most popular.[60] In this plan, the state hospital would consist of a series of detached houses connected by covered walkways. Each of these smaller facilities would have dayrooms and dormitories. These large institutions resembled small towns and often consisted of from 1,000 to 3,000 people—patients and staff—who lived together.[61] The large institutions would often have gardens, farms, and shops; places where patients could work, produce goods, and buy commodities.

In the early twentieth century, many of the reform efforts directed at large institutions were focused on the staff who worked at those hospitals. Physicians began to realize that staff were the primary caregivers at large institutions and that the quality of care could only be as good as the quality of staff. There was an emphasis on training nurses and paying them well, as well as a call for shorter work shifts and better staff-to-patient ratios, with individual staff members assuming primary responsibility for individual patients.[62] In keeping with this emphasis on training for hospital personnel, nineteen psychiatric institutions funded fully equipped training schools for ward attendants.[63]

While at an institution, a patient could expect to be treated with the same array of drug therapies, hydrotherapies, and electric therapies that had existed in the late nineteenth century. There was, however, a deemphasis on the use of mechanical restraint, and a more general belief that individuals needed humane treatment while they were in the throes of a psychotic experience. Practitioners emphasized holistic treatment that would respect a patient's individuality while acknowledging that the state had a responsibility in helping the individual to become whole again.[64] In keeping with this focus on more holistic treatment, institutions began to include programs of employment for patients, entertainment such as movies on the hospital grounds, and outdoor recreation and camps specifically for patients.[65]

Perhaps the most significant change in treatment during the first decades of the twentieth century came as a result of the new profession of social work. With social workers available to provide care and supervision for patients in the community, psychiatrists began to call for after-care programs, outpatient treatment, and outreach efforts that might focus on the prevention of mental disease.[66] Social workers were assigned to coordinate discharge planning and to provide environmental care for patients who were newly discharged to the community. In many cases, these social workers functioned like modern-day case managers, finding suitable housing and employment for patients who were discharged. Financial relief, in the form of short-term benefits, was also offered to indigent patients discharged from the hospital.[67] In general, after-care included follow-up visits, interaction with the patient's network, and general advice-giving and companionship. After-care services served a preventive function, assisting people to maintain themselves in the community.

In addition to working with patients who were newly discharged, social workers worked in outpatient clinics to help patients who did not need long-term inpatient stays. It was estimated that up to 35 percent of the patients treated in institutions could be seen satisfactorily in outpatient departments. Practitioners assumed that these patients would be far happier if they remained in their homes while receiving treatment. City administrators were quick to recognize that by diverting hospitalizations, outpatient departments might ultimately be cost-saving as well as therapeutic.[68]

In the first decades of the twentieth century, some avant-garde practitioners began to experiment with the psychoanalytic treatments that were being devised by Freud and his followers.

The debate thus began, within this country, as to the efficacy of the "talking" therapies. While there was a general sense that rational conversation might be a boon to hospitalized patients,[69] practitioners debated whether or not the specific approaches of the psychoanalyst were actually helpful to patients. Specifically, some questioned whether talking about sex might actually do more harm than good.[70] This was the beginning of a debate that occupied American psychiatry for several decades.

Not surprisingly, the treatment of the mentally ill did not escape the attention of reform-minded individuals at the beginning of the twentieth century. In 1909 the National Committee for Mental Hygiene was founded; it served as a clearinghouse for information on nervous and mental disease.[71] The mental hygiene movement received a boost from the first-person account of psychiatric illness published by Clifford Beers during this period. It is worth noting that despite the many accounts of mental illness that had been published by women in the preceding fifty years, it was the publication of Beers's autobiography, *A Mind That Found Itself*, that drew attention to the mental hygiene movement.

In part because of the work of advocacy groups, patients were given the right to admit themselves to psychiatric hospitals during this period.[72] Many of the women who wrote of their experiences prior to the turn of the century had complained bitterly of the process whereby they were involuntarily committed to hospitals. Voluntary hospitalization was now an alternative to the painful and often humiliating process of commitment.

Firsthand Accounts

1891–1920

The six women who wrote accounts during this period continued the reform spirit of their "sisters" in the previous period. Reform movements within the mental health establishment corresponded to the demands put forth by these women for better treatment and for the repeal of unjust laws and practices. With the increase in psychosocial and psychodynamic treatment interventions, women in this period wrote in greater depth about the actual treatments they received.

The women whose accounts are presented here are as follows: Mrs. H. C. McMullen, who from April 6, 1894, to November 3, 1897, and Alice Bingham Russell, who from February 26, 1883, to June 20, 1883, and again from April 28, 1903, to June 5, 1906, were patients at the First Minnesota Hospital for Insane, renamed in 1902 as the St. Peter State Hospital (St. Peter, Minnesota); Kate Lee, hospitalized at Elgin Insane Asylum (Elgin, Illinois) from June 7, 1899, to October 10, 1900; Margaret Starr, a patient at the Mt. Hope Retreat (Baltimore, Maryland) from September 6, 1901, to November 27, 1902;

Sally Willard Pierce, who between September 1919 and July 1923 was taken care of at five private psychiatric sanitariums, one neurological hospital, two nursing homes, and three different hotels with private-duty nurses (all facilities were in New York State except one private sanitarium in Connecticut); and Jane Hillyer, who does not divulge the names of the hospitals that provided her care and treatment for a five-year period.

Mrs. H. C. McMullen

(1894–1897)

Laws for Protection of the Insane (written while an inmate in a violent ward at St. Peter Hospital)

1. Homes of detention in each county before commitment are made so as to allow patients to notify friends regarding their interests.

2. A society for patients to appeal for protection and the proper enforcement of the law after commitment.

3. Members of the society shall have the right to go and visit the asylum in the interest of their charges on the receipt of reasonable complaints.

4. Patients shall have the right to correspond with whom they please as long as they have intelligence enough to address an envelope, the state paying for two letters a week, their own income or their friends paying for any extra ones. This amuse-

Alice Bingham Russell, excerpts from A Plea for the Insane by Friends of the Living Dead, *1898.*

ment will divert the mind and be a source of improvement and pleasure.

5. Friends shall be allowed to see patients at least for a few moments whenever they feel interested enough to call.

6. Letters written by patients shall be by them dropped into a letter box provided for that purpose and the officials should in no case handle them or control the patients' mail, there should be a United States delivery. Letters do not hurt the patients. It is the disappointment of not getting them or the knowledge that their letters have been opened that exasperates the patients. I have been an inmate three years and know whereof I write.

7. All rules and laws for the protection of the hospital inmates should be posted up and enforced, it would be a relief of mind to know what rights they can demand.

8. As the state pays equally for patients in the asylum, those who work should be allowed compensation for it, that would give those having no resources an opportunity to buy extras, work would then become a pleasure even if the amount received was small, patients would do more and the asylums would need less help.

9. All new attendants should be over thirty years of age, years of experience are worth more than training, remaining as long as adapted for service. It is unjust to compel elderly people to submit to the judgement of the young and giddy.

10. Patients shall have the right to select a guardian of their property, provided the guardian be a responsible citizen, also a right to change if dissatisfied. The society in their interest shall be allowed to advise in this matter when the patient requires it done. There should be fixed terms for service rendered thus preventing unjust bills from guardians.

11. Those in charge of the asylum should allow a patient about to leave to abide by the judgement of the persons having their interest at heart such as personal friends whom the patient may choose. Those patients leaving the asylum should select their residence where they have the means to do so. No bonds on leaving asylum should be required. We are free born and money should not be asked to protect the helpless, we do not demand it for helpless children or infants.

12. Harmless patients should be allowed to board in families and be permitted to change when dissatisfied. Should they become objectionable through frequently requiring restraint they should be returned at the recommendation of the society to the asylum.

Alice Bingham Russell

(1883, 1903–1906)

*D*ear reader, just stop a moment and think this is yourself. A sheriff calls in the early morning; you are at your accustomed duties; have had no sickness to prevent you from your usual labors; he reads you a warrant for your arrest; to be examined for insanity. The complainant is your husband, or your wife who, has pledged himself or herself, in the presence of a minister and invited guests, to cherish you who have become as one flesh, and whose interest should be as one person in sickness and in health, for better or for worse. Just stop and think of the shock from such a source. The sheriff does not tell you what to do to protect yourself; that is not his duty, so you have to leave your duties undone in the midst of some previous important arrangement, for the performance of the sheriff's duties demand that you go at once. If you resist and say it is unjust, and a conspiracy, that does not change matters with the sheriff. The

Alice Bingham Russell, excerpts from A Plea for the Insane by Friends of the Living Dead, *1898.*

arraignment has been made and time set for trial. Your trial comes off, and by the assistance of friends you go free for a time. If there is no stir in this matter how long can you have the assurance to your freedom? All that is required is to catch you off your guard and better evidence. The court's record shows you have had a trial, as to your sanity. The court does not have to demand why a sane person should be thus outraged, and should another complaint be brought, his duty for the protection of the sane demands that another trial be had. This is a legal crime, and once in the asylum, who is there amongst us, that sees we are kindly treated, that we are not detained when it is detrimental to our interests? When there is a guardian appointed, who else troubles themselves to know that his reports are correct as to our condition? The keepers become accustomed to suffering. As long as the slave master of these patients is satisfied, little interest do they show for their future welfare. They soon know who the friendless patients are. If some crime gets into the papers, it is soon suppressed, and gives no warning to arouse the sane to look after the oppressed. It is not their business, there are paid officials to attend to these matters.

I have been four months an inmate of an asylum under these unjust laws, and I can tell you the needs and requirements of the afflicted as though they were my own. I was a sane woman committed that others might control my property as I have records and proofs to show. To content myself until friends could reach me, I took to studying the needs of these poor victims of our insane laws, and heartless indeed he would be who could refuse these poor oppressed people the little that is required to do them justice. While we have the right use of our reason there are many thousands we know have not. Let us do by them as we would want done by us if in their place. Insanity is on the increase. Our asylums are enlarged at the expense of the tax payers, and still their misfortunes go unremedied. If we would band ourselves together as Christian workers, and let those in charge know that the inmates have friends, the keepers would become more human, and we would have done nothing more for them than we would want done by us if in their place. Therefore, let us not work for reward, but each as for himself, and let God judge our merit.

To the Readers of the Times:

Who are subjects of insane asylums? Answer, at times, everyone. This is to some of you a repulsive decision, but readers, if you will but make even so little investigation into the methods used to commit people, you will with terror admit that you or no one is safe. Can you not recall times in your life when you have done or said things that others with a motive to deprive a person of their freedom might have committed you to the asylum, perhaps for life? For there is no limitation on being adjudged insane, nor is there a higher court to appeal to or a society.

Your past record, your financial standing or social relations are of no importance. At your commitment you are without lawful rights, for you are legally dead and without influential interference if maliciously committed it can be life long: or if at the time of commitment you are friendless, a stranger from other countries, you may become an asylum drudge, without compensation, the victim of the most hardened and unmerciful attendant at the asylum. Your complaints are compensated by additional abuse or removal to more violent wards, till from despair you will submit to the most unreasonable demands without a murmur.

Unjust Uses of Insane Asylums

I have devoted twelve years of my past life to a study to improve the conditions of the insane. I visit many who have been inmates some time of their life in asylums, for it is the suffering who have been cured, who can give the best remedies for prevention or cure. To prevent a disease if possible should be our duty to the public, as well as to our family and friends, as insanity is largely on the increase and dreaded by all. It would be well for our good citizens to give this matter more than passing thought, for, as the sins of the father can come on the children, so neglect of paternal interest at this time when this question is being confronted can bring this in future to you or your dear ones.

True there are some cases that require restraint, and some cases of actual necessity, but let us investigate a few unjust commitments and common sense will admit that a horror is not a needful charity.

Here is the case of a young woman not informed as to the methods used to entice the ignorant into a madhouse. She refuses to sell her property to suit the caprice of her husband. He, acting on the advice of a lawyer, has her declared insane, first enticing her to the courthouse to examine their taxes; then in private court, with no friends at hand nor opportunity to notify them, while the judge, two doctors and her husband are under oath to faithfully perform their duty, this young and capable woman who has been doing, up to the very hour before, all her housework, including the care of two children, leaves a good home and property worth $20,000, to become a public charity and mingle and associate continuously with maniacs. Charity, where is your benefit to that unfortunate woman?

Another case: a woman and her husband quarrel; the wife with independence accepts a position as janitress, hoping her absence will prove her worth at home. She returns to secure some clothing, and learning from a neighbor that a housekeeper is in possession, and being refused admittance, she, in her haste to get justice, takes some of the washing from the clothes line, including some of the husband's and housekeeper's to give evidence of their living together. That evening she is arrested, but has not the least fear but that she can vindicate herself. To her surprise she is without friends or counsel committed to the St. Peter asylum.

Again, a wife, who is physically ailing and anxious about how her family are to live, the husband being out of work and credit stopped, undertakes to borrow money and go with her children to her relatives. She is taken without mercy before the court, not even knowing which of her persecutors is the judge, and is committed to the asylum with no friends at hand to interfere.

Next, a young girl, from disappointment, becomes tired of life and makes an attempt to end her existence. Kind friends would have sympathized and reasoned with her to change her views of life, but instead, she too, is sent without mercy to an asylum.

Again, a young woman, suffering from the relapse of fever, is sent needlessly, unjustly to a hospital for the insane.

Again, a man deserts his wife, and children; the wife demands support and is committed to an insane asylum by her heartless neighbors, and the children are scattered around.

Another case: a Norwegian preacher falls in love with a school ma'am, cruelly treats his wife, and, with only the clothes she has on, has her sent to the asylum. Her other clothes are bundled up to be cut over for the children who are sent to a relative.

Again, a woman who has been wronged out of some property is about to take steps to recover it when she is falsely accused and sent to the asylum by fraud.

Then a man becomes tired of his wife because she has had a stroke of paralysis. Yet she continues to do her housework without help. He secures her committal to an asylum and installs another housekeeper, whom he marries, claiming that the former woman with whom he had lived six years is not his legal wife.

Each of these cases were in our own state asylum.

The greatest of all needs is a society to visit and befriend them [patients in asylums] against injustice, to prevent designed incarcerations and desertion, leaving them to the mercy of the hospital. It is the friendless patients who are victims of the greatest injustice. If those who have suffered injustice would write on this subject these wrongs would soon be righted.

ASYLUM ABUSES (THE EXPERIENCES OF OTHER WOMEN RECORDED BY MRS. RUSSELL)

To the Public

About 18 months ago I was committed to the state hospital for the insane at St. Peter, where I was kept for six months. I was sent because of family troubles, but was not insane, and was as strong and well as a woman could be. I was given no opportunity to get my friends to testify in my behalf.

Upon arriving at the asylum I was put to bed for three days, as I was perfectly well I refused to take the medicine furnished me.

After three weeks, during which I refused to be crazed, I was placed in the kitchen; where I cooked for the physicians doing the pastry work, etc. The people lived well, having fine foods, wines and other liquors, on their table at all times.

The patients, however, fared worse, having cheaper food, and not so clean as it should have been. Occasionally, they were given plain cake, and on Sundays, they had dried apple pie.

Delicate women were compelled to take what was placed before them or go without. Sometimes patients were forced to eat. I have seen them fed by inserting a tube into their throats through which food was forced. I understand that they were liable to have their food drugged at any time at the will of their physicians or attendants. Dr. Baker told me that he saw I was not insane, but was placed there for other reasons. He said he could send me to some of my relatives until the time came that I might be legally discharged, but none of them were convenient.

At one time I ran away, but was persuaded to go back, thinking I would soon be allowed to go free. Some of the doctors did not wish me discharged as my cooking suited them. The patients were not permitted to have anything left from the tables of the officials, although much food was thrown away.

Patients were compelled to do drudgery which was the duty of the attendants, being told they must do it if they wanted to get out. That was about all the encouragement most of them got, the doctors very seldom giving any, sometimes insulting or sneering at them.

The superintendent, Dr. Tomlinson, sometimes insulted or laughed at women who begged of him to be allowed to go home to their children. I heard him tell a German lady who begged to go home: "Your husband don't want you; he told me so; you're no good at home."

People are sometimes driven insane by treatment and despair in the hospital. A Mrs. Carroll became so while I was there. She recovered, however, and is now out. Some people are kept there who are no more insane than the people who send them, and should be at liberty.

Violent treatment is not very common, there is some. I have seen three or four women attendants get upon a woman in bed to hold her down.

One woman, a Mrs. Murray, was brought to the asylum almost dying of paralysis. They made her walk the floor and beat her to make her dress herself, saying she was stubborn. I protested against such treatment and dressed the woman myself. In the morning she was dead and the doctors called it by some long name, which I cannot remember.

Dead people are carried, like animals to the dissecting room or the bodies sold.

Patients are locked in their rooms at night, sometimes ten or twelve in one room.

Upon entering the asylum their best clothes are often taken away and never returned. It seldom does any good for them to complain as they are not given credit for what they say, and, sometimes, being afraid of the attendants, they dare not say anything.

Sometimes women, worn out by hard work, are sent to the

hospital "to rest." As if a person could rest amid the noise, confusion and misery of a madhouse!

For exercise they are given a half hour a day about the grounds, sometimes more, sometimes less. But very few of the 1,300 patients there have the freedom of the grounds. It is literally a hell upon earth, with "weeping, wailing, and gnashing of teeth." It is bad enough to keep violent maniacs herded together, but for sane persons, or those slightly peculiar, it is terrible. Patients have little privacy in their correspondence. They can have but one correspondent at a time, and cannot change oftener than once in three months. Letters which they receive are or may be opened by the asylum authorities.

Visitors see but the best side of things, places which they see are put on dress parade, and cleaned up for the occasion. Some wards they are not allowed to see at all.

I make these statements voluntarily in the hope that I may do some good to the unfortunate people so unjustly confined, or cruelly treated.

I could say much more on this subject.

—Mrs. H. H. Hanley, Minneapolis
Penny Press, July 25, 1896

Horror

When we hear of a respectable, sane woman being kidnapped from her home into an insane asylum and bonds demanded for her release, we might well wonder whether our condition is any better than was that of the slaves in early times. We should be aroused to a sense of justice to have this legal kidnapping, this asylum despotism abolished.

—Martha Brand, Linwood Park

Unjustly Deprived of Liberty

I would like to call the attention of the public to a couple of ladies who are unjustly confined in our insane asylum at St. Peter. One of them is Mrs. Harms. She has recently returned to the hospital after she had been at her home in Norwood about three months. During this time her husband treated her brutally, and not only her, but her daughter also. Her son left home a year ago.

When Mrs. Harms came back about the first of September, we hardly knew her, as she was a mere skeleton, and her face was beaten black by her husband. She was anxious about her daughter, whom her father had threatened to knock senseless more than once. The daughter, learning of her mother being put back into the asylum, started from home on foot to St. Peter, which is about fifty miles from her home. Upon entering the hospital she asked to see her mother, and stated the truth about the case, as her mother had already told. Having no place to go, and not desiring to go back to her home, Sheriff Block took her in and finally procured a place for her in a hotel, where she now is.

Mrs. Harms is as sane as she can be, and wishes that something might be done so she and her children can live happily at home on the farm. She has stated things that her husband has done which any person would not do if they had their right mind.

If either of them is insane it is her husband. This woman is not the only one who is put in the asylum sane. Mrs. Kirby was committed by her children and did not see her daughter for two years. To all appearance she seems sane and is a perfect lady. She cordially welcomed the reformers last winter when they visited the asylum. Dr. Chilgren told them, in her presence, not to pay any attention to her story, as she was insane and could not be credited.

Mrs. Russell demanded the right to talk with her on the grounds that she was not a slave. Learning her plausible story, she [Mrs. Russell] visited Mrs. Kirby's daughter in Minneapolis and begged of her to go and see her mother. Though they are people in good circumstances, the lady waited two months for a railroad pass before going. At the asylum she gave directions that her mother be not permitted to see Mrs. Russell or correspond with her in the future. Four months afterwards she took her mother out for a short visit, and returned her before she was given a discharge.

Mrs. Kirby was sane when I left the hospital, and she had the privilege of the grounds, which is given only to favorite, reasoning patients.

She begged of me to intercede for her freedom. There are a great many there, who if they could go to friends of their choice, might never have to return to the hospital, but the superintendent and others controlling them prevent what might be to them a great blessing. Mrs. Russell, who is working to help these poor people, surely deserves the sympathy and assistance of the public in doing what is so badly needed. These people cannot help themselves, and need the help of others in their trouble.

—Mary Peters
Times, Sept. 28, 1896

Kate Lee

(1899–1900)

I will ask of all who may recognize the story, that my own name may forever remain unknown to the world; to the public it can make little difference, as one name is as unfamiliar as the other; and a compliance with this request will greatly oblige.

The people on B. 3. are very queer looking wrecks. One woman kept walking up and down, singing over and over,

"Jerusalem, Jerusalem," to a little tune of her own.

Some of the women were strapped to a seat. One wore a "muff," which is a contrivance something like a pair of leather mittens with steel attached, so buckled as to hold the hands together.

When the doctor was at liberty I was taken into the examining room, which is on this ward. Dr. Foley examined me. He asked me a number of questions, not apparently having much connection with insanity, though these were among them:

Kate Lee, excerpts from A Year at Elgin Insane Asylum, *1902.*

"Do you hear voices when you are alone?"

"Do you see unusual sights?"

To these I readily answered:

"No."

He tested my eyesight by various methods, and finally examined my heart with an instrument, and found me in good health.

He then said he would have to keep me for a time in order to find out whether I was insane or not.

I asked him:

"How long a time?"

He said he would make no promises.

About a month later he told me that he did not find me insane.

Patients who are somewhat disordered sometimes speak of having been "kidnapped," when they were brought to Elgin; and the word is suggestive even to those whose minds are clearer.

In the asylum the inmate becomes part of a great iron machine, which continues to revolve, carrying her with it. Very little attention is paid to her in particular; and inquiries in regard to leaving meet with no response.

The tax on the mind is greatest for the first month. It might be much lessened if those who are merely suspected of insanity could be kept for a time in some safe, quiet place, no more disturbing than the Center, which is never used for inmates. And if they were not required to eat, work or sleep, nor even to attend chapel with the really insane until they had become accustomed to the idea of being in an asylum, the dangerous mental strain would be further relieved.

One may have dark thoughts and recover from them several

times in a year, while the wheel of the Asylum continues to revolve, and new faces come and go.

On the Monday following (the fourth of July) I was transferred with Mrs. Carver to A. 2.

This was called the convalescent ward. It is rather dark, but is furnished better than the others and is considered the best ward.

The side rooms are alike throughout the building, but on A. 2. they are carpeted, and each contains, beside the bed, a good dresser, a table with two shelves, an iron contrivance which serves as a washstand without taking up space, a comfortable low rocker, and another chair.

One side of the alcove, which is carpeted and contains a good table and writing desk, is devoted to the library. Here books are given out by the attendant every Saturday afternoon, inmates being brought from other parts of the building by the attendants.

Across the hall from the alcove is the show case. Here are displayed quantities of crocheted edging and other fancy work, made by the patients. The proceeds from sales go to the institution, and are used for various purposes.

A. 2. is always a smaller ward than the others. When full it has room for but nineteen ladies at night; and often the number runs down to ten or twelve during the summer. These ladies dress and appear much like others elsewhere.

There were just then several inmates on the ward who expected to go home soon, and the group that scattered about the A. 2. grounds was more lively than usual.

There was one well dressed, fleshy lady who left soon after, but returned twice during the year. She was of a cheerful, hearty disposition, and never appeared to be insane.

Miss Holden is another lady in perfect bodily health, who has been in Elgin for about fourteen years. She maintains very good spirits, although the place is exceedingly irksome to her, and although she expects every week to go, and is every week disappointed.

She is tall, and may wonder why she continues to grow fleshy on what she has to eat. She is a sensible, cheerful lady, undoubtedly a prominent member of the church to which she formerly belonged, and in which she was one of the choir. She has been a music teacher, has friends and money, and would like to travel.

"In fact," she says, "I intend to have some good times after I leave here."

In the meantime her hair is growing gray, in a captivity which she deeply resents. She often tells the doctors or others:

"The court has discharged me! You have no right to detain me here;" or,

"My liberty belongs to *me*, and all my rights!"

Of late years she sometimes says these things aloud, when alone, or in conversation with others. If this habit may be called insanity, it is the only sign of it that she exhibits.

The doctors say she has a delusion. If so, she seldom mentions it. In all other respects she appears like any other lady, and as far as could be judged in a year's acquaintance, is entirely capable of caring for herself.

Among the young ladies on A. 2. who were soon going home was Florence Marsden. She was transferred from A. 1. to A. 3., and then brought down to the ward between; and having worked in the dining room had come to be beloved all over the building.

Florence was apparently the pet of an indulgent father; but

although a picture of her former home showed it to be a stately manor house, surrounded by beautiful grounds, yet her manner was always that of a simple Christian girl, with high principle and philanthropic aims, whose friendly and sympathetic manners made her a favorite with every one. When she played and sang it was always some old song, showing deep feeling, rather than a more operatic production.

"My songs are all so old, doctor," she said as Dr. Whitman came into the parlor for a short time one evening, but he responded:

"The old songs are often the best."

On the A. 2. lawn she was a typical "summer girl." She did not remain long, as her father was anxious to get her away.

During July Mrs. Hyman came and after the second night was brought up to A. 2.—a lively Southern young woman, the granddaughter of a wealthy Georgia planter.

Mrs. Hyman was witty, good natured and vivacious, and will long be remembered by some of the attendants, for she made herself one of "the girls" at once.

She was a graduate of Vassar, had traveled with an opera troupe, and finally lived in Chicago with an uncle. She had a guitar, sang a great deal in what was called a "sympathetic" voice, and differed from all others in having apparently come for "a lark."

She was soon sent out to the Cottage. There she remained during the summer and fall, and was one of those who gave no evidence of insanity while at Elgin.

Mrs. Golden was on A. 2. throughout the year—a little German Jewess, getting old, who in her despondent seasons walked the floor and wished she was dead.

"Work hard all your life and bring up a family of children, and then come into the crazy house to die, ain't it?"

The trees pleased her, for they reminded her of forests near her old home in Germany, where she went berrying when a girl. But little else about the Asylum was pleasing to her.

She would recount the benefits of home.

"Only had a little bit of a home, but always had a nice clean table cloth, and a little bit of something good to eat. Didn't you, too, have it so?"

"We ought never to have come here in the first place, is it not so?" she often inquired.

"If we once get here we never get out again."

"It's far better we're all dead, ain't it?"

These despondent periods lasted for a month or two, and then she would become bright and lively. She was naturally very observant, and often amused the attendants and others by her sharp remarks about people and things. What she had, or rather did not have, to eat, was a frequent theme with her.

Whatever treatment is given at the Asylum seems to consist of regular hours, long nights of sleep, low diet, a daily walk and discipline. Very few of the ladies, apparently, take medicine. Dr. Whitman is reported to have said that the term hospital, which is frequently used for the Asylum, should be changed, as only the sick ward and infirmary are properly a hospital; and the term "patient," so often used there, is evidently misleading, as the inmates are not patients in any true sense of the word.

It seems to be a widespread delusion, that may lead to the sending of many persons to Elgin, that the inmates are given treatment for insanity, except that mentioned above. This does not appear to be true, unless it may be on the back wards, or in some cases not known. Ladies who are sick are given medicine, as would be done elsewhere (and at Elgin there is no charge made). But many take little or no medicine, and it is not given to all who are called insane. If regular hours and low diet, with plenty of sleep and outdoor exercise, are desirable, they can be had anywhere, at least in the country. And if it should be required by law to give those who are not plainly out of their heads the alternative of leading this regular life or going to an asylum, it may be that many would live by the clock with great regularity rather than lose their freedom.

As to the discipline, all who are at Elgin do not need it, and it may be even suggested that some would be far better off, in mind as well as body, to be out in the world, and employed at some congenial occupation, of which they could have control, than to be under the control of others. Then it may be remembered that they are supported at public expense, and that it would be an advantage to the State if they were not admitted.

It would seem that persons who have not attempted suicide are sometimes sent to asylums for being low spirited although not otherwise deranged; yet the conditions of such a place are so depressing that it might prove too dangerous to put one among them who was already disheartened. The melancholy might be deepened into madness at any moment.

To be on parole now means to have permission to go about the grounds at certain hours, and under certain restrictions, not very stringent. A promise is given not to go outside the gates; and ladies who are not in before the doors are closed, that is before the ringing of the first bell for dinner, or supper, are liable to lose their parole.

With few exceptions the inmates of the Asylum were like birds vainly beating their wings against a cage in the effort to get out. To be given the liberty of the grounds was as if the cage had been opened, and the bird had been let out into a room. It was an advantage, but it was not freedom, and the bird might still pine for its native air. It was said that the men were less likely to run away than the women.

To those who feel that they do not need to be there, one of the leading objections to the life at Elgin is its aimlessness.

"We do not *live* here," as a lady expressed it, "we only get through the time."

"You know how aimless the life is here; yet we try to make the best of our unhappy lot," said another.

The things that may be done at Elgin even at a disadvantage, are extremely limited. Dressmaking would disarrange the rooms too much to be allowed; and any one whose occupation was that of a milliner, a storekeeper, a clerk, stenographer, housekeeper, teacher or music teacher would find herself entirely out of work.

Yet she might be in perfect health, and the days would drag very monotonously without employment, aside from the work for the State, and a little crocheting.

And not only can no *work* be done, but everything else must be abandoned. No business can be carried on, no trips taken, no visits made.

Occasionally it must happen that there are punishments which seem revolting to an outsider, but perhaps they cannot be helped.

The punishments seem to fall most severely on those who will not work. Thus, a woman in one of the work rooms claimed for several days that there was a holiday in her church, and she would not work. Finally she was brought into the room by two attendants, who laid her back in a chair, and both, putting their hands around her neck at the same time, choked her.

A few days later she again declined to work, and was taken by two employees into a dark closet, and the door closed. Cries and screams were heard, and the woman was brought out in tears and taken back to the ward. She did not come to the work room again.

This was the most disagreeable scene witnessed.

The same day another woman was tied to a chair by a sheet, because she refused to work, and wandered around the room.

Quite often patients were wrestled with for declining to work.

The ladies who were most often met came for various reasons.

Some became insane after sickness, especially typhoid fever.

Some came for overwork or overstudy.

Some from grief at the loss of friends.

One because an "unprincipled girl" stole her lover away, just before they were to have been married.

Another because:

"My boy learned so many things that I did not want him to."

One became insane from witnessing a tragedy, in which her betrothed shot and killed his brother.

One came because the husband whom she married late in life ran away with her savings.

Some are "insane on religion."

Then there were those who were sent for family troubles of various kinds. Of these there were a number at Elgin.

An old lady who did not appear to be insane, claimed that she was sent to Elgin by a son-in-law who wanted her out of her house, so that he and his family could live in it.

Then there are the maiden ladies living with married sisters, or other relatives, who do not fit in well with their environment. Some of these think themselves ill treated in their homes, and so are sent away. Of one who has been there three or four years it was reported that her sister said to her:

"You may stay till you rot before you will be taken out."

It would appear that there are also other forms of family differences, which may lead to an asylum. Occasionally an incompatible husband or wife is put in; or young people who desire to marry, without their parents' consent. Although there were no examples of it at Elgin during that year, this last is apparently considered a real form of insanity.

One who had large possessions might be thought fanatical or insane if she desired to devote her life entirely to Christian service, and might be put into an asylum in order to get her money into the hands of a conservator, thus preventing a course that appeared eccentric, but that might have proved beneficial.

It is probable that in the course of the world's history a number have been considered insane whom posterity would not regard in that light. Among these are reformers, inventors and others who might be mentioned.

It is said that there is less insanity in countries which have a despotic form of government than in those that allow more freedom of thought; and it is perhaps on this principle that the rigid military discipline of an asylum is maintained. It may be imagined that those whose minds are wandering would be steadied and controlled by the tone of command; but with others, who do not need it, the case is different.

As the medical profession recommends that all who are afflicted with insanity, even slightly, shall be separated from their surroundings and placed in institutions at the earliest possible opportunity, both for their own good and that of those around them, it is not only natural and right, but the duty of families to commit those whom they think insane.

But where nearly everything is called insanity, there is another side to the question, which there is no space here to discuss.

But it is difficult to leave the subject without intimating that if those who are "not apparently insane" should be taken up by law at all there should be an entirely different place provided for their detention; and one that would be helpful to them as well as to others.

In such a Home,—which might be called a "House of Peace,"—there could be, if desired, the same discipline, regularity, fresh air and low diet, or other treatment that would be obtained in an asylum; but the strain on the nerves which is connected with living in an institution intended for the insane, would be entirely removed.

In such a Home trades could be taught and a living earned; and when a sufficient sum had been saved the inmate might be both allowed and required to leave, regardless of either the authorities at the place, or any outside parties.

And if the institution could also operate as a home-finder and employment bureau, securing homes and occupation on leaving, and thus giving each inmate a new start in life, it might thus do a further good work, and in many cases entirely remove the symptoms of insanity.

Margaret Starr

(1901–1902)

I sat down wondering over the events that had landed me
here; for a short while my memory was crowded with my past
life.

As a schoolgirl I spent nine years at a boarding school. Having graduated, I not only visited my former teachers, but I made
friends with other Communities; so I am familiar with Institutions. My mother's sister had been a Madam, for sixty-eight
years, so my friendship for the members of the Community under whose roof I now am, is part of my very existence, while
this knowledge I have of Institutions and Community life will
both guide and console me, I am not pleased with my position.
The country home of our family was on the property adjoining
an insane asylum: a Mad-House. I visited and saw the insane
frequently; their indoor entertainments, their sorrows, and af-
flictions, as well as their outdoor sports, were familiar to me; so
the knowledge that I am confined on a hall, with several decid-

Margaret Starr, excerpts from Sane or Insane? Or How I Regained My Liberty, *1904.*

edly deranged persons, does not unduly alarm me. Just then Madam Pike came to speak with me. During my conversation with her I remarked that "I trusted we would cement a personal friendship." I was about to enter no further conversation when she interrupted me by saying: "Now go to bed, and be quiet, Miss Starr; you need a rest." Saying these words, she closed, then locked the door of my room.

I first pleaded for, and then demanded, my rights as a citizen, for the opportunity to regain my liberty. "What will you do for me, Madam? Whatever has been told you about me, having been captured, not having knowledge of my effects, or of myself, may not be, and is not, your fault. But to keep me here for a rest, against my will, is your fault." While I was speaking the door of the Hall was opened by Dr. Salt. After the usual courtesy, he enquired after my health.

I answered: "I am filled with anxiety; *and it is unmercifully cruel not to give me a proved cause for my detention. It is also cruel not to give me information of the power which gave them the right to receive and detain me.*" A few words about those who brought me here were given in answer. I interrupted the remark by declaring that I considered the Institution responsible for my *stay*.

Day after day passes. Nothing but the same routine. My life is a hardship as much as it is a blank. Of course, in the morning, and at noon, when the sun was bright, I could enjoy watching the glories of the day; and in the evening of such a day I could watch the broad sun sink down in its tranquility. And after the twilight I could see, through the iron bars of my window, "the Pleiades, rising through the mellow shade," and look on great Orion sloping slowly to the West; and view the scenes about me, as they were under the light of "The Fair Daughter of the

Night." But these nocturnal beauties could not compensate for the deprivation of one's liberty.

I am making an effort to win my dismissal. I am docile; I make efforts to be industrious as well as to entertain myself and others. I have several waists here, but Madam will not permit me to use them. As the sleeves I wear are in a ragged condition, I have patched them with figured lace. The heavy design of the lace served to hide the notes I write, in hope of being able to send them to outside friends. The notes to which I now refer were sewed in black ribbon bags, by the light of the moon. Three or four times Madam Pike loaned me the use of scissors; later she refused to let me have them. I failed to account for her refusal, as I had always returned them to her without delay. In consequence of this refusal on her part, I treasured more than ever a big darning needle which I have. It served me as a pair of scissors, to embroider notes to outsiders, for my cobbling work, and other odd jobs. As the nurses would at any moment remove any and all the effects from my room, I tried to keep this one possession by using it as a hairpin, when it was not in use otherwise. Once I had the use of a bottle of glue. By the use of my darning needle I managed to cut out letters in words, from a magazine, and then arranged them in a message to a friend asking her to visit me, and to secure my release.

The natural laws of self-protection are instinctively and practically carried out, even by persons without memory and reason. More than once, when Madam Pike would irritate the patients, they would strike out with their arms. Such an act, even if not endangering Madam's person, would be seized by her as an incentive to treat the patient unmercifully, and finally to put her in a straight-jacket. That not being enough she would then tie a pillow-slip over the head of the patient.

I asked so frequently to be allowed to return home that Madam Pike ordered a straight-jacket to be put on me. This is a close-fitting garment made of strong linen. Its sleeves are of sufficient length to cover the entire hand, and are sewed up as mitts, or a bag. By means of lacing down the front, and strapping the arms across the body of the patient, she or he became helpless. I was then put in a side room, and, as good fortune favored me, I found myself in the room adjoining that of the blind girl, who was talking at that time to another patient. She announced that she had been in the one room for four years; was not allowed to enter church, nor to take outdoor exercise. She was trying, she said, to save her soul and be reconciled to her imprisonment. That Madam kept her well dressed, but doomed her to live alone. I had a way of watching my chance to converse with her. She did not seem crazy, but at times she was very cross. She frequently expressed a wish to leave the insane.

One day in the month of February Madam Pike, in a rough, coarse growl, screamed at me, her voice sounding as though her soul was suffering and the scream gave her relief. Being in her presence she handed me the receipt for a registered letter from the certified accountants of the city where I lived. She also showed me a note which, she said, was written to a postmaster of a near station. The signature to this note was covered by the use of a piece of paper, so I inquired: "Who wrote this letter?" Again she screamed: "Sign the receipt; sign it." The part of the letter she showed me read as follows: "As Miss Starr is an insane inmate of Mt. Anchor, and is not able to leave," etc., "kindly send the registered letter to the Institution." I refused to sign the receipt, saying as I did so: "I am an inmate of Mt. Anchor, and I am not *able* to leave it; but only, Madam, because I am not *permitted* to do so." Again, if I sign it, Madam Pike may use the signature to her individual advantage, and then let me out of the Institution. For under the circumstances I was entirely under her control; so, if I *pleased* her, I might gain a dismissal. In *despairing hope* I signed the receipt. I had no sooner given my signature than Madam's manner and voice changed to a decidedly more normal condition; and as I walked through the dining room, in obedience to her order, to go to my room, I heard her laughing.

These acts on her part gave me additional fears for my chances for a speedy dismissal from the Institution. In almost a fainting condition I went to my room. When there, the following questions came to me: What object had Madam Pike in covering the signature of the letter? Had she signed it? Had the doctors signed it? Had the Head of the House signed it? Had it been signed by those who brought me here?

Laws concerning the loss of personal liberty, especially of a partially diseased mind, should be of a quieting character, but in talking with and watching the facial expressions of many of the patients, I *found that the mere knowledge that they were to be kept until called for was maddening!* Even the most loving patient grew suspicious and they suffered in proportion as they had mental force, fearing lest a circumstance, rather than an illness, should be the cause for detention. Certainly, from my standpoint of suspicion, it gives an Institution power to intrigue criminally with outsiders. It gives a criminal a chance to carry out a scheme by influencing weaker, or trusting minds. Several times I have been informed that lawyers were those who had assisted, or been instrumental, in having me committed here. Now, I wonder what that means. I wonder whether the lawyer who failed to file the paper which was intrusted to him, and which was for my protection in an estate in which I had a share, had any part in the proceedings?

The better mentally-balanced patients, frequently, asked me to tell, to the Head of the House, of Madam Pike's cruelties, but as I had learned that Madam Pike is an own sister to the Head of the Institution, and as I was stamped with lunacy, and there was no reasonable hope for giving relief by interference on my part, there was nothing left for me to do, but to suffer with others, and for myself.

Through my friends I learned that the lawyer with whom I had been on friendly terms, and who had boarded at the same place I did for several years, had within a few days after my sudden disappearance, presented a petition to the Court, asking that he should be permitted to see me. The petition was signed by two physicians whom I had known and frequently saw before I was spirited away. The Court refused to favor this petition. Other petitions followed, with the same results. Within a few weeks after this lawyer had volunteered to give me his services, my friend Mrs. R., whom I met at the Mad-House, had addressed him by note telling him that in her opinion I was sane. I also learned that my friends who had seen me immediately before my incarceration, had called but were denied an interview with me.

Within a short time my lawyer's efforts to gain further information, other than he had learned from me, developed statements and facts as follows:

"Not unlike a romance reads the life of Miss Starr during the last fourteen months. She knew nothing of the proceedings which adjudged her a lunatic, until after her escape. Her friends declare that her faculties and her mind are clear and lucid on all subjects. They believe she has been victimized without cause; and so far, without hearing. Her lawyers claim that they were never permitted to see her when they went to Mt. Anchor for that purpose. While they do not claim that she was treated unkindly at the Institution, they say it was a great injustice and indignity to confine a woman, of her mental calibre, in such a place. The Management of Mt. Anchor refused to make any statement whatever in regard to Miss Starr's confinement and her escape."

THE TRIAL

A lawyer who had boarded for two years in the same house where I resided, testified to my sanity; he informed the court that he had on several occasions played cards with me, and had noticed that I was attentive to gaining points in the game, and had displayed a certain suspicion which in his opinion showed the sort of judgment necessary or essential in the management of property or business affairs. He also, incidentally, mentioned that he had heard me perform on the piano. This remark, from him, caused the Court to inquire about my musical ability. The lawyer was somewhat taken by surprise, but he rose to the situation, and said: "The lady in question plays better than I do." As, by his manner and voice, he invited a laugh there was a moment's relief to the suspense of the occasion. A large number of witnesses, including several lawyers who knew me, testified in favor of my sanity. The testimony of the physician, a specialist of throat, chest and nose, whom I frequently saw socially, said that in his opinion I was perfectly sane. The other physician, a general practitioner, whom I knew socially, and had seen the day before I was incarcerated, pronounced me strong-minded.

The star witness was a noted expert on mental diseases.

In laying a foundation for his testimony, he said he had studied medicine for twenty years, making a specialty of nervous diseases. His studies had been pursued at New York, and also in the University of Vermont at Gottingen, Paris, Berlin and Vienna. "Miss Starr," the doctor continued, "has been under my observation for the last few weeks, and I have made a thorough study of her case. Six times I have talked with her an hour, or an hour and a half, at a time; and, in these conversations, I tried to develop, what has been told to me were Miss Starr's pet hobbies. The hobbies failed to develop; and she talked of the subjects only so far as she was drawn out by me. I found her to be of a neurotic temperament; but that is a trait of the American woman, especially the American woman who is high strung, sensitive and intelligent. In fact, the whole American nation, in my opinion, is made up of neurotics. This does not mean, however, that Americans are subjects for mad-houses, but that they are active, alert and energetic, not likely to sit down and wait, but to push on toward the goal of their ambition. Mild hysteria," the doctor continued, "is another characteristic of Miss Starr. Hers is not the hysteria that gets up and howls, and raises ructions generally. That is what I call violent hysteria. Mild hysteria," the doctor continued, "is an indication that a woman is active, energetic and ambitious, one likely to follow ideals, or purposes to the end." "Does this mild hysteria," asked the lawyer who represented Miss Starr, "lead to insanity?" "Never," answered the doctor, emphatically, "it has nothing to do with insanity. Insanity is a disease of the brain. I found Miss Starr mentally far superior to the average woman. But the average American woman is hysterical." The expert doctor then went into an illustration of the neurotic, as contrasted with the phlegmatic temperament.

The letters which I had written surreptitiously, and which had been intercepted by Madam Pike and her successor, were submitted to, and read by, the Court. When those which were written on pieces of muslin were seen in court, it caused a ripple of amusement. The latter were those which I had sewed in the hem of a patient's underskirt; and of which Madam Pike had said, if I intended to sue the Institution she meant to bring them to Court. The lawyer who had defended a citizen, whom I legally attacked, said he thought there was some mental disorder. I was so persistent, he said, that though he had advised me, again and again, to give up the case, I would not take his advice. The lawyer who had failed to file the paper, concerning an estate in which I had an interest, had been strongly instrumental in my commitment; although I had not seen him, or spoken with him, for five successive minutes in the last three years.

Another lawyer testified that I was perfectly rational, except in my legal affairs which I had instituted against a certain citizen, as he said I had raised my expectation of what was due me, in that case, to various large sums of money. As his facial expression gave evidence of his truth, I realized that I had wearied him by talking of the case, and that he had misunderstood my talking of numbers of pamphlets, instead of money. He was the Court Examiner. My visits to his office were in reference to papers filed in that case. Among those persons seen in court were my friend who had sent me the Christmas card; another lawyer, the husband of the friend who sent me the box of fine candy; and the policeman who assisted in putting me in the carriage the day I was taken to the Institution. When I was called to the witness-stand I took the oath. I told the Court, and those present, that the legal proceedings which I had instituted against a citizen had, by my request, been dismissed four months before my commitment: I having done so through the advice of a leading lawyer, whose name I gave to the court.

That I borrowed a small sum of money from a friend of my father's and had yearly, in secret, been allowed an income from a friend who lives in Ireland. I had not, I said, spent one dollar of my inheritance in these law matters. That I lacked experience in money matters. I wound up my testimony by saying that I forgave all persons connected with my incarceration, and I asked the Court for my liberty. There were other witnesses summoned, but the Court brought the case to a close.

The Decision of the Court

According to Pindar, Law Is King over All

The only question before me, said the Court, is Miss Starr's present mental condition. Her condition previous to her commitment to Mt. Anchor, and during her incarceration, in September last, has nothing to do with her present case, except in so far as it throws light on her present condition. I consider the lady at present sane and capable of managing her own affairs. I will therefore sign a decree accordingly, etc.

Through this decree I became financially responsible for the cost of the proceedings.

My friends, I promised to tell you of my "durance vile."

IT IS DONE

Sally Willard Pierce

(1919–1923)

Sally's trouble was merely a little matter of wrought-up nerves, which, for the time being, had tipped her over emotionally. It was temporary and it was far from serious; these little flare-ups were happening every day. All she needed was a short period of rest and quiet, some simple tests just to check up on her physical condition, a bit of judicious questioning when she was ready for it, and a few of his small lay sermons to start her moving in the right mental direction once more. If I took his advice, I'd send her up on the Hill for a while; she would be better off there than at home, and she would not have to remain long.

Sally Willard and Jeffrey T. Pierce, excerpts from The Layman Looks at Doctors, *1929, reprinted by permission of Harcourt Brace and Company.*

CASE HISTORY

It was a week later and it was eleven o'clock in the morning. Dr. Reginald Bolls, swinging into the bedroom of my suite, paused just over the threshold to greet me with an airy gesture—the sweeping salute of a hand that touched his forehead, curved outward in a wide arc, and dropped smartly to his side.

"Good morning, Madame Pierce!

"Physically, you're as sound as a bell—which simplifies the situation considerably, I'm glad to say. For now all we have to do is turn our attention to those foolish little foibles and fancies of yours, straighten them out, and send you back home to your good husband again, as well as you ever were."

"Dr. Bolls—" To my own ears, my dead voice gave indication of the hopelessness enshrouding me like a pall—"it's unfair for you to speak of my . . . my symptoms as just 'foibles and fancies.' They—"

"But what else are they, milady?" He laughed indulgently. "Since your trouble is not physical—or organic, as we medicos call it, then naturally it follows that it must be functional—or imaginary. And what are tricks of the imagination but foibles and fancies? They aren't real and they haven't any foundation in fact, then naturally it follows—doesn't it?—that they must be fancies; nothing but silly little tricks played on us by an imagination which is temporarily out of kilter. When our nerves get frayed and overwrought for one reason or another, then our imagination begins cutting capers, that's all.

"Just learn to look on them as so many harmless little mental demons which have got possession of you for a while—and which, after a bit, will get tired of you and go flitting away. And the quickest way to make them flit is to fill your mind with other things. Bright, happy, positive, true things—like your home, and your husband, and your good father."

PART II—DR. COZZENS!

A young man with beetling black eyebrows and fierce black eyes and a Method. A "personal and individual method of treatment" (sic) based on a "personal and individual theory of human nature" (sic).

"You've never really tried—not once since you set foot inside this cottage. Lying round in bed day in and day out, coddling a perfectly sound arm, babying a perfectly healthy body—I should think you'd be ashamed. Where is your sense of shame, anyway? Haven't you ever had one?—If you were physically sick, there might be some excuse, perhaps. But when a strong young woman with negative test-reports, persists in lolling under bedclothes and making people wait on her and staging giddy fits of hysterics—

"Everybody's been too confounded good to you around here, Mrs. Pierce—that's what's wrong with you now, and it's all that's wrong, too. Everybody's given in to you, and been s-s-so sorry for you, and wept great hot salt tears over you.

"How about giving a thought now and then to your husband, for instance? Or your father? It wouldn't hurt you any to wake up to the fact that you're doing them harm—with your 'troubles.' You've managed to make them both half sick.

"Getting the stage all set for a few hysterics, I see. Arranging a gratuitous skit for the special benefit of Dr. Bruce Cozzens.—You may as well save your breath, Mrs. Pierce. You won't get any pity—or any paraldehyde, either—out of me, hear? Stage one of your shows, and you'll stage it alone—to an empty room. Yes, and on an empty stomach, too. It happens that Dr. Cozzens is just out of pity and paraldehyde this morning."

Part III

There is something very impressive, if not downright resplendent, about the term Neuro-Psychiatrist. The former at once suggests Knowledge—which embraces all the complexities of the nervous system and all the intricacies of the brain. The latter suggests Scholar—a finished product of that intensive sort of study which keeps its devotees up at night. While both of them together—twelve rolling syllables, spoken in the same breath, the same sentence—

. . . There was something very impressive, if not downright resplendent, about Mohawk Towers. High above the Hudson it sat—a huge, solid, vine-hung building of gray stone—turreted and balconied as to exterior, formally luxurious within. All around it undulated the many acres of its own parkland; far below it, the river moved slowly toward the sea.

The place, in years past, had been a private estate, built and owned by one of America's famous "oil men." It was now a private sanitarium, owned and run by Dr. Allen Littlefield—as famous, in his way, as the man of oil; and more justly so.

For he—Dr. Littlefield—was a really fine man, honest, well-intentioned, and brave. He had his own convictions, and the courage of them.

The minute he crossed the threshold of my Louis Quinze bedroom on the afternoon of my arrival, I knew I was going to like him.—Not as I had liked Coles Farwell, of course; and yet admiringly. He was so erect and so carefully groomed, his mouth and chin were so strong, his voice was so firm, his hazel eyes were so straightforward and so serious. . . . Here, I said to myself (remembering Father, and Dr. Trotter, and, although with less assurance, Bruce Cozzens), here is sincerity again; here is a man with a Code of Ethics and a Purpose . . . not to mention Knowledge and Scholarship.

He shook hands, soberly, with Miss Severn and with me. (At Mohawk Towers you were allowed, encouraged even, to bring your own nurse with you.) Then he sat down near me, in a satin-upholstered chair. Miss Severn hurried out of the room.

His first request, like Coles Farwell's, was for an account of my past history, from childhood up until the time of my illness. But, unlike Coles Farwell, he did not specify that the account be limited to important items only. On the contrary, what he wanted, he explained, was everything—the Minor as well as the Major, the Little as well as the Large. . . . (Here, I said to myself, speaks the Neuro-Psychiatry in the man. And in spite of past disappointments, in spite of discouragement, depression and despair, hope, which is seven-lived, stirred feebly and raised its weary head. . . .)

Once more, then, I told my story—from beginning to end.

He cleared his throat. "And what—?" he asked gravely—"of Adaptation?"

(What indeed.) "I . . . I beg your pardon, Doctor?"

"Adaptation, Mrs. Pierce. That is to say, your personal ability or capacity as an Individual to fit yourself into, and become a part of, your personal Environment. How did you succeed, there?—You tell me that your life has been an unusually happy and peaceful one, but what about you yourself, in that life? How did you Adapt—to parents, to friends, to the whole workaday world of stern Reality?"

"Why . . . very well, I should say, Doctor." (What a command of words he had. Impressive words. Resplendent.)

"You were conscious of no outstanding Obstacles to your becoming a part, an integral part, of your Environment?"

"No, Doctor. None that I can think of." (And how inadequate, how childish, my own words sounded by comparison.)

"You were aware of no outstanding Conflicts—occasioned, perhaps, by Maladjustment?"

"No, Doctor. I don't remember any."

"But did you, perhaps, confine yourself too exclusively to some one rutted and inelastic manner of living?—thus negating, every day, the Equipoised Existence?"

"I . . . beg your pardon, Doctor?"

"Let me explain. The Equipoised Existence is a wisely equalized mode of living wherein the Individual combines—But wait. Possibly I'm going too fast for you. We'd best continue for a little, I believe, with the question of Maladaptations—their resultant Conflicts. . . . Tell me, Mrs. Pierce, did you never experience a yearning for another, a dissimilar, kind of life? An explicit dissatisfaction with Reality as such?"

"No, Doctor. At least, no more than anyone does in a while, I suppose. And the feeling always went right away again.—Until I was taken sick, I had a pretty happy life, you see."

(Was he looking—or was I only imagining it—just a shade chagrined? Baffled . . . ?)

" 'No explicit dissatisfactions, other than any one might have experienced. . . .' Must have been implicit, then. . . . Possibly you were a dreamer, Mrs. Pierce? Possibly you found your happiness in a series of Phantasies—day-dreams, in other words—wherein you Escaped From Reality by re-molding it a little 'nearer to the heart's desire'?"

"No, Doctor." It was getting to be a regular rubber-stamp; a stereotyped reply. I was failing him every time I said it. And he was—he unmistakably was—looking a shade chagrined. . . . Oh, to be able to say "yes" to him once, just once. But—"No, Doctor, I can't remember having had any particular day-dreams. . . . except"—(here was a thought)—"about my music. I mean, I did use to dream—day-dream—that some day I'd be a concert pianiste."

It fell flat. "Such day-dreams are not anti-Reality, Mrs. Pierce; they are pro-Reality, a very piece of Reality. . . . Nevertheless"—(Not to be beaten, not to be gainsaid)—"nevertheless, Maladaptation and Conflict were present somewhere; they always are. Somewhere in your life—either in connection with your friends (some one special friend, say, who disturbed you and grated on you); or with your parents (although that is less likely, loving them both as devotedly as you did); or with your schooling, or your adolescence, or your marriage. . . . Think, Mrs. Pierce. Think hard.—I'll just sit here quietly and say nothing, while you think back, review your whole life again, and pick out for me any outstanding isolated instances or examples which appeal to you, yourself, as Maladaptive."

So he sat quietly (he really was a fine man), while I thought back; thought hard; racked my brains. . . . How stupid, to have had a happy life. . . . "Well, of course, Doctor, there were some little things, such as any one . . . every one—"

"Yes? Yes?" All encouragement, all eagerness. Naturally he wasn't beaten. You couldn't beat Neuro-Psychiatry.

CONCLUSION

Psychoanalysis

In looking back, she said, over her past unhappy experiences with doctor after doctor, it seems to her now that the trouble had been that in every instance a cure had been sought either by means of palliatives, or the doctor's personality, or some one passionate conviction or aim, which, by its very violence, left out of consideration the individual needs of individual patients. Dr. Littlefield and his neuro-psychiatry had been "warm," but had failed through an unwillingness or an inability to recognize the necessity for getting at causes through the unconscious, rather than through the conscious, mind; he dealt with effects, not with causes at all; and in the apparent absence of either, he generously supplied one, such as Sally's supposed over-specialization in music. There could be no doubt but what the majority of these men had done, and were doing, a vast amount of good for a vast number of patients; but such patients, then, must be people to whom the answers of whys were not essential. Palliatives and personalities and passions were enough for them, at least temporarily; perhaps they were fortunate, or again, perhaps not.

For her own part, with the answering of her whys so nearly completed, she was eager to go home and begin all over again on a new basis. She was confident, she told me, that she had already changed "inside"; and that she would continue to change, and improve.

And so, during the first week of July, 1923, Miss Severn was dismissed with joy and yet with regret, for we had all grown very fond of her, and Sally came home to stay, exactly three years and ten months from the time she had first been taken ill.

Jane Hillyer

(Date Unknown)

I was locked in. It was I that the nurses had been discussing. Filled anew with a restless, gnawing misery that had brought me to the place a few days before, my moment of respite gone, I bunched myself into a knot upon the bed, burning with renewed struggle. I was locked in! All my fears were certainties; there was no escape from them; I had given up; I had done it to myself. Doubt was no longer possible. For many hours I had forgotten where I was and why. Exhaustion had been mercifully complete. Now I began to remember, hazily. The locked door recalled it all. I was soon the victim of a stinging swarm of inconsequent recollections which I could neither drive from me, nor ignore. They came as they would, and went when they chose, directing their own course as if I had not been there at all, save as a medium for them to play upon.

I was swept back to my early childhood in a stream of confused, crowding thoughts. With fatal directness the current

Jane Hillyer, excerpts from Reluctantly Told, *1927.*

paused and swirled about a bronzed October day some ten years before. It had been a tragic autumn. My father had left home. He had gone, they said, in the hope that such a move would brace him; more truly he had gone because life was becoming intolerable for the two children in the house. An older brother hovered on the edge of a breakdown as the result of a prolonged attack of rheumatic fever but recently past and I was quivering from head to foot most of the time with tension and anxiety. The outward mechanical part of life went on as usual. Every morning at nine fifteen I started for school with a book open before me, saying last minute Latin declensions to myself as I walked down the shaded street. Having been away from home all summer, I had not seen my father for many weeks. He had been pleading for only so much as a glimpse of me, but my brother was hot in his opinion. I must not—it would be too difficult. I was more than willing, but the interview had been postponed.

I looked up from my book—one day—as I came to the end of the block. My father was coming toward me down a side street which I was about to cross. Did I imagine it? I do not know. I never shall. But I thought his face was flushed, that his gait was not so sure as usual, that he looked at me with hesitation in glazed eyes. I stood, turned to stone. All my faculties left me. It would have been so simple to go to him and say "good morning." Had the meeting proved hard he would have been the last to prolong it. Yet, I did not go. I was overcome with a sudden, inexplicable animal fear. I had never known anything like it before nor have I known anything like it since. All the bits of terror I had ever felt, all the anguish of suspense, amalgamated and fell upon me like a mantle of lead. I was bound in every muscle. I could not move. He smiled—if the essence of tragic realization can be called a smile—and waved his hand indicating that I was to pass. I did so *without* speaking to him—such was my terrified confusion. I fairly raced down the street and arrived at school panting and out of breath.

A week later I came in from school, dropped my books, threw my hat into the "old brown chair" and fell wearily onto the window-seat to watch a humming bird, with enameled throat and vibrant wings, mine deep in a red lily searching out the last sweet meagreness of summer honey. I became conscious of my mother's voice at the telephone. As a rule she let nothing interfere with her music lessons. Something in her tone made me sit up straight. She was calm, as usual, but there was a deadly distinctness to her words that held my attention as in a vise. She went to the next room, dismissed her pupils very quietly, then told me that my father had been found dead in his hotel that morning, a glass beside him. They thought it was suicide.

I grew quiet; yes, I had done this thing; there was not the slightest doubt of it. But, though he was dead, I was still alive. We should see, we should see whether mistakes of this kind were to be the determining factors of the days that were to follow, or whether I could in some way make partial amends. I formed a compact with myself then and there. No slipping, no weakening was to be allowed. I went downstairs, calm and self-possessed. The family maid had left a day or so before, most inopportunely. My brother and I started luncheon together. All these years afterward—locked in, lying hunched upon a stranged bed—I remembered how small details had been indelibly fixed by shock, how yellow the sunlight was on the butter balls I rolled between two wooden paddles. Strange that they had looked so like yesterday's butter balls.

Now here I was locked in! The compact was utterly broken. I had made a second error hardly less serious than the first. This, then, was to be the determining factor; the inner structure was faulty; I *had* failed—just as he, my father, had failed before me. Mine was not so clean-cut and releasing as his had been, though I had tried desperately to make it so. I had *failed!* How that thought battered me. All those years of effort had been in vain. A constant repetition of this idea reduced me to an abject creature tearing with its teeth at a pillow case and calling for veronal in loud, strident tones. I had had only three nights' experience with veronal but I knew what it could do. I had felt the blessing of its oblivion.

More and more I began to object to the intrusion of those about me, to "resist," I think the term is. I did not want to go for a walk with my kind, capable little nurse. I did not want to sit on the lawn with the "ladies." I did not want to get up and dress in the morning. Why should I, what was there to dress for? I wanted nothing they had to offer me. Why didn't they let me alone?

It was time for my medicine.

"Why do you give it to me?"

"To make you well, so you can go home to your family."

"But I don't want to get well; there's no place for me, there."

"They said yesterday, they wanted you to come home as soon as you were well, and stay right there."

What was the use of explaining? There *was* no place for me there, not the "me" I had become. I emptied the medicine into a flower pot. A second glass was brought. Again I emptied it. "You are to take this." A third time I tipped the glass. It began to be amusing. I wondered if the plant would die. A second nurse entered the room. She held my hands while the first nurse tried to pour the stuff down my throat. I fought. How did any one dare to *touch* me? What did they think I was, a wild animal in a cage? I struggled harder. With a quick movement I was put flat on my back and the medicine somehow went down between clenched teeth.

I had been right. This was not my world.

I sat stiff on the edge of my bed. They tied us, did they? I had begun to identify myself with the inmates, a thing I would have burned at four days before. The nurses were "they," people apart. What kind of place could it be where people were tied? I thought of mediaeval tortures. "But she said it wasn't tight," I pondered; "it didn't seem to hurt." I became confused. It was so unnatural, this place where one group had such power over another. It brought thoughts of "enchantment and witchcraft." The world became less and less real. An element of ghoulishness crept into my consciousness. The voice went on. I lay down. It lost all meaning for me, ceased to convey a sense of sorrow. The monotony was lulling. I was quiet and nonthinking for a long time. That was, I suppose, the beginning of extended periods of stupor which were to come.

My mind balked at the difficulties; you can't get very far trying to rationalize the workings of a sanitarium for the insane. "I like the old way best," I said under my breath. "Do they really think I can endure it?" I bit the pillow case and tore it a little with my teeth. I gave the sheet a pull. "Stop tearing the bed clothes." I continued joyously in a purely infantile revolt. "Leave that sheet alone; there is no sense to what you are doing." I gave the sheet a skillful jerk; it, in turn, gave a grand muslin whistle and nearly halved. The Head Nurse entered. A band was slipped over my chest. My hands were bound; my feet were tied to the foot of the bed with a cleverly made noose. I watched the process with interest. I did not mind. It was something new; broke the monotony. It was a bother to my "keepers" and I was in a mood to appreciate that fact.

It is baffling business trying to explain the activities of patients in an insane asylum and it is little wonder that under the pressure of a constant effort to do this I became more and more confused. There was no reality here to help me. Conditions were so far removed from normal living that they actually aided my sense of cleavage, rather than cleared it up, as they are supposed to do. The few habits of ordinary living that remained with me were broken down by a new and rigidly enforced routine, having no connection with any phase of life I had ever known. My last moorings were cut.

I had quite forgotten my whereabouts, till some sound recalled me. I looked up. A procession of nude women were walking down the hall to be put to bed in the "dormitory." A nurse or two followed them. I was not shocked. All possibility of shock had been removed; I had had all I could take in the last months. I did not even wonder at those tragic figures, bent and huddled, too confused to protect themselves from the cold blast of exposure. There was not a lively line in the whole group, not a redeeming hint of beauty. They were all old and shrunken, with sagging flesh and knotted muscles like Rodin's infinitely pathetic and ironic "La Pucelle."

The why of this procession was apparent. It was easier for the nurses to handle the patients in herds. I looked out of the windows again. The pattern of the branches was dim and grey; the stars were bright, one yellow, one blue. How *could* the world lend itself to such sordidness as that hall contained? I heard some one gasp. The Doctor was standing beside me, also looking down the ward. She had been in the hospital only about as long as I had, and had apparently never chanced on the ward before just at this hour—though she went through it three times every day. I was a little astonished at the shock on her face, a little envious. There were some things to which she could object; I had objected all I could and was pretty well dead to horror. . . .

I resented suggestions of activity of any kind, particularly having to "go for a walk." And no wonder! The "Ladies" were lined up like a prison gang, a nurse in front and one in back, and perhaps an extra nurse who kept her eyes open for any signs of unruly behaviour. Somehow the patients looked worse outdoors than in, wrapped in old shawls, faded sweaters, jackets and coats of a previous generation. In the bright sunlight they seemed, somehow, more dead. I knew myself one of them, and it burned deeply. There were no fair Ophelias in that straggling line; insanity and beauty do not go together, at least, as I saw it. No one liked those walks. We were kept out a stated length of time, about half an hour, and no doubt the exercise was good for us, but in my case, at least, it took many hours before I ceased to tingle with resentment and humiliation after one of these excursions. "It's bad enough to be here," I would whisper, "without having to take part in a circus procession." After the first time there was nothing to see, plain red brick buildings, plain cement sidewalks, plain everything! It was the essence of dullness and institutionalism.

The one thing that made the long weeks pass at all was the fact that I was still so far from strong that I spent a large part of my time on the couch in a sort of half-stupor. I would rise for my meals and return to my couch, asking only to be quiet. I was partly asleep, partly too lacking in energy to remember what I had been thinking about two minutes before. The effort at adjustment to even so simple a situation as that which Cottage B presented was all I could manage. A half hour's activity with a number of people about me was enough to make me more than eager to "lie by" for the rest of the day. A visit from my guest often completely exhausted me. Even the Doctor's coming was, at times, fatiguing, simply because it was a bit unusual and was always heralded by a stir.

When spring came I was given my privilege. My nicest nurse put her hand on my shoulder. She unlocked the door and gave me a playful push. I stumbled down the steps and out onto the sidewalk. It was one of those "blue days" of May. The sky was blue and bright, flecked with small clouds, soft and downy; the air was filled with a moist blue haze that crept into the shadows to deepen them and clung like a garment about any little hidden distance. I looked up and filled my eyes with the blueness, breathed it in, absorbed it through every hungry pore. I started to move; it was the first time I had been out alone for three years, save for that one walk when I had managed to escape from Ward No. 13.

My powers of observation became very acute, more acute than they had been before—or have been since. This was partly because I had unlimited leisure to look. There was absolutely nothing to interfere. I had all the days of summer to keep filled; and, as yet, there was nothing to fill them with but looking. I looked and looked and *looked*.

At night I went to bed with these things in my mind. I had something to think about. Often the day's pictures would quite shut off the animal-like snarls and curses of my neighbor on the right when she was "disturbed," or the penetrating moans of the woman on my left, crying for her daughter. Often I went peacefully to sleep, still in the garden or thinking myself back under the branches of my favorite great oak. But I was not always so fortunate. There were times when nothing could hold me. I wanted to go home. I felt so caged there in that little room. We had to go to bed at eight *in summer*. It was not yet dark. It would be hours and hours before I was really sleepy. When outdoors failed me, I had no defences.

One morning the Doctor said, "Jane, would you like to have charge of the library?" I was on the top of the wave. It was as musty, dusty, ill-assorted a lot of books as ever came into the care of enthusiastic hands. But they were mine. I had the key to the shelves in my pocket. I pinned it on my pillow at night; and walked with my hand dug deep into the wool of my sweater where it lay comfortably nested.

Now I had some place to *be*. I did not have to stay out of doors until I was blue with cold or sit in the cottage listening to things I hated to hear. I could curl up on the window sill of the library and be quiet and alone—to be alone was bliss. "And no one will fuss about me or question me; they know I am here." My measure of peace was complete, though still greatly coloured by unhappiness and doubt as to the outcome of my experiment. In spite of this doubt and the harrowing uncertainty of every day, something kept me *trying*. I could not have stopped if I had wanted to. Something had got to work within me; down in the engine room the pumps were throbbing. Whether or no, the whole being had to respond, had to move. The signal had been given; up somewhere in some unknown chart room of my being the course was set.

RELEASE AND AFTER

Much time had to be spent in general rehabilitation. It took all the skill of a hairdresser and much of my own time to reduce my bushy shock to any kind of submission and a new way had to be found "to do it;" I had grown much older in those years. There seemed no end, but it was all pure delight. I constantly interrupted myself with excursions to the refrigerator. It was impossible to stay fed. I ate constantly and at the end of three weeks had gained fifteen pounds and approximated my normal weight. I came up from my dark hole like a Jack in the Box, getting better oriented with the passing of each day. Of all the things that gave me pleasure there was none more potent than doors. I could lock and unlock them myself. No one ever asked me where I was going. I fairly hugged doors!

My first dinner party was an event, not too simple. Fortunately the group was made of people who knew each other intimately; little was required of me. And that was well. No, I hadn't read the latest Galsworthy novel. No, I hadn't seen the last Broadway "hit." No, I had not visited the Nicholas Roerich "show" at the Museum. No, I hadn't heard the Philharmonic on its last trip West. As to fashions I had no ideas, only a very queer feeling in my brief, scanty skirts—quite new. I sat still and intense, committing all topics up for discussion so that I would have ammunition to use upon the next person with whom I had to talk. For some time I fired only interrogations, and though my remarks were of a rather inquisitorial type, they served to keep my head above water until I had a chance to live a little myself, until conversation could again become an unpremeditated activity.

One of the first things I did was to straighten out my attitude towards other people's opinion of the hospital experience. Of course any one who cared to think about it would know. One does not drop out of sight completely—no letters, no anything—and suddenly return save for about one reason. I knew it would make no difference to my most intimate friends and that most people were too busy with their own affairs to think much about mine. Still I was perfectly conscious that the attitude towards insanity was still one of recoil on the part of a large portion of society; it is a disgrace, a thing to speak of in whispers. An old aunt of mine, who would have done anything in the world for me, who greeted me with the greatest kindness, could not quite conceal the fact that she considered me a blot on the family escutcheon. Well, I would stand and take it. It had happened to me; there was no use cavilling with the experience. What I had in hand for the future, my adjustment, was my own job. It concerned no one but me very much.

A very good friend said one day: "There is a man in the University who helped me when I was terribly down. Maybe he might make things easier for you. He's a psychological expert . . ."

"Oh, I am all right," I answered. Then I began to wonder: "Was I?" How did I know danger signals, when to stop because of fatigue, when to go on for fear of developing an attitude of hypochondria, which I loathed. How did I know anything? I decided I simply did not know. I called the doctor and made an appointment. "It will not be easy to go all over this mess," I thought wearily.

It was a dull November day when I entered the office. The doctor was busy with his notes. As I stood at the door he looked up.

"Hello," he said simply, "sit down."

It took all the poise I could summon, and a little more, to go through the formalities of greeting; I wanted to tell him so very much that it was quite as it should be, that his task was done, in a sense, before he had begun. I knew from the first second that I had made harbor. I dropped all responsibility at his feet as I said haltingly: "Yes, it's dark, but I love these late fall days." In my heart, I was singing a hymn of relief and thankfulness. I need not go another step alone. I perceived at once the penetrating quality of his understanding, the bracing draught of his sympathy. He said afterwards he felt as if he were the Woodsman in the fairy tale who finds the lost Tinker's daughter in a darkly enchanted forest. I hope that good Woodsman knows, as I do, that the Tinker's daughter would still be wandering there, had it not been for his leadership. I could not have gone much longer without help. I am sure the necessity of intelligent aftercare cannot be sufficiently stressed. The convalescent is not able to make his own personal adjustment and handle his own case. The responsibility is too utterly crushing. Even with all his help there were times when I felt my feet slip on the rope, the distance below me looked unbelievably great.

The Woodsman's devotion and persistence were marvelous. He worked at the cost of incalculable fatigue and loss of time. He pressed onto an end where no end seemed to be. As the months went by, however, I became less and less tense. He could bring up new difficulties and be met with no resistance. He could take me back over old ones and we both came out smiling. For three years I talked, unburdened every fear, every horror, every despair, that I had been conscious of and many that I did not know, save as they *affected me emotionally*. A certain concrete terror of early childhood was "excavated." In itself it proved to be unfamiliar, but the emotion of which it was the hidden center was as old as I, as new as yesterday.

At last it was done. I and all things connected with me had been so discussed and "hashed over" that there was nothing secret, nothing to inspire curiosity or dramatics. It was all commonplace and human. I became to myself not so much an individual as a mere unit in a species—and not a very exciting one either. Emotional reactions had become very largely subjected to reason. What the Woodsman finally succeeded in doing—in a word—was to make me feel with my mind, not to think with my feelings.

The relief was indescribable. If ever one human being went down into the farthest places of desolation and brought back another soul, lost and struggling, that human being was the Woodsman—and the fringe of crisp white hair behind his ears is his halo, here and *now!*

PERIOD IV

1921 – 1945

Reprinted with permission of Butterick Company, Inc., New York, New York.

WOMEN'S LIVES

*T*he country's flirtation with the image of the sexualized woman continued with the Flapper. The Flapper, a woman who was sexy, attractive, and young; who went from adventure to adventure, challenging societal taboos and celebrating her own experience.[1] The Flapper presented women with an image of a restless and excited personality who was aggressively feminine, yet desirous of being recognized for herself. She was a young woman who wanted to have it all: she wanted both a career and a marriage and she wanted to express her own personality and find self-fulfillment.[2] The Flapper became the embodiment of the restless energy that characterized the country's mood during the Roaring Twenties.

The growing film industry immortalized the Flapper in several films that presented images of a hedonistic, uninhibited young woman who was clearly enjoying herself. Film star Clara Bow, who was widely identified with the Flapper, became known as the "It" girl.[3] "It" combined sexual charisma and carefree self-indulgence. If one had "It," one knew it.

Despite her sexual and spunky persona, the Flapper still wanted the traditional pleasures of marriage and family. Although Flappers enjoyed and indulged themselves, like their more traditional sisters, they were headed for marriage and homelife.[4]

The image of the Wife/Companion took the Flapper into married life. Before the wide acceptance of birth control practices, wives were necessarily mothers. To be married meant to produce children. Once birth control became acceptable within middle-class families, however, wives could be sexual companions without necessarily producing children. The Wife, like the Flapper, was an attractive woman, and her attractiveness reflected on the success of her husband. As a Wife, a woman became a sexual trophy for the man she had married.[5]

During the period between World War I and World War II, two additional images of female possibility emerged: the Idealized and Libidinal Mother and the Happy Homemaker. With the development of psychological knowledge about parenting, and about mothering in particular, the image of the Ideal Mother emerged as the perfect nurturer. She was a woman whose greatest happiness came from caring for her child. She had no needs and desires of her own; rather, her pleasures were inextricably bound with the joys and pleasures of her child. The message conveyed to women by the image of the Idealized and Libidinal Mother was that if women did not want to be mothers, something was wrong with them.[6]

The Happy Homemaker was a second traditional image that flourished in the thirties and forties. The Happy Homemaker was fully satisfied doing housework and household tasks and showed her love of her family by taking care of her home. She was depicted as being happy, cheerful, even elegant, as she went about the mundane tasks of keeping her family fed, clothed, and clean. It was part of the Happy Homemaker's persona that she rarely worried and never felt angry.[7] One can clearly see what a heavy burden this idealized image might have placed on ordinary women who could hardly be expected to be creative and cheerful as they went about stretching the family budget. For many women, especially during the Depression and the war years, it was difficult to avoid worrying or being angry and frustrated. The Happy Homemaker thus represented an almost impossible ideal for ordinary women.

In 1937 Emily Post referred to the Happy Homemaker as "Mrs. Three-in-One," the woman who was cook, waitress, and hostess at her own dinner party. Advertisements in the popular media often made women feel guilty and ashamed if they could not live up to the characterizations of the Happy Homemaker.[8]

In the decades of the twenties and the thirties, the advertising industry clearly fostered certain images of womanhood. The consumerism that swept the country encouraged women to purchase products to make their homes more livable and more modern.[9] The image of the Happy Homemaker was actually fostered by the advertising industry, since homemakers were the primary purchasers of the consumer goods that began flooding the marketplace.[10]

Home economists and other experts filled the popular media with data that left women feeling guilty for not having perfect homes or raising perfect children.[11] Similarly, the cosmetic industry perpetuated an idealization of the attractive woman.[12] Women were encouraged to purchase a raft of products that would make them more beautiful and help them to approximate what was becoming a cultural idealization of femininity.

In keeping with the idealized images of the 1920s and

1930s, most women deemphasized their involvement in human-itarian causes and social reform during this period. They no longer saw their primary concern as trying to fix the society; instead they were more preoccupied with fixing their own lives. Although there were some social movements that caught the attention of large numbers of women, the extent of women's involvement was far less than in previous decades.

The American Birth Control League, founded by Margaret Sanger in 1921, stood out as the exception. Yet, even the Birth Control League, which sought to promote women's reproduc-tive autonomy by challenging the legal barriers to the dissemi-nation of birth control information, was clearly in keeping with a woman's desire for more personal freedom and more self-ex-pression.

The failure of the National Women's Party to obtain the popular support that the National American Woman Suffrage Association had known reflected the mood of the period. With suffrage secured, the National Women's Party turned its atten-tion to the passage of an equal rights amendment that would end discrimination in divorce, marriage, work, and property. This agenda, however, brought the party into heated conflict with reformers who had made great strides in passing legislation to offer women protection in the workplace. Protective legisla-tion, which provided special benefits to women and children, would have been negated by the passage of an equal rights amendment.

The National Women's Party had difficulty garnering wide-spread support for several other reasons. The women involved in the party, unlike past reformers, were seen as an elitist group who were more invested in their own accomplishments than in perpetuating an agenda that was truly broad-based.[13] The National Women's Party also came under suspicion for having Bolshevik leanings. While the truth of this accusation was dubious, the party fell victim to the "Red scare" that swept the country in the 1920s.[14] The most important reason that the National Women's Party failed to achieve much influence had to do with political power. Following the passage of the Voting Rights Amendment, mainstream politicians came to realize that women were not going to vote as a unified special interest group.[15] Rather, they were going to vote in patterns similar to those established by their husbands or by their families. Consequently, politicians had less reason to pay attention to a feminist agenda.

While women as a group were not especially active on the national scene during the 1920s, 1930s, and 1940s, a few individual women achieved a level of influence and prominence that had been previously unknown.[16] Eleanor Roosevelt, in particular, became a powerful proponent of the rights of women and children. She was a strong advocate for a women's agenda and was instrumental in the appointment of Frances Perkins as the first female member of a president's cabinet.[17]

The forces affecting women's lives during the period from 1921 to 1945 were far more global than parochial women's movement issues. This period was bracketed by two world wars and contained the most devastating economic depression that the country had ever known. Women's lives, their families, and the country's expectations of them changed dramatically.

It was in the workforce that women most felt the impact of these monumental national events. The Depression that began in 1929 brought with it a backlash against workingwomen. Laws were passed making it illegal to employ married women in certain occupations. During the 1930s, twenty-six states had laws prohibiting the employment of married women.[18] The "married person's" clause in the Civil Service Act proposed that the spouse of a federal employee should be the first to go during a reduction in personnel.[19] These legislative actions were based on the assumption that married women took employment away from men, and moreover that families would fare better overall if women stayed home and men worked.

A 1936 Gallup poll revealed that 82 percent of respondents believed that married women should not work, because they not only took jobs away from men but also undermined a man's place at home.[20] During the Depression, business leaders and Labor Department officials emphasized a family wage rather than an individual wage in order to guarantee a certain minimum income to each family.[21] This served primarily to keep women out of the labor force and away from higher paying jobs.

Employment opportunities, among other things, changed with the beginning of World War II. The war took men away from heavy industry and allowed women to enter the labor force in record numbers. Despite the patriotic depiction of Rosie the Riveter, the vast majority of women worked in light industry and in clerical positions, not in wartime industries.[22]

During World War II, eight million women went to work, increasing the size of the female labor force by half. It is significant not only that women went to work in record numbers but that the profile of the average workingwoman changed as well. By the 1940s the average woman in the workforce was married, over thirty-five years of age, and working to help support her family.[23]

The period from 1921 to 1945 was one of great social, political, and economic upheaval. There were dramatic changes in what was considered acceptable behavior. A sexual and moral revolution that expanded the way women thought about themselves was followed by a shattering economic depression that caused the entire country to retrench. Both of these in turn were followed by the events of World War II, which once again rewrote a woman's role and redefined acceptable behavior. While most women were able to adapt to rapidly changing expectations, some were not. Some women found themselves confused and overwhelmed as the images of acceptable womanhood changed more rapidly than at any time in the past.

The Psychiatric Establishment

During the period from 1921 to 1945, there was an emphasis on personal development and the fulfillment of the self. Psychiatrists became interested in personality development, mental adjustment, the social life of the family, and the inadequacies of the educational system.[24] The field of psychiatry subdivided into several specialties, with practitioners focusing on such areas as child development, industrial psychiatry, and psychoanalytic psychiatry.[25]

The new field of mental hygiene emphasized mental health even more than it did the cure and prevention of disease. Mental hygiene was defined as the "promotion of the best development of the individual mind and its mental capacities."[26] The field of mental hygiene focused on preventing impairment to natural capacities and skills, and restoring capacities if they became impaired.

During this period, psychiatry began to define its domain more clearly and specifically. In 1928 the American Psychiatric

Association joined with twenty-one other professional organizations in writing the Standard Classified Nomenclature of Diseases.[27] This standardized work attempted to articulate the disease entities that were the specific purview of different medical specialists. Psychiatrists focused their attention in particular on the illness of schizophrenia, or dementia praecox, which by 1930 accounted for 22 percent of all first-time psychiatric hospital admissions. Schizophrenia was believed to be the reaction of an "inadequate personality" to his or her environment. The individual diagnosed with schizophrenia displayed a disorganized personality and had a history of educational, vocational, and social failures. The prognosis for an individual with schizophrenia was not good, since practitioners generally believed that schizophrenia resulted in a progressive deterioration of the individual's cognitive capacities.[28]

By the end of 1936, 566,000 patients were housed in institutions or asylums.[29] When one considers that in 1870 the figure stood at 45,000, the increase is rather dramatic. Several practitioners began to speculate on why it was that so many patients seemed to be in need of long-term institutional care. Some hypotheses focused on the changing demographics of the United States population: people lived longer, urban density made it more difficult for an aberrant person to go unnoticed, families could no longer afford to provide a home for unproductive members, and family tensions were on the rise as economic hard times increased.[30] Some practitioners, however, speculated that the increase in hospital admissions was due to the increase in hospital beds.[31]

During this period, Freudian thought began to affect American psychiatry. Psychoanalytic theory emphasized the instinctual life of the individual in the causation of psychiatric illness.[32]

Instinctual conflicts that were unsettled made themselves manifest in the disturbed psyche of the adult. The unconscious mind became a new dimension in the theoretical framework of American psychiatry.

Causal factors of mental illness that were specific to women waned during this period. References to menstrual, puerperal, and climacteric psychosis disappeared from the literature, and there was a general recognition that routine biological processes did not in and of themselves cause mental illness. Instead, practitioners looked to biological transitions as being problematic for particular women. The difficulty that some women experienced with menopause, in particular, was seen as being related to the fear and anxiety that many women had about menopause rather than to the impact of the biological changes themselves.[33] Similarly, menstruation was believed to cause problems only in women whose attitude toward it made it an especially difficult transition.[34]

While there was less of an emphasis on causes of mental illness that were specific to women, Freudian theory did focus some of its attention on women's psychology. There was speculation, for example, that the sexually assertive woman was really a frustrated man, a woman uncomfortable with her own sex.[35] Lesbianism, which was linked to feminism, was also declared to be deviant.[36] Freudian psychology defined both narcissism and masochism as particularly feminine characteristics;[37] some psychoanalysts concluded that feminism threatened a woman's happiness because a woman could not be herself when she was "imitating a man."[38] These psychoanalytic explanations of a woman's psyche served to stigmatize and condemn independent and professional women, rather than to genuinely further the understanding of psychic causality.

Despite the emphasis on psychological determinism by practitioners, the period from 1921 to 1945 saw some of the most radical physical interventions in the treatment of mental illness. During this period, psychosurgery was introduced and prefrontal lobotomies were performed on individuals thought to be "especially refractory."[39] A lobotomy surgically severed the connection between the thalamus and the prefrontal regions of the brain.[40] This procedure was believed to lower emotional responsiveness. It was performed in cases in which worry, anxiety, or apprehension seemed uncontainable.[41] Practitioners were aware, however, that psychosurgery resulted in a loss to the individual of spontaneity and "sparkle."[42]

Some practitioners suggested a prolonged narcosis or sleeping cure for individuals who had acute schizophrenia and were depressed or overly excited. Long-term sleep was believed to break through the patient's autism and emotional disturbance.[43] Several procedures were developed to shock the individual's metabolic system. Insulin shock in particular was designed to produce a coma by creating intense degrees of hypoglycemia.[44] Practitioners believed that a profound shock to the system would change the patient's affective state dramatically. The development of insulin shock was quickly followed by the advent of Metrazol-shock treatment and then by electroconvulsive therapy (ECT). ECT became the treatment of choice because it was safer, simpler to administer, more economical, and apparently less noxious. A single physician, using ECT, could shock thirty patients in under two hours.[45] The prescribed treatment often called for a series of twenty shocks in order to adequately treat patients thought to have schizophrenia.[46]

Another physical intervention designed to treat mental illness, albeit indirectly, was the enforced sterilization of mental patients. Twenty-four states introduced sterilization policies during this period; legislators believed that the best way to "treat" mental disease was to prevent its spread.[47] This practice bespoke an underlying assumption that mental illness was genetically transmitted and could be controlled by preventing "carriers" from reproducing.

In addition to these aggressive physical interventions, the 1920s and 1930s saw several new social treatments applied to the seriously mentally ill. Psychotherapy, or the "talking cure," was a method whereby the patient could talk about his or her symptoms and come to understand the meaning of particular behaviors. The more specialized psychoanalytic technique focused on a reconstruction of early childhood memories and an analysis of the transference that developed between patient and therapist. Harry Stack Sullivan in particular attempted to apply psychoanalytic principles to the treatment of schizophrenia. Both psychotherapy and psychoanalysis focused on reconstructing the chronology of the patient's psychosis. Sullivan believed that there was meaning in the psychotic utterances of patients and that free associations should be encouraged to uncover the true meaning of the psychotic process.[48]

In order to treat patients whose garbled talk was now considered to be meaningful, ward personnel needed to be sensitive and aware of their own personalities and their own dynamics. For the first time, practitioners suggested that perhaps the underlying personality dynamics of the treater were a factor in the treatment.[49]

Several practitioners offered modifications in psychoanalytic techniques normally applied to neurotic patients, in order to treat psychotic patients. With more disturbed patients, psychotherapists needed to be more active, to assist the patient in reestablishing contact with reality, and to work to develop rapport between the treating physician and the patient.[50] Psychoanalysis needed to be combined with advice-giving and reeducation in order to treat very disturbed patients. All of these psychotherapeutic techniques, even the more educational ones, focused on an attempt to understand the forces that shaped the disturbed personality.[51]

In addition to the new practices of psychotherapy and psychoanalysis, the field of rehabilitation therapy assumed prominence during the period after World War I. In past decades, rehabilitation and occupational therapies had been limited to craft and hobby activities; the new focus was on social rehabilitation and on the preparation of an individual for return to the community. Psychiatric rehabilitation stressed the "restoration of a handicapped individual to the fullest mental, emotional, physical, vocational, and economic usefulness of which he or she was capable."[52]

Sheltered workshops in the community were designed for the partially rehabilitated patient who was in transition from the more structured environment of the hospital to the more normalized environment of the community.[53] Occupational therapy was designed to help an individual control his or her emotions and to direct appropriate responses in healthy directions. With a successful rehabilitation effort, a patient might learn to direct his or her actions toward socially useful and acceptable modes of living.[54]

The family or home-based care movement, begun at the beginning of the twentieth century, became more widely prevalent in the 1930s and 1940s. Under systems of family care, patients who no longer required inpatient treatment were placed in homes in the community. This plan reduced the overcrowding in hospitals and promoted the socialization of patients. Family care provided a bridge between inpatient treatment and total release to community life. In that way it was consistent with the practice of "trial release" begun during this period, and it afforded the state a less costly form of residential placement while patients awaited full release.[55]

Family care was not only seen as a residential alternative to hospitalization; it was also viewed as a successful form of treatment in its own right. Family care was especially useful in the treatment of homeless patients who might otherwise be undomiciled. Practitioners believed that by having patients live in normal neighborhoods, the general public would become educated about psychiatric illness and thus would be more receptive to the plight of recovering patients.[56]

Most individuals, however, were still receiving the majority of their treatment in hospitals. This widespread use of hospitalization and the state's presence in the mental health care system led to the establishment of standards for psychiatric hospital treatment. The standards established for mental hospitals proposed that the chief operating officer be a physician or psychiatrist and that all hospital employees be subordinated to that chief administrator. These standards contained provisions to free hospital administration of partisan politics; the medical mission of the hospital was made paramount, and hospitals were removed from the political patronage system. Standards addressed doctor-to-patient ratios and prescribed the contractual arrangement between consulting physicians and the hospital administration. The reporting structure within the hospital as well as issues of recordkeeping and staff education was also specified in this new standardization of care.[57]

Despite these somewhat utopian standards, hospitals during

the 1920s and 1930s continued to suffer from the overcrowding of previous decades. Overcrowding reached such new dimensions that patients slept in attics, basements, and hallways.[58] An examination of the demographics of the hospital population revealed that patient length of stay was represented by a bimodal distribution.[59] Some patients stayed a very short time while others stayed a very long time. The average length of stay was 3.7 years for men and 4.7 years for women.[60] The issue of why women remained hospitalized longer than men was not addressed in the literature of the time, although a lack of economic and family resources that would permit a woman to return sooner to care within her home may certainly have played a role.

During this period, some practitioners became aware that long-term institutional care was in itself detrimental to the mental health of patients. The syndrome of "institutionalization" was described in the literature. Some writers referred to a "prison stupor" in patients whose social contacts diminished and who became passive and unmotivated.[61] Hospitals, while beneficial in the early stages of an illness, seemed to become detrimental after a while.[62] Institutions promoted conformity, deprived persons of individual interests, and obstructed individuality. The conclusion of the psychiatrists who identified the syndrome of institutionalization was similar to the criticisms leveled by women inmates over the years—namely that institutions promoted conformity and actually worked against the free expression of an individual's healthy personality.

Firsthand Accounts

1921–1945

*U*nlike the women who wrote during the two previous periods, the six women whose accounts follow were concerned with their personal experiences of asylum care and not with broader issues of reform. They wrote of the many personal indignities they suffered at the hands of sadistic attendants and of the terror they felt when they received "hydro" and wet pack therapies in particular. Some also described the changing hospital milieu, which now emphasized predictable schedules, social and recreational therapies, and a greater emphasis on "talking cures."

The women whose accounts are presented here are as follows: Marian King, cared for in an unnamed private psychiatric hospital in the Washington, D.C., area in the 1920s; Margaret Isabel Wilson, hospitalized from December 24, 1931, until the end of April 1937 at an institution she pseudonymously refers to as "Blackmoor"; Lenore McCall, who between 1934 and 1938 spent two years in a midwestern sanitarium and one and one-half years at the Institute of Living (Hartford, Connecticut);

Mary Jane Ward, who spent nine months of 1941 in a public psychiatric hospital in New York City; Margaret Aikins Mc-Garr, a patient at Manteno State Hospital (Manteno, Illinois) from October 13, 1943, to July 29, 1944; and Frances Farmer, who after a few days' stay at Los Angeles General Hospital starting January 20, 1943, and a subsequent nine-month stay at the Sanitarium at La Crescenta (California) was a patient at the Western Washington State Hospital for the Insane (Fort Steilacoom, Washington) from March 24, 1944, to July 2, 1944, and again from July 5, 1945, through March 23, 1950.

Marian King

(1920s)

A NUT!" I exclaimed.

"Yes," she replied. "Where do you think you are?"

"I am in a general hospital, but I do not know the name of the place yet."

"Like Hell you are! You are in the Bug House!"

A sudden clutching darkness closed in on me. My breath came short and quick and I opened dry lips. But words would not come.

How long I lay motionless I cannot tell, but when I came to myself, I was alone.

During the second week there was nothing different in the schedule except that we were ordered to take "Hydro." One went down into the basement for the treatment. Needle showers, packs, vapor baths, and salt rubs are given, continuous tubs and rubdowns. There are little dressing-rooms, where one un-

Marian King, excerpts from The Recovery of Myself, *1931. Reprinted by permission of John M. King and Joseph B. King.*

dresses and puts on some sort of a piece of sheeting tied from the neck and hanging in a straight line to the ankles.

One patient refused the Hydro point-blank as she did not think that it was sanitary. I think that she had a germ complex. Another patient who came for the treatment thought that she was married, so when she was summoned by her own name she would call another name back. She would write letters to this so-called husband of hers and would give everyone the name of a bird with a Mrs. attached to the title.

As Thanksgiving drew near I heard the nurse say that there was going to be a bridge and a tea, as well as a dance for the patients. A dance for the patients and the men were to be there too! I don't know why I had that fear because the men were going to be there. I used to dance with the girl patients but I considered that I did not know the men well enough.

As I became more familiar with this little world which I had entered for a time, I rapidly learned the complex technique in the process of restoring us to normal vigor. Just one illustration of this was the vigilant recording of almost everything we patients said or did. When I asked one of the nurses about it, she answered that all these notes go on the individual's chart. I was not much worried about what went on my chart as I knew that I was there to get the drug out of my system and get rid of the habit of taking it. If you said anything that sounded as if a doctor should know it, it was jotted down, so after a while we used to give the nurses a regular line of fictitious impressions. Then the doctor would come around and ask why I said this and why I said that. I told him truthfully that some of the nurses never gave you credit for having any sense whatsoever, and no matter what you said they would give it back to you in the words on your chart. Sometimes some of the things that were written there were quite amusing.

Just "ten days"—as I might have received sentence—had I passed in this little "mental" world of real bolts and bars.

And then the sudden announcement to me: "Full Parole."

Freedom once again—within the boundaries of the "estate."

But a queer sensation came over me. Can you understand that my heart sank?

I was getting to know some of the patients, and here I was going into another ward where I would have to go through the same thing again of learning to know the people, and not only that, but some of us had been there together from the very first day of our admission.

The next day I was handed the daily schedule which I followed for the weeks to come. Here it is:

7–8. Being awakened and getting dressed.

8–8:30. Breakfast.

9. Doctor makes rounds.

9–10:45. Writing or reading.

10:45. Club. Sometimes there were conferences with the various doctors during club and free times.

12. Dinner.

1–1:45. Hydrotherapy.

3–5. Free time. Walks, tennis, teas, library reading, etc.

5. Supper.

5:30. Back in ward and free until 10.

10. Lights out and bed.

Every Sunday the laundry was collected and everyone was asked what she wanted brought from town. One could smoke, if permission was granted by the doctor, so cigarettes could be obtained, but the usual allowance was three a day. Smoking only in the conservatory. All material of this kind was kept in the chart room and every chart room throughout the whole hospital was locked, except when the nurse was in there. One had money in the financial office and this was drawn according to one's own asking for things.

There was always a tea on Thursday and Saturday afternoons. Some of us also got the librarian to let us come to her in the library on odd days and have extra parties. There were always plenty of cookies left from the regular library tea day and, besides that, one could always obtain them from the chart room in the Parole Ward from the nurse in charge.

At intervals there were bridge, dancing, and games. There was usually some amusement on Saturday morning whenever there was not the regular gymnasium. Bowling, tennis, walks, and the like were substituted.

The whole aim of the place was to keep us occupied with interesting activities of wide variety. And every possible provision was made for keeping us busy in a normal and at the same time restorative manner.

I played tennis as often as the weather permitted and I soon found out that I was spending much time on the courts and out of doors in general.

But amid all the pleasant diversions I was looking for the first time into the depths of myself. Just how far had I been turned from a normal, healthy inner life? Even more searchingly did I ask, "Just what kind of person am I?"

Sometimes I would think that the nurse would make some of the others think that I was mentally ill. Well, if I was then, all right, she had reasons to call it a mental sickness. I kept trying to tell her that I was not mentally ill, and the doctors had told my parents that I was not and told me that I was not, too. She told me the reason for saying that I was ill was that if I did not get my own way one way I got it another; said that I was spoiled and, being spoiled as I was, was a mental illness. That I had never had to combat with anything as far as desires were concerned.

PSYCHOTHERAPY

"Dearest Mother and Dad:

"To celebrate New Year's Eve we had a circus in the ward. Our program consisted of a clown-act, a tight-rope walker, a ballet dancer, a bearded woman, and two wild women; the latter was the most appropriate in my estimation considering who we are! No getting away from it.

"I was busy all New Year's Day untrimming the Christmas tree and removing trimmings from the ward. And now all that remains of the holiday is the memory we all cherish.

"The pond is frozen! And those of us who are fortunate enough to possess ice-skates or who could borrow them had a real winter's treat, chaperoned by the gymnasium teacher. The pond is so near the entrance of the hospital grounds that a number of outsiders had gathered and we skated along with them. They never for a moment knew who we were any more than we knew about them. There did come to me a realization that they were on the outside in reality while we were not. But we had a good time anyway.

"Do you know that it is so cold here that the leaves are all curled up in masses and the ground is hard and stiff and in many places very icy?

"I had just been figuring that it was five days since I had a conference with my new doctor when I was sent for to come into his office.

" 'Well, how's the temper?' he inquired pleasantly.

" 'So far, all gone,' I replied.

" 'Do you know that this sudden outburst of yours has been the first opportunity for you to display that selfish desire as well as determination to have your own way? And,' he continued, 'the thing that loomed the largest in your horizon was the desire to go home and with that you were determined to have your own way. You thought that all you had to do was to express your wish in an overemphatic way and that it would be granted.'

" 'But,' I interrupted, 'I soon found out that I did not have anything to say in the matter.'

" 'You had not given yourself a chance, much less the doctors. This certainly should have happened sooner. If you had been on the outside, more than likely you would have sought refuge in the drug by letting it numb your discontentment in sleep. Here, where you could not seize that means of escape, you sought refuge in an outburst of temper. And just where did it get you?'

" 'Nowhere,' I admitted.

" 'Now you are beginning to know your inner self,' he continued. 'Have you read "The Doll's House," by Katherine Mansfield?'

" 'Yes,' I answered.

" 'Now just compare yourself with these little waifs.'

" 'I guess I have got something to think about,' I responded. 'Both the story, and the characters.'

" 'Yes,' he interrupted, 'you have had everything that your heart desired. But these waifs had hardly anything. They were satisfied with the glimpse they had of the doll house, while you on the other hand have had so many beautiful and lasting glimpses that when the time came for you to stop and really look into your inner self, you passed on and let something else get ahead, something that you have to fight. Selfishness, wilfulness, and resentment are your chief obstacles. Now fight them off. Conquer them as you have the drug. Let them find a way out of your system—a natural way.'

" 'But how?' I asked.

" 'By really facing the facts of yourself. Search out the facts which seem hidden from you. Bring them into the light where you can see them. Don't be afraid. And now are there any other questions in particular that you would like to ask?'

" 'Yes, there is one thing that has been constantly puzzling me. Why is it that the talk of sex and sex relations, especially homosexuality, becomes a regular diet with the patients? No sooner does any group of patients gather than someone breaks in with some absurd question about sex.'

" 'Because in some of our conferences the questions that are asked deal with sex problems and those who talk about such problems are the ones who have had the questions asked them. They are eager to discuss this question with anyone who will listen. It is like everything else. It has its beautiful side as well as a vulgar side, but it is you yourself who must decide which it will be for you.'

"An announcement of a new patient being admitted shortened our conference but I guess I have enough to think about until I go to him next.

"Your loving daughter."

It was Sunday, and the day was cold and raw. The outside had no attraction for many of the patients and I found myself a lonesome traveler along the woody paths. I was well and heavily clothed but somehow or other the cold seemed to penetrate through my body. By the time I came back I was chilled and achy all over.

After being in the building some time, I found that I could not get settled down to reading or anything that would afford me my usual amusement. So I decided to get out the big puzzle of twelve hundred pieces which was a map of the city of Washington.

Some of the patients gathered around the three tables we had put together and started in to help find and locate the pieces. We worked on it nearly all the afternoon and by evening we had only a small part finished. Some said that we couldn't possibly do it; that there were far too many pieces and that none would have the patience to do it. But I was not going to give it up as I knew that it had been put together before and it could be done again. I also realized that there was enough work there to occupy many minds and hands for some time.

For two days we worked. Everyone who passed by came over to put a piece in and the doctors were as much interested in it as the patients.

Just as we were getting into the formation of the map, I was taken with bronchitis and the flu.

What a gloom came over me! I wanted to finish the puzzle, I wanted to work like the rest of them at it. But fortunately, I had the first room in the ward and that led out to the living-room. I could hear the various ones working on it and every time someone would get a piece, they would yell in to me and tell me about it. And that was consoling.

While the patients were at dinner, two of the doctors came to work on it. I could hear them say: "I found a piece, now look at this—who would ever have thought? Doesn't this go there?"

The next day found me worse and for a few days all I could do was to listen to my friends shout whenever they found the right piece; and I shared all their excitement and elation from my bed. I felt that I was vicariously helping to reconstruct the national capital with them.

Day after day they worked while I listened. All the while at intervals the heads of my fellow workers would bob in sympathetically at my door and ask what they could do for me.

Then one evening during a dance a friend who was also confined to her room escaped with me to the puzzle tables. Only a few pieces remained. Eagerly we bent over them. In a few moments I had put the last piece into its place. Then we fled back to bed in triumph.

The next morning in came the doctor with an approving smile.

"So you have solved the puzzle," were his first words.

"Yes," I replied, "but I have the most uncanny feeling about it."

"How's that?" he asked.

"That puzzle seems to me like myself," I replied. "There were many pieces all jumbled together. Then many hands and minds have helped to put each part into the whole design so that one could see it as a complete picture."

The doctor smiled thoughtfully. "That's just about what we try to do here," he said slowly. "To help people solve the puzzles of themselves."

"But will the puzzle stay together?" I asked. "Will I, when I go back into the world as something reconstructed, fall apart like the puzzle with the first shaking up or will I meet my problems squarely with the confidence of my new knowledge of self?"

"It is up to you entirely," he rejoined. "You are young, which is a great asset. You have everything that you can wish for. Here you have had to submit to all kinds of discipline and strange experiences. And you have proved yourself.

"Now that your eyes are opened, keep away from that drug. You escaped this time, but you probably would not again."

"Do you really mean that?" I asked soberly.

"I mean every word of it," he answered. "And now"—he went on in a less serious tone—"you can get up as soon as you like. You have only two more days here. We feel that you are ready to go back. Remember that we are all your friends ready to help in the future."

Margaret Isabel Wilson

(1931–1937)

*I*t is not my aim to give a "sob story" of my experiences. I shall simply try to tell how and why I became a voluntary patient in a mental institution, and to give some idea how you might think, act, and feel in my place.

In 1923 I was a teacher in a large college in the South, where I was making a visit to a state hospital for the insane, which was considered second in reputation in the United States. I was impressed. But had I known that eight years later I would be a patient in just such a place as that, I should have been astounded. I was then comparatively young, a modestly intelligent person and a teacher of youths. I had already spent considerable time on the behavior of normal adults, and the study of the abnormal mind did not particularly interest me; but my five years in Blackmoor taught me more among borderland minds than I had ever learned during my long teaching years.

It was a stream of unforeseen circumstances that took me

Margaret Isabel Wilson, excerpts from Borderland Minds, *1940.*

out of normal life into a collapsed world where every value was wrong—into an asylum for mental cases. Looking back, I can easily see how I unwittingly forged the chains that were to bind me for five long years, and how my mistakes and wrong decisions led me into a maze from which escape seemed impossible.

On Christmas Eve, 1931, I arrived at the sanitarium, ostensibly for a temporary stay. The head nurse of the institution escorted me politely upstairs to the second story, as we exchanged a few trifling remarks. As she unlocked the massive door at the top of the flight, I was arrested by loud talking and incoherent expletives.

Another surprise, half an hour later, was a new bathing process. The head nurse ordered a seasoned patient to give me a bath. I demurred, saying that it was my old-fashioned method to take my own bath—a private one—preferably. Miss Lawrence told me firmly that the girl would have to bathe me in a tub and wash my hair. I got the idea at once, for I saw I had to. I was thoroughly scrubbed and weighed. As I stood there shivering, I said, "Miss Lawrence, may I have my nightdress?"

She replied curtly, "Stand still; yours will have to be marked; I'll give you a hospital nightdress."

The ward was thoroughly aired, cleaned, shined, and the walls and ceilings were nicely painted; the corridors were covered with durable, dull linoleum, which was polished daily; the brasses shone; the woodwork was dusted and oiled; and the windowpanes washed well. Indeed, Welcome Ward was immaculate; but also unappealing.

From the very first, I did not like Blackmoor; in fact, it took me only about an hour to decide that it was a poor place for me to take a rest cure as a recuperating person, and before the end of the first week, I felt that the hospital was simply the limit of human endurance. You see, I did not then foresee that my limit of endurance would be more than five years. I was like the famous elastic cat—she was frozen, burnt, boiled, and poured out of a bung-hole—and then the cat came back!

For the new patients, the lesson was taught at once. There was no liberty at all for us. We learned to jump up briskly at the sound of the rising bell, and to dress speedily without answering back. I tried to dress as quickly as I could, for I did not wish to be called "fresh." Some had to be forced, and others were not able to clothe themselves, for they could not think. The rest of the incapables were conducted to the toilet en masse, while we, the more capable ones, would voluntarily make our hasty toilets and were ordered to go directly to the sitting room after the bath room was locked. We could not go back to get a bit of privacy; it was against the ordinance.

After an hour's morning fast, we went to breakfast. There were no morning prayers. Conversation during the meals was taboo.

After breakfast, some of the working patients had regular jobs—no pay, of course. The rest of us were escorted to the toilets again, twenty-five or so. There were three toilet seats, without doors. We waited in turn until the toilet was unlocked. We were supposed to use the seats, whether we needed it or not.

The only warm spot in Welcome Ward was the kitchen, whereas the corridors, toilets, dormitories and the sitting room were inadequately heated, particularly if the patients were compelled to sit in the same chairs most of the day.

The weekly schedule ought to be good discipline for some; the monotony was killing for others, physically and mentally. There were bells, bells, bells; orders, orders, orders. We arose by the bell; ate breakfast by the bell; used the toilet after the bell; occupied the sitting room chairs until the school bell would ring again. After the morning session, another bell would ring to take us back. The supper bell and then the night bell would ring, accompanied by the attendants' raucous orders. Any infringement of a rule would follow curtailment of liberty, if we had any at all.

Here is a specimen of the weekly program. On Sunday, were church services; morning or afternoon, alternate, Protestant or Catholic. The Jewish did not attend, as there was no temple near. During my first months in Welcome Ward there were about seven Protestants. Whether church service was compulsory or not, I cannot recall, but I am sure it was considered desirable. The visiting hours were from two to four on Sunday. After supper, the "medication" (as they termed it) a purge was administered to every patient—a large dose of salts.

The effects of the laxatives kept us patients busy in the toilets during the morning hours. There was school forenoon and afternoon.

Tuesday was the weekly kerosene procedure—soaking the hair with carbon oil to prevent lice; then the bed mattresses were washed lightly with a disinfectant liquid, and afterwards covered with rubber blankets, as soon as they were dry.

I wish you could see the bath; presumably it still goes on. Each Wednesday would be devoted to a half day for the weekly group bath. At nine A.M., the nurse would call in about eight persons in relays; they would undress (some couldn't); then they stood in line and were bathed two by two in a shower, where the older inmates rubbed the patients vigorously, scrubbed the feet and hair, rinsed them and turned them out, while another inmate brought towels, hustled them to the other end of the toilet, while the nurses handed them their clean clothes, made them dress themselves, if they were able, and rushed them into the sitting room.

I believe that the Thursday and Friday schedule consisted of school mornings and afternoons; afternoon dances from two to four—not compulsory, though advisable; baseball in summer, and football in the fall. A movie picture every week. These amusements were really compulsory if the patients were fairly sane.

Every third week was the time to take our group to the beauty parlor. It was well equipped, in charge of an attendant, and had several patients as assistants.

The cold pack was considered one of the hardest ordeals for some. They dreaded it. Even a threat would pacify them and keep them quiet. First, there was a rubber blanket, then a dripping wet sheet placed over it. The attendants laid her down, held her, and tied her hands and feet as she lay on her back. If she were very troublesome, the nurse would get some of the older patients to hold her. Next, another wet sheet, then a wool blanket, two if it were bitter cold; then they were tucked up neatly, a hot bag placed at the feet and an ice bag at the head, if the patient had a temperature. Usually the subject would get warm and sleepy, and finally go to sleep. To be sure, I had seen some patients being treated unfeelingly, and mental abuse is extremely difficult to prove. If your husband abuses you mentally, and you can prove it, you can get a divorce, but it's hard to divorce yourself from an insane asylum.

Some of the inmates did escape, but only a few got away to any distance. During my first year, I heard the siren very often. One man disappeared in the woods and was never found. The authorities then saw to it that the patients were guarded more vigilantly than ever. One woman traveled across to a separate state, spent a carefree week-end, and did some shopping and sight-seeing, for she had some money in her purse. Her husband found her somehow, and persuaded her to go back to Blackmoor.

The result of a runaway is rarely serious; but a suicide would be regarded as one of the gravest injuries to the reputation of a mental hospital. The insane could not be blamed; they should be protected. Mrs. Kendall, whom I met in Welcome Ward while she had been "packed," had been improved so that she was promoted to Ward A. She planned her suicide there, and executed it successfully. Just a few weeks before we had been discussing trivial topics, and then touched on our mental conditions. It appeared to her that she was existing in a "flat land," stationary, in a changeless plane.

Gradually, however, Mrs. Kendall got out from her slough of despondency in part, through her cooperation with the doctors and nurses. She had begun to take a little interest in doing some chores in Ward A. She had always been quiet and aloof. Then I was shocked by the news that Mrs. Kendall had taken her life. Some of the other patients had found her dead, hanging on the bars in one of the corridors, where she had been cleaning.

We had no wholesome activities, no work and no play. There was nothing to talk about except our own pasts. In spite of my apparent self-control, I had actually reached the point of terror and despair, yet none of the attendants realized it. I abhor the word "fear," and I hate to admit that I am afraid. I do not mean that I was obsessed by some obscure phobia; I was afraid of incarceration; I had seen too much of the deadly effects of institutionalization; and I knew that any neurotic subject might break down utterly under the strain. I thought of Mrs. Kendall.

In the early spring of 1935, after we had been housed up all winter, I was persuaded to take a walk with a few hardy patients. My heavy coat had disappeared, so I was forced to take one of the county coats, a thin one. We went two by two; a nurse led the file, and the others followed up the rear. It was a queer procession, a grotesque imitation of an old-fashioned walk in the old private school days, when I was a teacher. We took the twenty-minutes walk through the penetrating wind. It was too much for me; it chilled me thoroughly and gave me a cold which settled somewhere in my back, and stayed there. To take a hot bath without a doctor's order would not be possible in Blackmoor; you would have to use a lot of ingenuity to get thoroughly warm without any means.

RELEASE AND RETURN HOME

When one has been sliding back steadily for over five years, it is a difficult task to climb up; but I have made some progress day by day. I was in bed in my relatives' home for a week or so, then I began to get up after breakfast and go downstairs by holding to the banisters. Afterwards I lay for hours in the sun parlor and looked up into blue sky, and relaxed. Through companionship, my appetite came back; I could sleep in peace, and there was nobody to annoy me. There were no maniacal shrieks to make me shudder; no attendants to yell out orders; no nurses to give me arsenic and physics; no doctors to terrify me by planning to operate upon me.

I was thrilled at the thought that I was free, and should

never have to be incarcerated again. "Never" is a strong word, but I have a conviction that I shall never be in danger again of going into an asylum, voluntarily or involuntarily. After a month of freedom I received a "permanent release" signed by Dr. Berry, the head of Blackmoor, and I have the original in my strong box.

I can count my many blessings, and can also look back at the things I sorely missed in Blackmoor: (1) liberty; (2) my vote; (3) privacy; (4) normal companionship; (5) personal letters and un-censored answers; (6) useful occupation; (7) play; (8) contacts with intelligent minds; (9) pictures, scenery, books, good con-versation; (10) appetizing food.

It took me months to get over the effects of my incarcera-tion. Then I began strolling around my sister's lawn; I took no medicine whatsoever; Nature was my doctor. Then, in July, I went, voluntarily, of course, to one of the larger cities to be examined physically. I said nothing at all to the doctor about my former experience, believing that a wise physician could diag-nose my ailment by observing me. He then reported that I had no organic disease at all, but was under-nourished, had pro-lapsed organs, and was extremely nervous.

To sum up the effects of my asylum experiences: when I entered I had sufficient money in the bank, some real estate, chattels and personal belongings; a position, a fine constitution, and a fair chance to go on with my teaching. My money was wasted, possessions lost, and friends disappeared; I was left with bad nerves, an impaired constitution, and a weakened heart. Courage remained. My compensation is to keep busy, forget and smile at my past, and remember my less fortunate friends. I am only one of the many in Blackmoor.

Lenore McCall

(1934–1938)

*M*y first months at Hilltop were bleak ones for I slid down into the deepest depression and most of my waking hours were spent in weeping. As usual I made a pattern of all my movements to avoid confusion and one of the upholstered chairs, that one which had its back to the bay windows and faced the door, became my special post. There I sat hour after hour, dissolved in bitter tears and racked by sobs. I wept for my lost world, wept in fear and horror, wept because I could see nothing ahead for me but life in this hospital, a downward progress which I was quite sure would end in Foster House, that large building across the grounds which became my bugaboo.

"What is Foster House?" I muttered.

"That's the large building across the lawn from Woodland Hall. It was the original hospital when Dr. Foster started it about forty years ago. It's named for him. He was the founder, you see." Mrs. Peters's mincing cheer had been restored as we once more climbed the hill.

"Yes, but what is it?"

"What's what, Mrs. Fowler?"

"Foster House—what is it?"

"It's a part of the hospital."

"I know. But the people—what kind of patients live there?"

"Well, the very sick ones. You see, each house has a different kind of guest; some are more ill than others. Now, Woodland Hall, where you are is—,"

"I know, but the others—you mean they're quite mad? That woman we saw just now—the nurse wasn't treating her very well."

"Don't you worry about that, Mrs. Fowler. They're all treated well. Only when they're stubborn, well, you see how it is."

Yes, I had seen. I had seen the shapeless bundle that had once been a woman. I had heard the cackle of senseless laughter. I had seen and I had heard and I would not soon forget. So this was it. Foster House. How long would it be before I would be an inmate there? God, why couldn't I have died at St. Luke's. Why couldn't that effort to escape have been successful? I can't go on living.

Bit by bit during the days which followed I learned to know the different buildings of Hilltop and the classification of their inmates. Men and women were both housed in Woodland Hall and their eligibility depended upon their comparatively normal conduct. If you could behave yourself, live peaceably and conventionally with others, carry on the outward semblance of normal living, then you were accepted in Woodland Hall. No one definitely psychotic was admitted.

As Dr. Fisk had told me on his first visit I was kept in seclusion for several weeks, and though I had glimpses of my fellow inmates as I went to and fro on my walks, it was some time before I was allowed any association with them. I did not mind this, for my depression was so deep and so persistent that I was in no condition for personal contact with others. The patients I saw as I traversed the corridor all seemed quite harmless, so normal, in fact, that I began to wonder why some of them were there. But that reaction was born of casual glimpses and I was to know later that each one of those patients carried his or her own private load and they were all fighting their individual battles.

Because I could control the dreadful paroxysms of weeping which, incidentally, had done much to spend me physically, and could conduct myself with more of an outward semblance of conventionality, it was assumed that I was improving. Dr. Fisk, on his occasional visits, did not attempt to discover the underlying cause of my subdued behavior, assured me that my condition was very encouraging and that I was to be given "privileges." This was the sanitarium's term for increased scope of activity. Gradually I took up the normal routine of living in Woodland Hall, though there was nothing really normal about it, save that the inmates ate, dressed and behaved in a perfectly acceptable manner.

I awoke one morning towards the end of May as the door opened and I heard someone come in with my breakfast tray. The shades were raised and then whoever it was came to the foot of the bed where I lay with my hand over my eyes to shut out the bright sunlight which was so agonizing to me.

When the nurse came in the room later I looked at her for the first time. She was neat and sturdy, her cropped red hair curled over her head and freckles spattered her nose. She went about the job of doing my room quietly and the results were much better than those produced by Mrs. Peters's slow-moving efforts. She made one or two casual remarks and seemed to know instinctively that I was not capable of, nor interested in, carrying on a conversation at that hour. Her manner was so unobtrusive and yet so reassuring that I could not resent her.

And so began a period which was the most salutary of all my stay at Hilltop. The young red-haired nurse was a godsend and the year that she was with me was the easiest in some ways of any of my illness. She was not a graduate nurse, very few of the attendants at Hilltop were, but she possessed inherently all the finest qualities so essential to the nursing profession. She had tremendous understanding, unflinching patience and her sole concern was the good of her patient. She established between us in a short time a bond of trust and she never once broke that bond. With her I came closer to piercing the wall that stood between me and my lost world than with anyone else throughout my illness.

I knew that I could count on her in every way. I continued always to insist upon doing what I could for myself, and she encouraged me in this practice. In spite of this, I became dependent upon her in many ways and while this was not to my ultimate advantage, still it quieted some of my fears and eased my tension. When she finally had to leave me a year later I was completely lost and my condition retrogressed steadily from that time. She had kept burning the tiny flames of ambition and energy that remained within me; had succeeded even in kindling a few sporadic sparks of hope in my sick mind and had stimulated me at every turn. I have never seen her since that dreadful day when I knew that she had left the hospital but I shall never forget her.

There was a room under the gymnasium which was known as the "Occupational Therapy Department," and my nurse had been urging me for some time to go there and see if we could not find some work to interest me. So one afternoon I finally agreed but it proved to be a fruitless expedition. From what I later knew of occupational therapy the effort made along those lines at Hilltop was very meager.

It takes a staff of skilled craftsmen and trained workers, tremendous effort and a good deal of capital to make a success of occupational therapy, as I was to learn later. I can only presume that Dr. Taylor's hospital was not able to acquire the personnel, nor did it have the means to set up a proper workshop. At least it made the gesture and Miss Jones, the elderly woman in charge of the department, did what she could.

It was that spring that a horrible obsession laid hold of me. I became convinced that an unpleasant odor emanated from me and it caused me unspeakable torture. I knew that I kept myself clean, for I bathed daily and I changed my clothes as often as was necessary. But I could smell this odor; it was real to me and I grew to loathe myself more and more. It was not my clothes that smelled, it could not be my body which I scrubbed violently every day. So what was it? Was it the odor of corruption? Was it the vile smell of sin? Had the heinous acts for which I was being punished left festering sores on my spirit that were now putrefying?

In shame and desperation I asked my nurse if she could smell the foul odor which I was convinced hung about me. I did not tell her the horrid thoughts that racked my mind in explanation of this imagined smell.

"Of course I don't smell anything, Mrs. Fowler. You're as fresh as a daisy. You're positively fastidious about your personal cleanliness. The only thing I ever smell is a hint of those bath salts that Mrs. Windham sends you. Whatever gave you the idea that you have an unpleasant odor?"

I refused to enlarge upon it any further, but I knew the smell existed. I knew it; there was no question of it in my mind and that delusion persisted until my recovery. It caused strange habit patterns which grew more and more pronounced. I avoided sitting or standing close to anyone else because I was sure that this smell would be noticed by others. I dreaded warm weather from then on because I was convinced that it made the smell stronger and more foul. Whatever room I occupied from then on was unbearably cold for my nurses and attendants because I kept the radiators turned off and always had a window open even in freezing temperatures to clear the atmosphere, as I thought, of the smell.

Transfer to a New Hospital

Heavily, unwillingly I struggled against awakening. I did not want to return to consciousness and face my first day in the Huntingdon Hospital. I did not want to live. I had drawn the window shade the night before but through it glowed the sunlight and I covered my eyes with my hand. I am sick—why can't I be sick enough to die? Don't fool yourself, your kind of sickness isn't fatal. You've got years and years ahead of you.

"Still asleep?" The voice was young and casual. "Your breakfast tray will be here in a minute. It's seven-thirty. You'd better get up."

Seven-thirty. I had never been disturbed before nine at Hilltop, and there my tray was brought in without a word and I was left alone to drag myself into the mists of the day's beginning.

I lay without moving. I can't begin another day. Why didn't I realize how lucky I was at Hilltop? I haven't the courage to face whatever lies ahead. I heard voices in the sitting room. The breakfast tray. I struggled out of bed. Better to get up than to have that nurse ordering me around. Or is she a nurse? She has no uniform. All the nurses at Hilltop wore uniforms. What kind of a place is this?

I took my bath, tears rolling down my face, and dressed myself. I wandered into the sitting room and stood by one of the windows. The spacious grounds of the hospital were covered with snow and there were many figures hurrying along the numerous paths.

There was a knock on the door and I dug my fingernails into the palms of my hands. Hold on, now.

"Good morning, Mrs. Fowler. I suppose you thought we'd forgotten you." Dr. Steward held out his hand. Why, he's young, much younger than the other doctors I've had. Take it easy, and don't forget what you're going to say. Dr. Steward drew up a chair and sat down. I did not speak and I had ignored his gesture of greeting.

"Then I'm sure you're going to find our life here very interesting. There will be plenty to absorb you and a daily schedule will be made out for you after you've been grouped.

"Mrs. Fowler, you're in an institution now where there are rules and regulations, just as there are outside this hospital. You will very soon discover that these rules and regulations are made for the ultimate good of the patients. You must learn the value of cooperation, otherwise your stay with us will not be as pleasant as we try to make it. You must conform to our standards which are no more stringent than the standards of the world to which we are going to return you. Do you understand?

"Now, I've been trying to tell you that you will go to the Science Building this afternoon for the first of your examinations. These examinations and tests are regular routine and will take three or four days. They're quite extensive. When we have all your data compiled, you will be transferred from this suite to another building which will be best suited to your needs and condition. You will also be grouped. Let me explain that the patients in the hospital are put into groups for their routine of activities. They range from Group One to Group Four and you will find that you are placed where you can most easily adjust yourself."

Insulin Treatments

"Mrs. Fowler, I can imagine that you want to know what we're going to do to you. This hypo contains insulin, just a small amount. You won't go into shock today; you'll just feel a bit drowsy. Tomorrow we'll increase the units and you'll feel more cloudy than today. The third day that sensation will increase and you may sleep a bit. By the fourth day you will go into shock. It's really not bad; rather like going under an anesthetic.

"You didn't perspire much today. When you finally go into shock you'll be dripping wet. Now, Mrs. Fowler, swing your legs over the side. Here, let me spread a blanket over them. I want you to sit up and eat your breakfast."

I looked at the large tray and put my hand over my mouth. I'm going to throw up. I stared at the outsize glass of orange juice, at the bowl of oatmeal, the plate of scrambled eggs, the four slices of bacon, the mound of toast swimming in butter, the saucer of marmalade. A pot of coffee stood on the tray, two pitchers of thick, yellow cream and a bowl of sugar. The tall glass of milk was like an insulting exclamation mark.

"I can't eat this—I can't."

"You have to." Miss Kelly stood over me.

"I can't."

"Now, Mrs. Fowler, we might as well get this straight from the start. You've got to eat every smitch of food that's put before you during this series of treatments and part of my job is to see that you do. I don't want to have any unpleasantness, but you're going to eat, do you understand? Go on, dig in."

Breaking through the first sodden layers of consciousness. Up, up, up. Slow, agonizing approach to awareness. I don't want to come out. I've been in oblivion and I don't want to come back. Don't make me, please, don't make me. Up, up, up, one more layer nearer the misery of living. My eye is caught by the gleam of the washstand at the foot of the bed. I close my eyes. I don't want to see. I don't want to look at the trappings of a life that is too horrible to believe.

"Don't uncover yourself, Mrs. Fowler. Stay where you are for just a minute." A thin faraway voice speaks.

My eyes open and I see the dark-brown linoleum floor. I am hanging over the abyss of the bedside. I've been hanging over the abyss of horror for so long. The smell of fresh wool. I am rolled over on the other side of the bed on to dry blankets. Up, up, up, another layer. I don't want to come back. I stare at the wall beside me and nausea grips me. They make me come back every day, day after day, back from the nothingness. The sickness, the taste of blood in my mouth, my tongue is raw.

The gag must have slipped today. The foggy pain in my head.

My night aide, Miss Hagar, who was still on with me, appeared at seven and Miss Kelly left us. Miss Hagar helped me into my coat and we left Ellicott and walked twice around the Little circle. I was exhausted when we returned to my room and I lay on my bed until the aide drew my bath. I undressed wearily, bathed myself and when I came into the bedroom I shuddered at the sight of the tray on the table with its generous sandwiches and its large pot of hot chocolate. Soon I was in bed, the lights were out and I knew another day was over.

This was my unbroken routine for three months and that period is very vague to me. Very little of it is clear in retrospect save the agony of emerging from shock each day and a fragment here and there. The effect of the daily injections of insulin never entirely wore off and I was cloudy and unaware during that time.

RECOVERY

I sat up suddenly, my heart pounding. I looked around the room and a sweep of wonder surged over me.

God in heaven, I'm well. I'm myself. This is I, Anne Fowler. My mind is working. I'm glad to see the day; the sunlight is beautiful to me. I'm well. I've come back from the dead.

That day as I came out of shock I was well aware of the difference in my reaction towards this ordeal. It was bad, yes, it was horrible, but I wanted to come out. I could hardly wait for the cloud to lift and as I struggled through each layer of semi-consciousness I knew that ahead of me lay the wonder that life now signified. I'm well. Up, up, up, this is bad, but it doesn't last long and I'm well.

As I ate my breakfast, feebly joking with Miss Kelly over the vast quantities of food I was obliged to stuff into me, and still a bit hazy from the effects of the insulin, there was a knock on the door and Dr. Felsing came into the room. He held out his hand.

"My felicitations, Mrs. Fowler. We are so happy for you. It is a great achievement and you will forgive me when I say that your recovery means much to me."

"Dr. Felsing, what can I say to you? May I please just tell you that I thank you from the bottom of my heart?" The Viennese made his formal little bow.

"I accept your thanks, Mrs. Fowler, with deep humility. It is wonderful to see you as you are. May I give myself the pleasure of calling upon you later in the day in your residence?"

I stayed in the hospital until the end of May and those four months were the most valuable ones I have ever spent. The knowledge I acquired during that time has taken me unscathed through many a crisis since then. The lessons which I learned in the art of living have enabled me to live a far richer and a more useful life than I had ever known before my illness.

Mary Jane Ward

(1941)

*T*he smoking was a chain proposition. You were allowed
three cigarettes but only one light. When Virginia had lit a
fresh cigarette from her stub she dropped the butt into the cone
and gave it a quick squeeze. You did this expertly and neither
you nor the cone became scorched. Vaguely you remembered
times when you hadn't had any paper, when you had to put a
cigarette out in the palm of your hand. You could spit into your
hand first. I must have dreamed this nonsense. . . .

The guard was shoving a sort of rack that dress shops use
for Special Values. Swinging from the rack were white sacks.
Miss Hart put the rack in the center of the room and the ladies
stopped smoking and began to undress. Virginia started toward
Miss Hart to ask where a telephone was but somehow she didn't
go through with it. She had a feeling that she was not a free
agent and that she had to stay overnight. This was absurd. She

was no criminal and no one could keep her shut up. All she had
to do was say she was leaving; she would not have to say it if she
knew the way out, or if she had one of those keys.

"Forty-three," said Grace. "You've got to remember it. I
don't know what you'll do when I leave. You never remember
your number."

Forty-three. The hangers on the rack were numbered. I am
forty-three. She found the hanger and took it from the rack.
The white sack was supposed to represent a nightgown. It was
enormous and made of material suitable for tents. The number
forty-three was stamped on the garment as sort of trim. The
neck was deep and wide and the sleeves were butterfly.

The system was simple. You hung your clothes on the
hanger and put your shoes under the place numbered forty-
three.

There were four washbowls and you waited in line to brush
your teeth and wash your face. Virginia found soap in her bag
and so could ignore the questionable piece that lay beside the
bowl. Next to her a woman sat in the washbowl to give herself
an intimate bath. Virginia rushed through her washing just in
case the plumbing should collapse. She supposed they wouldn't
blame her but it was as well to be in another part of the room.

"Meditation, ladies," announced Miss Hart.

This was too much. You would not join them in evening
prayers. Virginia had nothing against prayers, but she did not
care to be included. She was extremely tired. The others could
run along and pray if they wished.

But the ubiquitous, mind-reading Grace spoke up. "You've
got to take medication, Virginia. You have got to take it as long
as you are on the list."

"Medication? I thought she said meditation."

"Sure," said a woman who was almost fat enough for the prison gown. "Come on." She had a Dutch bob, always the favorite cut of square-faced, dark, fat women. She looked as if she might make trouble if you didn't come on, and although Virginia felt she would almost rather meditate than medicate, she came on.

They and several other women went through the hall to a room they called the office. At a desk was a woman in white uniform and cap, just as if she was an R.N. She was serving something in lilycups.

Sue graciously let Virginia go ahead but fortunately she was not the first in line and so was able to watch the procedure. The guard poured something into a lilycup and the prisoner drank it down. While the victim choked and sputtered the guard refilled the cup from another pitcher and this was drunk gratefully. One woman just ahead of Virginia knocked the cup from the guard's hand, but the white uniform simply filled another cup and said, "You drink this." The prisoner drank it.

And so did Virginia drink what was handed to her. It was a worse drink than she had expected.

"What is that stuff?" Virginia asked Grace when she met her in the hall a moment later.

"Formaldehyde," said Grace.

"Jesus," said Virginia. If she hadn't been so weary she would have gone to the washroom and put her finger down her throat.

She and Grace went to a sort of dormitory. Grace got into one of the cots and Virginia got into the one next to Grace's. No one threw her out and so it must have been the right cot. She had put her bag under the bed but now she leaned over and dragged it out. It was getting too dark to read but she did not intend to try. She slipped one of Robert's letters from the packet and put it under her pillow and then she felt safer. They are doing their best, but it will take more than formalde-hyde.

Outside of the dormitory someone was screaming. The dormitory, like the toilet booths, had no door and so you heard things easily. Drowsily Virginia imagined running down the hall to rescue the screamer. But then there was quiet.

After a while a guard came and took one of the robed women away. There was pink in the sky now. The pink was turning to red when another woman was taken away. It was nearly light when Virginia was taken.

She was taken down the hall to a little room and the moment she saw that room she knew she had been shocked previously and that she did not care for another helping. The room smelled like her old electric egg beater and there was a dull red glass eye in the wall. "I think I'll go back downstairs," she said.

They put a wedge under her back. It was most uncomfortable. It forced her back into an unnatural position. She looked at the dull glass eye that was set into the wall and she knew that soon it would glow and that she would not see the glow. They were going to electrocute her, not operate on her. Even now the woman was applying a sort of foul-smelling cold paste to your temples. What had you done? You wouldn't have killed anyone and what other crime is there which exacts so severe a penalty? Could they electrocute you for having voted for Norman Thomas? Many people had said the country was going to come to that sort of dictatorship but you hadn't believed it would ever reach this extreme. Dare they kill me without a trial? I demand to see a lawyer. And he—he always talking about hearing voices and never hearing mine . . . He, pretending to be so solicitous of me and not even knowing my name, called me Jeannie. If I say I demand a lawyer they have to do something. It has to do with habeas corpus, something in the Constitution. But they and their smooth talk, they intend to make a corpus of me—they and their good mornings and how are you.

Now the woman was putting clamps on your head, on the paste-smeared temples and here came another one, another nurse-garbed woman and she leaned on your feet as if in a minute you might rise up from the table and strike the ceiling. Your hands tied down, your legs held down. Three against one and the one entangled in machinery.

She opened her mouth to call for a lawyer and the silly woman thrust a gag into it and said, "Thank you, dear," and the foreign devil with the angelic smile and the beautiful voice gave a conspiratorial nod. Soon it would be over. In a way you were glad.

You bathed twice a week. You lined up for the showers. There were two stalls for the forty or fifty women who lived in Ward Three and in order to speed things up you were told to soap yourself before you got under the water. You reached a hand into the spray and caught enough moisture for a lather and in that way you could spend your bath time rinsing. You might almost get completely rinsed before the nurse would tell you to get out. Virginia had not, as yet, ever had a shower stall to herself even for a moment but she understood that this could happen. It was indeed rarely that she had only one other woman in her bath.

Once a week was fine-comb night. You squatted at Miss Hart's feet and she went through your hair with a fine comb. Beside her on a stool was an enameled pan of some clear fluid that you hoped was a strong antiseptic. She dipped the comb in that pan. The same comb was used on everyone. She combed you quickly and efficiently, if roughly, and that was that.

These two processes, the showers and the fine combing, were the only organized efforts in the direction of personal cleanliness. Otherwise you were on your own. You did not have to wash or comb at any other time unless you chose. As far as Virginia could tell, all of the ladies chose. The four wash basins and the strip of mirror above them did not give much chance though. When the way was less crowded you washed your pants and bras and stockings. You hung your washing on your private hanger and if it was not quite dry in the morning, well, there was nothing else to wear.

Looking at the ladies of Ward Three she was again conscious of the terrible odor that always clung to the place. The room was very clean and so the smell must come from the ladies. They did not look so very dirty but on the other hand they did not look so very clean. How could they? If there was any laundry service Virginia had never heard of it. She did not know how long it had been since she and Grace had sat in the park or how long before that she had worn this old dress but she did know that the dress had not been washed since that day in the park and that it certainly had not been clean then. She had worn it every day since then. She had tried to wash off several spots she had got when the Nose in the dining room had flicked gravy at her but the dress needed more than a sponging; it needed throwing away. All of the ladies needed washing and ironing and something done to their hair instead of fine combing. Why fine combing? Was Miss Hart hunting something when she ran that comb through your hair?

The nurse took Virginia into a cubicle where there was a tub. "Not a bad idea," said Virginia. The perspiration was still running down the backs of her legs.

She stepped into the tub. She was not able to get all the way down into it, though. "There's something in it," she said to the nurse. "Cloth or something."

"Never mind the gags, Society Lady. Just lay down."

Virginia lay back in the canvas hammock that was for your head. The tub was filled with water but the tap was still running. "I'd like it a little warmer, please."

"I never saw one for being so cold," said the nurse. She pulled a wooden gadget out of the tub and looked at it. Then she dropped it back into the water. "Right on the nose. Body temperature, Society Lady."

"My body is cold. More hot water, please."

"You lay back and relax." The nurse threw a sheet over the top of the tub, as if it was a bed, as if the sheet would warm the wretchedly tepid water. "There now, take a little shut-eye."

"Sleep in a tub? That's a very dangerous thing to do. Don't you know that more accidents happen in the bathroom? Not that this is a bathroom but . . ."

"I'll keep an eye on you. Just you relax, Society Lady."

"What society?"

"Hm? Oh, Ultra. Very Ultra. Look, I can't hang around and chin. I got my work. But I'm keeping an eye on you, so don't you worry none."

"The person whose blood they measured to find out how much to warm this water," said Virginia, "was a fish. A dead cod."

She [the nurse] had forgotten to turn off the water. At first Virginia thought she was going to be drowned. She was tied into the tub in some way and could not get out. Then she realized that her head was higher than the tub and that the whole room would have to start filling up first. And the little room was only a part of a long hall that had lots of little nooks like this and they would have to fill up first.

She heard water running elsewhere and she heard voices. If the water filled the whole spa then it would run down Juniper Hill and into the sea, the cold water, the wet always and the skin sloughing from the palms of my hands. I am very tired of the water cure.

Wrapped in the robe she was led into another cubicle and the nurse said to get into the tub.

"Is it different water?"

"Yep."

"It looks the same. I thought medicinal waters were colored." She got into the tub. She did not want to. If my hands keep on peeling I will have no more hands. But anything to avoid the ride. "I didn't wash before," she said. "Could I have some soap?"

"You're clean as a newborn babe."

"Are they clean?"

"Don't go technical on me, Society Lady."

"I think I would like to go to the bathroom."

"Well, go ahead. Don't mind me." The nurse spread a sheet over the tub.

"I have to go to the toilet, nurse."

"Go ahead."

"You'll have to help me out."

"Look, Society Lady, if you gotta go, go."

"In the tub!"

"The water's changing all the time."

"I think that's perfectly disgusting."

"Don't give me that, Society Lady."

"What's the point of changing tubs?"

"It's the law," said the nurse. "We are getting around the law, but don't you worry about that."

"I am tired of being in a tub."

The nurse went away and after a while she came back. She was talking to someone with her. "Of course you aren't supposed to be in here, Mr. Cunningham," she was saying, "but we thought . . . Virginia, your husband is here. He's going to give you your lunch now. Isn't that nice?"

The man sat on the low chair beside the tub. Virginia looked at him long enough to see that he resembled Robert very closely. Then she turned her head away. They had fooled her once, but they could never fool her again. They had put her head into a sack the last time. I remember. I remember very well that they fooled me about him coming and then they put my head in a sack. I am not utsnay enough to fall for that trick again.

The man talked and talked. She would have told him what she thought of anyone who made a business of masquerading as other people's husbands, but she knew if she opened her mouth he would stick food into it. She was smart. She kept her mouth and her eyes shut tight and after a while he went away.

When she opened her eyes another man was there. It may have been the same clever impersonator; it may have been himself as himself. This time he was not calling her darling as he had done before; he was calling her Jeannie now. But he was harping on the same subject. Food. She would throw up in his face.

They had let the water run out of the tub but the bedding

was sopping wet. They had taken the tile walls away and enlarged the cubicle to make it look like a room. They had even put a window into it. Oh, the trouble they went to. They couldn't be satisfied with electrocuting you and choking you; they had to bundle you up in icy wrappings and then torture you with food. Say it again and I'll scream.

You wanted to get well. You never had a conscious moment in which you were not aware of being sick. You could no more, while conscious, forget your sickness than you could forget to breathe. Asked your greatest wish in life you would have replied at once—sanity. How remote was the world in which sanity was taken for granted. In the world outside, people longed desperately to be millionaires, movie actors, club presidents and even, tell me little gypsy what force creates this one, even novelists. True, a bad cold, a touch of heartburn, an allergy to a favorite dog could blot out for a time the desire for money, power and fame. During the period of the running nose, the stomach ache or the asthmatic wheeze physical well-being would stand alone in the spotlight of yearning. But nowhere, nowhere save the madhouse, did mental health get its share of prayers.

At Juniper Hill there was one real god, one real goal, one real love. The patient who possessed the smallest seed of sanity cherished it tenderly.

Two women in civilian dress assisted at the party. Virginia had a sickening conviction that they were church or club women earning merit badges and the privilege of telling their acquaintances over teacups about exotic and dangerous adventures among the insane. In loud saccharine voices these amateur social workers explained that there was to be a very gay game with prizes. Virginia was unable to concentrate on anything but the bitter difference between her clothes and the costumes of the hostesses, but the other patients got through the game of lotto without effort or enthusiasm. They played it as if it was a chore to be got out of the way. When a lady filled a row she announced it and she took her prize, a candy bar, and divided it among the other players at her table. The hostesses were upset about this dividing and would try to explain that when you won you were entitled to keep the prize for yourself. The sick ladies looked at the well ladies and did not understand; they had quite forgotten the ways of the world.

I am nearing non-patient status. The softness is leaving. The sympathy. Yes, and the generosity . . . I no longer distribute cigarettes the way I used to. It is a queer way to judge your sanity. I shall feel better about this return of selfishness if I consider it a return of antlike wisdom. I am able now to take heed of the day to come. I have three cigarettes and if I look ahead I'll see that I cannot order more until the day after tomorrow. Therefore I shall not share my supply but I shall hoard it so that each day I can be sure of having one smoke. That, dear lady, is sanity. An insane woman would give all three cigarettes away and then wonder why she hadn't any for herself. And sit off in a corner with a roll of newspaper . . .

Margaret Aikins McGarr

(1943–1944)

*T*his is my story—a tragic one. Most of it is true—but I have in most parts given fictitious names to persons and places to safeguard the living—many of whom still live in "The Institution"—or other such so-called "Mental Institutions." It is the story of how I, too, came to suffer mentally and was incarcerated "for my own good"—*supposedly*—in such an institution.

I was then a young woman—well preserved, tall and dignified; yes, and I may truthfully say, fairly good-looking and cultured. I say this candidly because it is the truth and not because I wish to boast, for there would be no good reason to boast.

I had been torn from my home, my loved ones—and borne away to "the institution." The worst that could happen to me, it seemed then, had happened. Death is easy; it is the end of things. There is no longer any suffering; there is peace of mind —rest, blessed rest. The body and the soul are at rest.

But, when taken to a "mental institution," it is only too

Margaret Aikins McGarr, excerpts from and lo, the STAR, *1953.*

often the beginning of a new and terrible life—a living hell instead of the rest and relaxation and cure it should be and is declared to be.

Yes, there I was—there I stood, looking sheepishly about me. I was shorn of the dignity of clothing—*my* clothing, which was being snatched from me and hastily tabulated on a record sheet by the white-clad attendants of this "Psychopathic Hospital" where I had been taken by people I had every reason to trust. People who, supposedly, meant only the best for me; wanted me cured of what was troubling me so that I could be speedily returned to them and normal society in perfectly normal, natural state—mentally.

But I could not believe then that I was not right. I was as sane as any of them; perhaps a little high-strung; my nerves a bit frayed, due to overwork and too much to think about. But certainly far, far from being mentally unbalanced.

It had all come so suddenly—this taking me away, bringing me here. What did all this mean? As I stood there I had a strange, uneasy feeling that I was being betrayed—especially when the person who had brought me there had suddenly left me. I felt so all alone—entirely deserted.

It is only fitting that I now tell somewhat more of my background than already told—that you may understand me and my story the better.

My little "prairie home" was built at the peak of prices in 1929—but I got all the breaks, for, when depression set in and the company that built for me crashed in market speculation, my payments were suspended for a year. In the end H.O.L.C. took over my account, however, reducing my future payments to less than half of what I had been paying.

Later, I sold the old homestead in Michigan after it could

no longer be rented without a great outlay of money and finished paying for my prairie home.

I have always said that God gave me my summer cottage. I got the 100 square feet of lake property when Wisconsin liquidated her taxable land, for forty dollars' back taxes. About that time, the school board paid the teachers their back salaries and having few debts, I spent half the money on a cottage. I built cheaply through the Best Built Company, but well—of second-hand lumber—vermin-proofed through chemical treatment. It had a stone fireplace, screened-in porch and plywood walls, stained. I had a small basement added and the plumbing installed. In the spring I added some interesting, useful, much-needed cupboards to the kitchen and corner dish cupboards in the living room.

I made a terrace from the dirt out of the basement. It gave me a grand view of a small, private lake and a country church.

And in my little prairie home it was pleasant on warm, sunny mornings to carry my breakfast tray to my back yard terrace, all screened in with shrubbery, with vines climbing over the rocks and trained against the house like a drop-curtain on a stage. It was delightful to gaze on such a scene.

There were always birds and gophers to watch. One season a baby gopher nibbled crumbs that I dropped for him at my feet. I named him Johnny Junior.

There came a time every season when it was necessary to cut down the thistles near the house to keep them out of the garden. It was great fun hunting and swatting down "Bengal tigers"—as we played. Sometimes I could induce the small boys in the neighborhood to help me—then the hunt was really exciting.

As the town house is located beyond all sewers, there was

great difficulty in curbing the seepage water from January until June. An electric pump carried off the water, but made the basement impossible to finish into the recreation room I had hoped for. Keeping the pump in order so that the oil burner would be kept running was always my greatest problem.

During the coolest weather of 1942, I was without heat for weeks. Fuel was almost impossible to obtain. No European had any greater housing and heating problem than I had. I would wear old coats and sweaters, bundle up with several blankets on the davenport where I sat and read with my mittens on. This experience did not help me mentally, though I made the best of it. That winter was followed by the great heat of the summer when I was stricken with my sunstroke.

Perhaps few would have noticed my change had I not had to try to carry on with my teaching—and then had the fainting spell which led me to the hospital.

It was while I was in the hospital, lying on my back viewing the crucifixion—the psychic picture of the Holy Family for several days—that I realized I had been remiss in my church relationship.

The psychic picture creates an illusion. You casually see only the Holy Family and saints, but on looking at it intensely you see a nude figure of a woman enter the circle and reappear fully clothed. It is the SOUL.

There in the loneliness of that room I confessed my sins again, before God, and felt I had experienced re-birth—being accepted within the family circle of God's own.

My resolution was to live a better, Christian life—KNOW THYSELF.

I had many sessions with the "psychiatrist." It did relieve my mind, telling my worries, my troubles, I must admit. I told her of how a gang of teasing young scamps whom I watched leave their games one time, crept through the grass Indian fashion to tap on the water-board around my house, hoping to frighten me. It was very aggravating the way they tried to turn my place into a "haunted home."

In my talks with my psychiatrist, I relived much of my childhood—days with Mother and Father. Father was always very fond of me. I would race to meet him evenings and take his hand, sometimes without even an exchange of words, depending on his mood. We would walk along in silent understanding. Father was what is known as undemonstrative. He was tall, straight and distinguished-looking in cropped beard, robust of figure, ruddy-complected and white-haired, after thirty. He had laughing Irish blue eyes.

When my brother was drowned at the age of twelve, I was nine, but I tried in a child's feeble way to take his place in their hearts. After more than fifty years I still have his little straw hat found on the river bank.

One night a group of us "inmates" were taken in "covered wagon" auto to our new wards. The run of the mill in this ward were older women: mothers who didn't fit into the modern house of some upstart west-sider, mothers of social climbers, mothers who had foreign accents, mothers whose families had deserted them in their later days. Some were elderly women like Rebecca, the Jewish woman who knew seven languages—but not even enough English to ask for things. She was quite attracted by the design on my blue and white print housedress. She was trying to tell me something pleasant and instructive about it. I was the dumb pupil. Later, I happened upon the fact that the design was a Jewish symbol of the brush used by the Jews in sprinkling blood on the lintels of the doors in the first

Passover. I discovered the same design on a grey and white dress I had with me; one of the four dresses I had been allowed by my conservator. Rebecca could sew nicely and might have earned her way with some Jewish family had the way opened up for her.

Then there was a lovely Swedish girl named Esther. She had beautiful clothes and a new permanent wave when she entered. She grew quite nervous and very frightened at being left there. She refused to eat. The attendants and the "strong men" of the ward, however, grabbed her and actually pulled her lovely hair out by the roots in "force feeding" her.

She clung to me for a long time and we became pals, trying to cheer each other up. I remember how we stood at the window in late October and she recited, "The frost is on the pumpkin."

She was finally sent to "Hydra." I had seen Hydra once when I had volunteered to let the nurse demonstrate "the pack" to a visiting nursing class.

This consisted of a patient being packed in cold, wet sheets —and I understand that in disciplinary cases the packed "mummy" is then put into a tub of ice cold water. Then they also get the cold water "treatment"—a shock treatment which is more an outlet for the viciousness of the attendant than a help to the patient. Most of the "Hydra" patients deteriorate very rapidly.

One of the strange, interesting interviews I had by a psychologist interviewer while I was there brought forth another new point which surprised me.

"Lady," he asked me, "do you think you are a saint?"

I looked at him in amazement. "I certainly am not a saint!" I exclaimed. "Whatever gave you the idea that I'd think that?"

He smiled indulgently and said, "Because you seem to think of yourself as a seer, an apostle, or a fortune teller; don't you?"

Again I indignantly denied each accusation. I tried to reason it out in my mind. I wondered if, because I had wanted *The Apostle*, by Sholom Asch, a book which had been reviewed and pushed by the bookstores—and I had written that this would be one of my first purchases when buying books again—if that had given this man the false impression about me.

Also—because, perhaps I associated my affliction with that of the apostle, Paul, he might have thought I considered it my biography, or closely akin to it.

A bit later in our interview, he mentioned "rebirth" to me. "Just how do you consider such an experience as rebirth possible?" he inquired.

I told him frankly, "Because I consider anyone who feels truly sorry for his sins and turns to God—while he may be found, asking forgiveness—is forgiven. And that one's sins are cast into the Sea of Forgetfulness.

"Yes—" I told him boldly, sure of my ground, fearless, "when one tries to do better in every way—that is *re-birth*—a Christian's rebirth!"

I had about given up hope that they would ever let me out of the institution, for I had tried a number of times in various ways to get out. Yes, I had even run away that time, and been sent back with added time tacked on as punishment.

But ever in my heart and mind was the hope that someday they would consider me "cured"—if, indeed, I had ever really been insane. I had merely had a touch of the sun. I would someday be released—and all would once again be well with me.

So it came finally as a distinct surprise to me when my release came—but a wonderfully welcome surprise.

Here is how it goes in most cases—and did in my own:

The patient is working away one moment at her regular work in the institution—and the next he or she is told to go back to the ward, and then, someone in authority gives out the wonderful news:

"You're going home!"

It is by then an almost unbelievable message. But it is nonetheless welcome. Hasty goodbyes are said and everyone is glad for you and sends you off with the best of wishes—seeming to be and acting sincerely glad for your good luck.

There are many things the patient of a mental institution is intent upon after release. Upon his recovery, the patient generally endeavors to account for the "urges" which came from being mentally ill. It would seem to be a reenactment of the various lives the patient has lived and familiar experiences like a rehearsed act. It lacks the piquancy of undirected movement, however.

The body expresses the thing that is in the soul. It is as though we came back many times to the earth—and retained some of our bodily, mental and spiritual characteristics, seeking perfection through transmission and reincarnation of the soul.

I thought of myself in spirit as a kind of Pegasus, the White Horse—the escapee from man. I had always been the runaway type. I thought of Peg being the nickname for Margaret.

Insanity, the psychologists admit, is an effort to escape from bitter reality, including a lot of roundabout thinking.

I remember how, while I was a "patient," I was constantly reaching out to friends on the "outside"—hoping I might interest them in my case. But, alas, only too often "outsiders" think a patient is getting the best of treatment and is in good hands—

so they do not concern themselves with the existing facts of whether the patient is well enough to be released or not.

Wartime measures kept many of my friends from coming to see me. They explained to me in their letters that they had to "watch their auto tires" even in taking an extra ride around the block. And gas, too, was a big problem.

The patient has no way to ascertain what may be holding up the progress of his or her release. Although I knew a lawyer had been engaged, I had not learned why my retained attorney was so slow in getting action in my case.

There are many laws relating to the release of "mentals" and many rules that the institutions must observe. The patient may be better versed on the laws governing his or her release often than his or her signee.

It is said that people who have had a "psycho" or "psychio" experience (I suppose "mentals" are all such), have a great awareness, a keenness of mind that causes them to so manage their affairs that they often become very wealthy and even make their friends rich at times through their suggestions.

And again—others become humanitarians, giving of themselves for the good of others. I am of this latter class.

Every book-reviewing magazine shows that more and more is being written to take the "hush, hush" out of the problems of the mentally ill. I want to do just that. My pride is not of this earth. Help is needed—and I want to do all I can to help.

Frances Farmer

(1943–1950)

For eight years I was an inmate in a state asylum for the insane. During those years I passed through such unbearable terror that I deteriorated into a wild, frightened creature intent only on survival.

And I survived.

I was raped by orderlies, gnawed on by rats, and poisoned by tainted food.

And I survived.

I was chained in padded cells, strapped into straitjackets, and half drowned in ice baths.

And I survived.

The asylum itself was a steel trap, and I was not released from its jaws alive and victorious. I crawled out mutilated, whimpering and terribly alone.

But I did survive.

Frances Farmer, excerpts from Will There Really Be a Morning? *Copyright © 1972 by Frances Farmer. Reprinted by permission of the Putnam Publishing Group.*

The three thousand and forty days I spent as an inmate inflicted wounds to my spirit that could never heal. They remain, raw-edged and festering, for I learned there is no victory in survival—only grief.

I can recall the twisting circumstances that eventually locked me into a world devoid of all hope, but I cannot rationalize why it happened. All that is left is the painful memory that it did occur and that somehow I managed to live through it.

The asylum was about thirty-five miles south of Seattle, and somewhere along that frightening drive, I regained consciousness.

There was no ventilation in the truck, and the close air was rancid with the stench of sweat and stale urine. How many others had been hauled into hell . . . lashed to that same hammock? Straining their flesh against the straps. Wetting on themselves. Befouling their bodies. Feeling chunks of vomit and sour bile fill their mouths. Helpless. Terrified. Alone. Some, perhaps, mad beyond reason but still alive. Still able to feel. Still able to care.

From the truck, they carried me to a small admitting ward, and despite my thrashing, three orderlies finally succeeded in strapping me into an armless wooden chair that was bolted to the floor.

Much later a nurse and two women attendants came for me. I was sleeping soundly, and when they untied me from the chair, I was unable to stand. My legs crumpled under my weight. I slumped to the floor and began to sob uncontrollably as needle-like pains shot up my legs and my calf muscles knotted in spasms.

The women dumped me back in the chair, but the nurse knelt in front of me and massaged my legs until I gradually felt my muscles relaxing, and I was able to stand.

They took me to a small infirmary, where the nurse washed off my face and swabbed and sprayed my nose with a medication that gagged me. She was impersonal but efficient.

I asked for a drink of water, and since I was still in the straitjacket, one of the women held a paper cup to my mouth while I greedily gulped down the tepid water. I wanted more, but she refused me a second cup.

The nurse made notes on a report sheet, stuffed it into a folder, and handed it to one of the women. From the infirmary I walked between them down a long dim corridor. We stopped before a double door with the words ISOLATION WARD stenciled across it.

One of the women pushed a buzzer, and the door was unlocked from the inside by a nurse. I was guided into a large ward which resembled an underground cave.

The nurse was a tall, lean woman whose hair looked like thick cotton pasted on her head. It was cut blunt and short and held back over her ears by black bobby pins that stood out like ebony spears.

The attendants shuffled impatiently while she fumbled through my record. She read a few lines, then peered curiously at me. Then read on. Finally she said, "Take her to the toilet, then we'll put her in seven."

They took me to a small room a short distance down the hall. It was about ten feet long and not more than six feet wide. When the door was pushed open, a hideous, deathlike odor streamed out with such force that I began coughing.

A dirty washstand, an ancient bathtub and two stools cramped the closetlike quarters. The room was filthy. Rusty iron rings were bolted to the floor on either side of each stool. From an unlocked wall cabinet one of the attendants took out a darkstained canvas strap with hooks on either end and an adjusting buckle in the middle.

The other woman stood me in front of one of the toilets, reached under my dress, and pulled down my pants. They were soiled and damp, and I felt a wave of embarrassment as they fell around my ankles.

My pants lay on the floor, and I strained until I was able to clamp my toes around the ugly, soiled material. I scooted my filthy foot back toward me and kicked them behind the stool and out of my sight.

I waited until every muscle in my body spasmed, and I started screaming and kept it up until the three of them came charging into the toilet. One of the attendants slapped me hard across the face and my nose started to bleed again.

"You'd better learn to keep your mouth shut 'cause there ain't nobody gonna hear you but us, and we ain't gonna listen."

"Ignorant bastard," I snarled, spitting out a flow of obscenities at her until she tried to shut me up by rapping the palm of her hand back and forth across my face with the rhythmic rat-a-tat of a machine gun.

When the other attendant stooped to unlock the strap, I started to get up, but the woman who had struck me pushed hard on my shoulders and shoved me back on the toilet. She leaned on me until my buttocks swam in the dirty water.

"Hold your horses, big shot, and spread your legs apart."

She had several sheets of toilet paper balled up in her hand and proceeded to grind the paper into me until I was begging her to stop. She stood up and with one hand clamped her fingers around my chin in a steel grip and pinched my jaws until my mouth was held open involuntarily. I was terrified at the look on her face, and when I saw her lifting the wad of wet paper toward my mouth, I tried to scream, but her fingers slipped down and clutched my throat in a painful vise.

I knew, perhaps for the first time, pure fright, but I was unable to speak. Only groans and whimpers came from me. I looked at the nurse, begging her with my eyes to help me, but she seemed busy at the wall cupboard. She was aware of what was going on, and I knew it, but she was removing herself from the episode. The other attendant looked away, and I caught a fleeting shade of sympathy cross her face.

"Open wide, big shot," the woman said. "You might as well learn now, 'cause in here sooner or later everybody eats their own shit."

The three of them took me to a cell near the center of the ward. Its only furnishing was an iron cot anchored to the wall. On the cot was a thin mattress, with a sheet but no blanket or pillow. The barred window was closed and the smell was as rank as the toilet, musty and rotten.

One attendant unbuckled the straitjacket and my arms fell limply to my sides. The other attendant, the one who had hit me, leaned against the door and frowned at me. When the straitjacket was removed, I tried to flex my shoulder muscles but flinched at the pain and stiffness. I had lost track of the hours I had been in it.

Dr. Conway pushed back his chair and locked his hands behind his head. "Do you realize," he mused, "that it was your mother who obtained the court order for your commitment and that she has already appeared before this board and given her testimony?"

He tapped a folder on the table in front of him. "From what we have here, she has not painted a very pretty picture, Mrs. Anderson, and I'm of the opinion that you are entitled to know the major charges she has brought out in her testimony."

"You listen to me, big boy. I couldn't care less what she says. So don't waste your breath. And don't ever mention her name to me again."

"Now, Mrs. Anderson," Dr. Browning (a female psychiatrist present at the hearing) interrupted, "you must admit that it isn't normal for a mature person to be so antagonistic toward one's mother."

"You silly woman," I blurted. "You absurd, silly woman. You lock me up in a crazy house and then tell me that I'm not acting normal. Jesus Christ!"

I slouched back in my chair and watched him [Dr. Conway] shuffle through the papers before him. "We'll discuss the testimony on page four, paragraph three. Dr. Rocky, will you handle the questioning?"

Rocky was a slight, middle-aged man, who chomped vigorously on the stem of an unlit pipe.

"Mrs. Anderson," he began, "Dr. Conway told you that your mother has brought some very serious charges against you. She was informed, by this board, prior to her testimony that whatever she said would be included in your records so please understand that she was well aware of the critical consequences of her charges.

"Now, we have no reason to doubt her, for she seems deeply concerned about your welfare. According to her, you were out of control and she therefore found it necessary to petition the court for a permanent commitment.

"Also, as your legal guardian, she has given us permission to prescribe whatever treatment we consider necessary to assist in your possible recovery.

"Furthermore, your mother has given testimony which indicates that you are dangerous to yourself and others. Therefore, it is no longer safe for you to be at large. She has testified that you have made violent attacks against her person, and she gave further evidence relating to your mistreatment of your dog."

Looking around at the other doctors for agreement, he said, "I think you doctors will concur with me that this patient should not be given open-ward privileges." They all nodded.

It was a critical time. Tax-supported institutions could not provide high enough salaries to entice people away from defense work, and it is an indisputable fact that during this period the asylums were operated by the inmates.

Where I was, wild-eyed patients were made trustees. Homosexuals wormed their way into supervisory positions. Sadists ruled wards. Orderlies raped at will. So did doctors. Many women were given medical care only when abortions were performed. Some of the orderlies pimped and set up prostitution rings within the institution, smuggling men into the outbuildings and supplying them with women. There must be a twisted perversion in having an insane woman, and anything was permitted against them, for it is a common belief that "crazy people" do not know what is happening to them.

Buildings crumbled in filth and decay. Heating plants broke down and went unrepaired. Rats nested in every ward, and it was not uncommon to see them leaping onto food trays, fighting with patients for morsels.

Decent food, clothing and supplies never reached the patients but were either bootlegged by the employees or enjoyed by the executive staff. Women hardly able to function were put to hard labor under the guise of occupational therapy. Old men worked the farm fields day in and day out until they stumbled and fell from exhaustion. Many men, already driven mad, spent ten to twelve hours a day in the slaughterhouse, killing pigs and wading in blood. All day long they clubbed and stabbed and gutted, and then, at night, they would scream in howling misery.

Wards were like neighborhoods, full of intrigue, graft and gossip. Cliques were formed. Enemies were made. Fights were constant.

The orderly unlocked my restraints, and the nurse told a dull-eyed trustee to take me to my cot, halfway down the room.

"Prep her for hydro," she called after us.

The trustee pointed to an unmade cot, telling me to remember which one was mine, then steered me through the ward into a small room fitted with three bathtubs.

Women were in two of them, their heads sticking out from the canvas sheets stretched tightly over the tubs. Their bathing caps made their heads look like skulls.

One woman was screaming, her voice hoarse. Her eyes popped and blazed, seeing nothing as she thrashed under the canvas. She kept screaming for someone named Arnold, then would sink into babbling.

Before I could organize myself, the trustee had taken down three canvas straps from a hook on the wall and looped one around my chest, pinning my arms against my sides until my breath was cut short. The second was buckled around my thighs, and the third around my ankles.

She left the room as I tottered to keep my balance. I tried to hop after her but tumbled headlong. My chin cracked against the floor and I felt a sharp pain as my teeth sliced my lower lip. I lay there screaming, flopping, trying to maneuver myself into a sitting position, but, tied as I was, I was unable to do little more than rock back and forth on my stomach.

The trustee returned with a student nurse and another attendant, who pulled me to my feet and stood behind me while the nurse checked my bindings, easing the one around my chest. I was still screaming and gabbling, spitting blood from my mouth, but the wound was ignored. They picked me up, one by the ankles, the other by the shoulders and dropped me into the empty tub, bruising my spine.

They pulled the heavy canvas sheet up to my neck, and while one tightened the neck drawstring, the other took a long dirty rope and looped it under the lip of the tub. The rope was wound around and around until it made a tight band that kept the canvas secure.

The first crash of icy water hit my ankles and slipped rapidly up my legs. I began to shake from the shock of it, screaming and thrashing my body under the sheet, but the more I struggled, the more I realized that I was helplessly restricted in a frozen hell.

I began to gnaw on my lip, flinching from the pain of my teeth digging into the wound but praying that it would take my mind off the freezing water that burned my body like acid.

Hydro was a violent and crushing method of shock treatment, even though it was intended to relax the patient. What it really did was assault the body and horrify the mind until both withered with exhaustion.

I lay there in the glacier grip until my mind had gone blank. I felt it slipping from me, but I tried to keep it active by thinking of addresses, phone numbers, nursery rhymes. I counted forward and backward. I became confused. I recited the alphabet, but everything was jumbled. I struggled, and screamed, and froze. Then, like the incoherent woman calling for Arnold, I slid out of awareness and tumbled into a gibbering, scrambled maze.

For the next twenty-four days I was depersonalized in hydro. The physical pain, the spiritual injury, the mental torture mashed one day into another, until all thoughts hinged on either being in or out of the tub. Nothing else existed.

Soon after the treatments started, I began to menstruate, and a trustee brought two small paper sacks and put them by my cot. In one was a pile of worn sheeting that had been torn into narrow strips. These were to be folded and used. When the rag was soiled, I was told to put it in the other sack, and at the end of my period, I was responsible for washing them out for reuse. There were no pins or belts of any kind allowed in the asylum, so the rags were simply held in place by keeping the legs pressed together. Later I learned that many of the women fashioned slings by tying a rag around their waist and one between their legs.

Hydro was prescribed for a three-hour duration, but seldom did the treatments terminate on time, and the endless hours in the cold water attacked my bowels and bladder. Lying in the water, with my nerves and system violated, knowing that my blood and waste were mingling with it, offended and grieved my spirit beyond description. My femininity was mauled, my power to reason or struggle vanished. I simply existed in chilling confusion.

I was unnaturally calm at the end of three weeks, for I had been systematically deenergized. All personality was washed away and all that was left was a water-logged robot.

I had been tamed.

During the third month, I was moved to another ward. I had graduated from shock, and as a reward, I was housed with the aged and infirm, the theory being that an inmate fresh from shock was incapable of any responsibility except the most menial. Those of us who were put on practical duty were expected to take care of the aged bedridden.

The old were pitiful in their wrinkled agony. Toothless and blind women, rotting away, were given only the most primitive care. We were to feed them once a day, on no particular schedule. We would wait until the soup cart was brought to the ward, for their one meal was always a weak, colorless broth, and those acting as pseudo-trustees filled buckets from the soup kettles and went from bed to bed, feeding with the same spoon, from the same bucket.

Patients were never washed or talked to. They lay on their thin, filthy cots and waited for death. No one ever visited them. No one ever inquired about them. Forgotten relics doomed to lie in a grave marked only by the state.

And they died, I remember, mostly in the wee hours of the night. They would slip away in the blackness, and we would find them in the morning, already cold. Their bodies stiff, and their sightless eyes open, milky and dead.

Just before Christmas, after seven months as an inmate, I was told to appear before Staff to discuss my parole.

Although I desperately wanted to be free, I was frightened by the news. My confined life offered a kind of twisted security. Rules were made, and if they were broken, the offender was punished. There was safety in routine. The thought of being thrown back into a world where money and ambition created a pressure pot terrified me. As I dressed for Staff, I was tense and nervous. I wondered whether I could remember how to act "normal," or if I had been caged too long.

Go to any state or county, and look into the ancient buildings or behind the modern facades. Search through the long dim corridors and peek into the grieved souls of the patients

. . . and then say to yourself, if you can, "Things are getting better." Indeed, in comparison to our times, they regress, and the terror of insanity still screams into unresponsive ears. And so, as I recall the five years that I spent locked in the violent ward of a state asylum, I do so with the knowledge that the same force of evil still lives in so-called hospitals.

Epilogue

The first-person accounts presented in *Women of the Asylum* constitute an important, previously missing part of the history of American psychiatry. As historical documents, these narratives tell the stories of women who were locked away, usually against their will, in order to receive treatment for mental illnesses, the legitimacy of which they often questioned and frequently challenged.

It would be reassuring to believe that these accounts exist merely as historical records, reminders of a now distant past. The truth is, fifty years after the events recorded in the last account, women are still decrying their oppression at the hands of would-be healers and misguided family members. The recent memoirs of Kate Millet, Barbara Noel, and Susanna Kaysen all describe the personal agony, the fear, and the tyranny that sometimes accompany even modern psychiatric treatment.[1]

Certainly, the past fifty years have brought significant changes not only in how psychiatric care is delivered but also in where it is rendered. Asylum care has given way to community-based treatment. The introduction of medications that control psychotic symptoms has decreased the need to use incarceration, seclusion, and gross means of physical restraint to subdue unruly patients. As a result, more and more women (and men) are able to receive all or most of their psychiatric treatment as outpatients.

The consumer and patients' rights movements, buttressed by first-person accounts of abusive or misguided treatment, have helped to mandate that treatment be delivered in "the least restrictive environment." Class-action court cases in many states, as well as more individual and personal attempts at advocacy, have helped thousands of women avoid unnecessary institutionalization. Economic realities have spurred health care planners to seek less costly alternatives to long-term inpatient hospitalization. All this has resulted in the closing of psychiatric hospital beds nationwide and the development of community-based residential, case management, and outpatient programs.

Does this shift away from inpatient care and the apparent demise of the asylum mean that the "women of the asylum"— those recipients of psychiatric care who view their treatment as oppressive personal and political tyranny—are vanishing from the scene as well? Regrettably not. What it does mean is that we must look elsewhere for this generation's women of the asylum. They no longer languish in institutions; instead they are crowded into psychiatric ghettos and warehoused in city shelters for the homeless.

The scars of psychiatric treatment are different in the 1990s. Overmedication has replaced long-term hospitalization as a way of exerting punitive control over unruly patients. The termination of parental rights and the absence of residential programs for mothers and children have replaced sterilization as a way to deny the sexual and maternal needs of women who are labeled as mentally ill. And social stigma and discrimination have replaced legal sanctions as ways of preventing women from returning to the mainstream of community and family life.

Whenever treatment is delivered in an environment that institutionalizes the power imbalance between caregiver and patient, attendant and inmate, or expert and novice, the potential for oppression exists. Sexual abuse, intimidation, and dehumanization—all described by asylum inmates—continue to exist in modern treatment relationships. The words of an anonymous woman patient written only a few years ago are hauntingly similar to accounts recorded in the last century.

> They broke into my room and got hold of me. They wouldn't listen. They were in a hurry. I started hollering, asking for help and nobody on the floor would help me. So finally they grabbed hold of me. They took me right into the wagon there. They brought me over here, sat me down, and went away.

The walls of the asylum may have come down, but the voices of the *Women of the Asylum* continue to echo. It only remains for us to hear.

Notes

INTRODUCTION

1. "Scene in a Private Mad-House," *Asylum Journal* 1 (1842): 1.
2. Letter, I. Ray to D. Dix, August 31, 1864, collection of Houghton Library, Harvard University. Cited with permission.
3. L. T. Ulrich, *A Midwife's Tale* (New York: Vintage Books, 1991).
4. L. Schlissel, *Women's Diaries of the Westward Journey* (New York: Schocken Books, 1982).
5. G. Allport, *The Use of Personal Documents in Psychological Science* (Social Science Research Council, 1942).
6. P. Chesler, *Women and Madness* (San Diego: Harcourt Brace Jovanovich, 1972).
7. E. Showalter, *The Female Malady* (New York: Viking Penguin, 1985).
8. Chesler, *Women and Madness*.

PERIOD I: 1840–1865

1. B. Welter, "The Cult of True Womanhood," *American Quarterly* 18 (1966): 151–74.
2. M. J. Buhle and P. Buhle, eds., *The Concise History of Woman Suffrage* (Urbana, Ill.: University of Illinois Press, 1978).
3. C. Hymowitz and M. Weissman, *A History of Women in America* (New York: Bantam Books, 1978).

4. M. Ryan, *The Empire of the Mother: American Writing About Domesticity 1830–1860* (New York: The Haworth Press, 1982).
5. Hymowitz and Weissman, *History of Women in America.*
6. C. Smith-Rosenberg, *Disorderly Conduct* (Oxford: Oxford University Press, 1985).
7. I. Ray, *Mental Hygiene* (Boston: Ticknor & Fields, 1863).
8. B. L. Epstein, *The Politics of Domesticity* (Middletown, Conn.: Wesleyan University Press, 1981).
9. R. Gundry, "Observations on Peripheral Insanity," *American Journal of Insanity* 16 (1860): 294–320.
10. J. McDonald, "Puerperal Insanity," *American Journal of Insanity* 6 (1847): 113–63.
11. Welter, "Cult of True Womanhood."
12. Hymowitz and Weissman, *History of Women in America.*
13. E. Jarvis, "The Causes of Mental Disease," *Journal of Mental Science* 4 (1860): 119–40.
14. Hymowitz and Weissman, *History of Women in America.*
15. Ibid.
16. D. Meyer, *Sex and Power: The Rise of Women in America, Russia, Sweden, and Italy*, 2nd ed. (Middletown, Conn.: Wesleyan University Press, 1989).
17. L. Schlissel, *Women's Diaries of the Westward Journey* (New York: Schocken Books, 1982).
18. M. H. Blewitt, *We Will Rise in Our Might: Working Women's Voices from Nineteenth Century New England* (Ithaca, N.Y.: Cornell University Press, 1991).
19. Smith-Rosenberg, *Disorderly Conduct.*
20. Ibid.
21. O. Banks, *Faces of Feminism* (Oxford: Basil Blackwell Ltd., 1986).
22. D. L. Rhode, *Justice and Gender* (Cambridge: Harvard University Press, 1989).
23. Buhle and Buhle, *Concise History of Woman Suffrage.*
24. Hymowitz and Weissman, *History of Women in America.*
25. S. M. Evans, *Born for Liberty: A History of Women in America* (New York: The Free Press, 1989).
26. Buhle and Buhle, *Concise History of Woman Suffrage.*
27. W. F. Browne, *What Asylums Were, Are, and Ought to Be* (Edinburgh: Adam and Charles Black, 1837).

28. S. Woodward, *The Tenth Annual Report of the Trustees of the State Lunatic Hospital at Worcester* (Worcester, Mass.: Barton, Dutton & Wentworth, 1843).
29. E. Jarvis, "Causes of Insanity," *Boston Medical and Surgical Journal* 45 (1851): 289–305.
30. Browne, *What Asylums Were.*
31. Jarvis, "Causes of Insanity."
32. J. Conolly, "Hysteria," in *Cyclopaedia of Practical Medicine*, ed. Forbes et al. (Philadelphia: Lee & Blanchard, 1845).
33. H. R. Storer, "The Medical Management of Insane Women," *Boston Medical and Surgical Journal* 61 (1864): 209–18.
34. Conolly, "Hysteria."
35. McDonald, "Puerperal Insanity."
36. Ray, *Mental Hygiene.*
37. Jarvis, "Causes of Insanity."
38. J. Bates, "Report on the Medical Treatment of Insanity, and the Diseases Most Frequently Accompanying It," *American Journal of Insanity* 7 (1850): 97–111.
39. D. Noble, "On the Use of Opium in the Treatment of Insanity," *Journal of Mental Science* 4 (1858): 111–18.
40. S. B. Woodward, "Observations on the Medical Treatment of Insanity," *American Journal of Insanity* 7 (1850): 1–34.
41. Ibid.
42. Ibid.
43. A. Brigham, "The Moral Treatment of Insanity," *American Journal of Insanity* 4 (1847): 1–15.
44. Ibid.
45. Browne, *What Asylums Were.*
46. J. Conolly, "On Residences for the Insane," *Journal of Mental Science* 5 (1859): 411–20.
47. I. Ray, *A Treatise on the Medical Jurisprudence of Insanity* (Boston: Little & Brown, 1837).
48. A. Brigham, "Insanity and Insane Hospitals," *North American Review* 44 (1837): 91–121.
49. "Hospitals for the Insane," *Boston Medical and Surgical Journal* 49 (1853): 86.
50. "By Laws, Established by the Trustees of the State Lunatic Hospital," 1845, Worcester, Mass.

51. E. Jarvis, "The Influence and Distance from and Proximity to an Insane Hospital, on Its Uses by Any People," *Boston Medical and Surgical Journal* 62 (1850): 209–22.
52. Ibid.
53. E. Jarvis, "On the Proper Functions of Private Institutions or Homes for the Insane," *American Journal of Insanity* 17 (1860): 19–31.
54. S. B. Woodward, Ninth Annual Report of the Trustees of the State Lunatic Hospital at Worcester (Worcester, Mass.: 1842). Barton, Dutton & Wentworth.
55. I. Ray, "The Popular Feeling Toward the Hospitals for the Insane," *American Journal of Insanity* 9 (1852): 36–65.
56. J. M. Galt, "On the Medico-Legal Question of the Confinement of the Insane," *American Journal of Insanity* 9 (1853): 217–23.

PERIOD II: 1866–1890

1. C. Smith-Rosenberg, *Disorderly Conduct* (Oxford: Oxford University Press, 1985).
2. Ibid.
3. N. Cott, *The Grounding of Modern Feminism* (New Haven, Conn.: Yale University Press, 1987).
4. C. Hymowitz and M. Weissman, *A History of Women in America* (New York: Bantam Books, 1978).
5. S. M. Evans, *Born for Liberty: A History of Women in America* (New York: The Free Press, 1989).
6. S. Rothman, *Woman's Proper Place: A History of Changing Ideals and Practices, 1870 to the Present* (New York: Basic Books, 1978).
7. Hymowitz and Weissman, *History of Women in America*.
8. T. P. Martin, *The Sound of Our Own Voices* (Boston: Beacon Press, 1987).
9. Hymowitz and Weissman, *History of Women in America*.
10. Cott, *Grounding of Modern Feminism*.
11. Hymowitz and Weissman, *History of Women in America*.
12. M. Ryan, *Womanhood in America* (New York: Franklin Watts, 1983).
13. B. L. Epstein, *The Politics of Domesticity* (Middletown, Conn.: Wesleyan University Press, 1981).
14. Evans, *Born for Liberty*.

15. D. Meyer, *Sex and Power: The Rise of Women in America, Russia, Sweden, and Italy*, 2nd ed. (Middletown, Conn.: Wesleyan University Press, 1987).
16. Epstein, *Politics of Domesticity*.
17. C. Smith-Rosenberg, "Beauty, the Beast and the Militant Woman," in *A Heritage of Her Own*, ed. Cott and Pleck (New York: Simon & Schuster, 1979), 197–221.
18. Hymowitz and Weissman, *History of Women in America*.
19. M. J. Buhle and P. Buhle, eds., *The Concise History of Woman Suffrage* (Urbana, Ill.: University of Illinois Press, 1978).
20. O. Banks, *Faces of Feminism* (Oxford: Basil Blackwell Ltd., 1986).
21. Smith-Rosenberg, *Disorderly Conduct*.
22. Cott, *Grounding of Modern Feminism*.
23. Smith-Rosenberg, *Disorderly Conduct*.
24. B. Ehrenreich and D. English, *For Her Own Good: 150 Years of Experts' Advice to Women* (New York: Doubleday, 1978).
25. "Provision for the Insane in the United States," *American Journal of Insanity* 33 (1876): 92–97.
26. W. Channing, "An International Classification of Mental Diseases," *American Journal of Insanity* 44 (1888): 361–80.
27. J. P. Gray, "The Dependence of Insanity on Physical Disease," *American Journal of Insanity* 26 (1869): 49–80.
28. "A Project of a System of Statistics," *American Journal of Insanity* 26 (1869): 49–80.
29. F. Pratt, "The Increase of Insanity in the United States—Its Causes and Sources," *Journal of the American Medical Association* 1 (1883): 668–75.
30. O. Everts, "Common Errors: Theoretical and Practical, Relating to Insanity," *American Journal of Insanity* 43 (1886): 221–42.
31. H. P. Stearns, *Insanity: Its Causes and Prevention* (New York: G. P. Putnam's Sons, 1883).
32. "Insanity and Uterine Disease," *American Journal of Insanity* 37 (1881): 443.
33. P. F. Munde, "Clinical Observations in Reflex Genital Neurosis in the Female," *Journal of Nervous and Mental Disease* 13 (1886): 129–39.
34. "Insanity in Menstruation," *Alienist and Neurologist* 5 (1884): 546.
35. "Female Hallucinations," *Boston Medical and Surgical Journal* 108 (1883): 358.

36. E. H. Van Deusen, "Observations on a Form of Nervous Prostration (Neurasthenia), Culminating in Insanity," *American Journal of Insanity* 25 (1869): 445–61.
37. E. C. Mann, "The Nature and Treatment of Hysteria," *Alienist and Neurologist* 1 (1880): 533–40.
38. Ibid.
39. Ehrenreich and English, *For Her Own Good.*
40. "Hydrotherapy in Mental Diseases," *Boston Medical and Surgical Journal* 117 (1887): 187. "The Abuse of Massage," *Alienist and Neurologist* 6 (1885): 627–29. "Electricity in Insanity of Seven Years Duration," *Journal of Nervous and Mental Disease* 11 (1884): 303–4.
41. H. M. Bannister and H. N. Moyer, "On Restraint and Seclusion in American Institutions for the Insane," *Journal of Nervous and Mental Disease* 9 (1882): 457–78.
42. W. B. Goldsmith, "Report on Progress in Mental Disease," *Boston Medical and Surgical Journal* 108 (1883): 369–70.
43. J. B. Andrews, "The Distribution and Care of the Insane in the United States," *American Journal of Insanity* 44 (1887): 192–205.
44. "Oophorectomy at Cleveland Asylum," *American Journal of Insanity* 43 (1887): 364–65.
45. S. W. Mitchell, *Lectures on Diseases of the Nervous System, Especially in Women* (Philadelphia: Lea Brothers & Co., 1885).
46. "The Treatment of Ovarian Pain in Hysteria," *Journal of Nervous and Mental Disease* 10 (1883): 720–21.
47. Mann, "Nature and Treatment of Hysteria."
48. "Cauterization of the Clitoris in the Treatment of Hysteria," *Journal of Nervous and Mental Disease* 10 (1883): 177.
49. "What Then?" *Alienist and Neurologist* 6 (1885): 446–65.
50. S. W. Mitchell, *Fat and Blood and How to Make Them* (Philadelphia: J. B. Lippincott & Co., 1882).
51. S. W. Mitchell, "Massage," *Journal of Nervous and Mental Disease* 4 (1877): 636–38.
52. S. W. Mitchell, *Doctor and Patient* (Philadelphia: J. B. Lippincott & Co., 1888).
53. M. A. Cleaves, "The Medical and Moral Care of Female Patients in Hospitals for the Insane," *Proceedings of the Annual Conference of Charities* 6 (1879): 73–83.

54. G. C. Paoli, "Female Physicians in Insane Hospitals: Their Advantages and Disadvantages," *Alienist and Neurologist* 8 (1887): 21–29.

55. "The Twenty-Fifth Meeting of the Medical Superintendents of American Institutions for the Insane," *American Journal of Insanity* 27 (1871): 503–4.

56. C. H. Hughes, "The Rights of the Insane," *Alienist and Neurologist* 4 (1883): 183–89.

57. O. Everts, "Treatment of the Insane as Related to Science, and General Conditions of Humanity Historically Considered," *American Journal of Insanity* 46 (1890): 354–62.

58. C. F. Folsom, "Recent Progress in Mental Disease," *Boston Medical and Surgical Journal* 105 (1881): 393–97.

59. "Training School for Attendants," *American Journal of Insanity* 42 (1885): 267–69.

60. H. M. Hurd, "The Data of Recovery from Insanity," *American Journal of Insanity* 43 (1886): 243–66.

61. J. G. Kiernan, "Contributions to Psychiatry," *Journal of Nervous and Mental Disease* 10 (1883): 26–35.

62. G. C. Palmer, "The Colony System of Caring for the Insane," *American Journal of Insanity* 44 (1887): 157–69.

63. "Hospital Treatment for the Insane," *Journal of Nervous and Mental Disease* 16 (1889): 596–99.

64. "Family Care of the Insane," *Journal of Nervous and Mental Disease* 12 (1885): 398.

65. T. W. Fisher, "Recent Progress in the Treatment of Mental Disease," *Boston Medical and Surgical Journal* 103 (1880): 490–93.

66. E. C. Spitzka, "Merits and Motives of the Movement for Asylum Reform," *Journal of Nervous and Mental Disease* 5 (1878): 694–714.

67. F. C. Barlow, M. B. Anderson, and T. Hun, "Report," *American Journal of Insanity* 29 (1873): 590–95.

68. B. Cushing, "The Commitment of the Insane," *Boston Medical and Surgical Journal* 102 (1880): 32–33.

69. T. W. Fisher, "The Commitment and Certification of the Insane," *Boston Medical and Surgical Journal* 102 (1880): 578–82.

NOTES

PERIOD III: 1891–1920

1. C. Smith-Rosenberg, *Disorderly Conduct* (Oxford: Oxford University Press, 1985).
2. D. Brown, *Setting a Course: American Women in the 1920's* (Boston: Twayne Publishers, 1987).
3. O. Banks, *Faces of Feminism* (Oxford: Basil Blackwell Ltd., 1986).
4. D. Meyer, *Sex and Power: The Rise of Women in America, Russia, Sweden, and Italy* (Middletown, Conn.: Wesleyan University Press, 1987).
5. S. Rothman, *Woman's Proper Place: A History of Changing Ideals and Practices, 1870 to the Present* (New York: Basic Books, 1978).
6. B. Ehrenreich and D. English, *For Her Own Good: 150 Years of Experts' Advice to Women* (New York: Doubleday, 1978).
7. M. Ryan, "The Projection of a New Womanhood: The Movie Moderns in the 1920's," in *Decades of Discontent*, ed. L. Scharf and J. Jensen (Boston: Northeastern University Press, 1987), 113–30.
8. R. Rosenberg, *Divided Lives: American Women in the Twentieth Century* (New York: Hill & Wang, 1992).
9. Ehrenreich and English, *For Her Own Good.*
10. Rothman, *Woman's Proper Place.*
11. Banks, *Faces of Feminism.*
12. T. P. Martin, *The Sound of Our Own Voices* (Boston: Beacon Press, 1987).
13. Brown, *Setting a Course.*
14. Rosenberg, *Divided Lives.*
15. Ibid.
16. A. Scott and A. Scott, "One Half the People: The Fight for Woman Suffrage," in *Women's America: Refocusing the Past*, ed. L. K. Kerber and J. S. DeHart (New York: Oxford University Press, 1991), 326–39.
17. M. J. Buhle and P. Buhle, eds., *The Concise History of Woman Suffrage* (Urbana, Ill.: University of Illinois Press, 1978).
18. Banks, *Faces of Feminism.*
19. Ibid.
20. W. Chafe, *The Paradox of Change: American Women in the 20th Century* (New York: Oxford University Press, 1991).
21. C. Hymowitz and M. Weissman, *A History of Women in America* (New York: Bantam Books, 1978).
22. Chafe, *Paradox of Change.*

23. Hymowitz and Weissman, *History of Women in America*.
24. N. Cott, *The Grounding of Modern Feminism* (New Haven, Conn.: Yale University Press, 1987).
25. A. Kessler-Harris, "Where Are the Organized Women Workers," in *Women's America: Refocusing the Past*, ed. L. K. Kerber and J. S. De-Hart (New York: Oxford University Press, 1991), 252–67.
26. Cott, *Grounding of Modern Feminism*.
27. Rothman, *Woman's Proper Place*.
28. Chafe, *Paradox of Change*.
29. Kessler-Harris, "Organized Women Workers."
30. D. L. Rhode, *Justice and Gender* (Cambridge: Harvard University Press, 1989).
31. Rothman, *Woman's Proper Place*.
32. Kessler-Harris, "Organized Women Workers."
33. Chafe, *Paradox of Change*.
34. W. L. Russell, "The Medical Services of State Hospitals for the Insane," *American Journal of Insanity* 66 (1910): 365–82.
35. C. F. Neu, "A Few Important Points in Regard to Nervous and Mental Diseases," *Alienist and Neurologist* 30 (1909): 42–62.
36. W. F. Drewry, "The Insane," *Alienist and Neurologist* 31 (1910): 36–53.
37. J. V. May, "Immigration as a Problem in the State Care of the Insane," *American Journal of Insanity* 69 (1912): 313–22.
38. W. A. White and F. M. Barnes, "A Plan for Indexing Cases in Hospitals for the Insane," *American Journal of Insanity* 69 (1912): 92–105.
39. W. A. White, "Schemes for a Standard Minimum Examination of Mental Cases for Use in Hospitals for the Insane," *American Journal of Insanity* 67 (1910): 17–24.
40. Ibid.
41. W. W. Hawke, "The Importance of Complete Records of the Insane and a Few Remarks, Concerning Chiefly the Preliminary Examination," *American Journal of Insanity* 67 (1910): 25–35.
42. F. M. Barnes, "Chemistry of Nervous and Mental Diseases," *American Journal of Insanity* 68 (1912): 431–72.
43. Ibid. S. D. Wilgus, "Remarks on State Charities Laws with Suggestion for a Standard Type to Cover the Needs of Present-day Management and Also the Mental Hygiene Movement Looking to Prevention," *American Journal of Insanity* 73 (1917): 499–517. J. Collins and

E. G. Zabriskie, "Neuroses in the Light of Our Present Knowledge," *Alienist and Neurologist* 28 (1907): 34–71.

44. "Neurasthenia," *Alienist and Neurologist* 28 (1907): 294–95.

45. W. A. White, "Psychoanalytic Tendencies," *American Journal of Insanity* 72 (1917): 599–607.

46. "Menstruation," *Alienist and Neurologist* 14 (1893): 486–87.

47. "Puerperal Insanity," *American Journal of Insanity* 59 (1903): 727–28.

48. J. G. Kiernan, "Kleptomania and Collectivism," *Alienist and Neurologist* 23 (1902): 449–55.

49. D. S. Booth, "Coitus Interruptus and Coitus Reservatus as Causes of Profound Neuroses and Psychoses," *Alienist and Neurologist* 27 (1906): 397–406.

50. "One of Those Erotopathic Women," *Alienist and Neurologist* 28 (1907): 245.

51. "The Farmer's Wife and Insanity," *Alienist and Neurologist* 28 (1907): 419–20.

52. A. Myerson, "Out-Patient Psychiatry," *American Journal of Psychiatry* 77 (1920): 47–74.

53. "Diversion of the Insane," *Alienist and Neurologist* 32 (1911): 345–46.

54. W. W. Ireland, "On the Physiological Feebleness of Women," *Journal of Mental Science* 49 (1903): 540–42.

55. J. G. Kiernan, "A Medico-Legal Phase of Auto-Erotism in Women," *Alienist and Neurologist* 31 (1910): 329–38.

56. L. P. Clark and H. P. A. Montgomery, "Suggestions and Plans for Psychopathic Wards, Pavilions and Hospitals for American Cities," *American Journal of Insanity* 61 (1904): 1–30.

57. M. S. Gregory, "Reception Hospitals, Psychopathic Wards and Psychopathic Hospitals," *American Journal of Insanity* 65 (1908): 63–76.

58. Clark and Montgomery, "Suggestions and Plans."

59. F. Peterson, "Twentieth Century Methods of Provision for the Insane," *American Journal of Insanity* 58 (1902): 405–22.

60. J. G. Rogers, "A Century of Hospital Building for the Insane," *American Journal of Insanity* 57 (1900): 1–19.

61. C. G. Wagner, "The Care of the Insane," *American Journal of Insanity* 59 (1903): 521–627.

62. "Ohio Insane Asylum Ex-Employees Indicted," *Alienist and Neurologist* 28 (1907): 239. A. C. Clark, "The Future of Asylum Service," *American Journal of Insanity* 50 (1894): 354–61.

63. O. Copp, "The Psychiatric Needs of a Large Community," *American Journal of Insanity* 73 (1916): 79–88.

64. E. Riggs, "An Outline of the Progress in the Care and Handling of the Insane in the Last Twenty Years," *Journal of Nervous and Mental Disease* 20 (1893): 620–28.

65. A. V. Goss, "Occupation as a Remedial Agent in the Treatment of Mental Disease," *American Journal of Insanity* 70 (1913): 477–86. "Moving Pictures for the Insane," *Alienist and Neurologist* 32 (1911): 344. C. F. Haviland and C. L. Carlisle, "Extension of Tent Treatment to Additional Classes of the Insane," *American Journal of Insanity* 62 (1905): 95–113.

66. C. G. Wagner, "Recent Trends in Psychiatry," *American Journal of Insanity* 74 (1917): 1–14. L. V. Briggs and A. W. Stearns, "Recent Extension of Out-Patient Work in Massachusetts State Hospitals for the Insane and Feeble-Minded," *American Journal of Insanity* 72 (1915): 35–43.

67. H. R. Stedman, C. L. Dana, and F. X. Dercum, "Report of the Committee of the American Neurological Association upon the After-Care of the Insane," *Journal of Nervous and Mental Disease* 24 (1897): 658–62.

68. A. W. Stearns, "The Value of Outpatient Work Among the Insane," *American Journal of Insanity* 74 (1918): 595–602.

69. J. M. Buckley, "The Possible Influence of Rational Conversation on the Insane," *American Journal of Insanity* 59 (1902): 117–27.

70. C. W. Burr, "A Criticism of Psychoanalysis," *American Journal of Insanity* 71 (1914): 233–48.

71. E. S. Abbott, "What Is Mental Hygiene?" *American Journal of Psychiatry* 81 (1924): 261–84.

72. W. D. Granger, "Review of Laws Regulating Voluntary Commitment of the Insane to Asylums," *Journal of Nervous and Mental Disease* 18 (1891): 132–35.

NOTES

PERIOD IV: 1921–1945

1. N. Cott, *The Grounding of Modern Feminism* (New Haven, Conn.: Yale University Press, 1987).
2. E. Showalter, ed., *These Modern Women: Autobiographical Essays from the Twenties* (New York: The Feminist Press at the City University of New York, 1989).
3. G. H. Douglas, *Women of the 20's* (Dallas: Saybrook Publishers, 1986).
4. S. M. Evans, *Born for Liberty: A History of Women in America* (New York: The Free Press, 1989).
5. S. Rothman, *Woman's Proper Place: A History of Changing Ideals and Practices, 1870 to the Present* (New York: Basic Books, 1978).
6. B. Ehrenreich and D. English, *For Her Own Good: 150 Years of Experts' Advice to Women* (New York: Doubleday, 1978).
7. R. Schwartz-Cowan, "Two Washes in the Morning and a Bridge Party at Night: The American Housewife Between the Wars," in *Decades of Discontent*, eds. L. Scharf and J. Jensen (Boston: Northeastern University Press, 1987), 177–96.
8. Ibid.
9. Evans, *Born for Liberty*.
10. Cott, *Grounding of Modern Feminism*.
11. R. Schwartz-Cowan, "The Industrial Revolution in the Home: Household Technology and Social Change in the Twentieth Century," in *Women's America: Refocusing the Past*, eds. L. K. Kerber and J. S. DeHart (New York: Oxford University Press, 1991), 372–85.
12. M. Ryan, *Womanhood in America* (New York: Franklin Watts, 1983).
13. Evans, *Born for Liberty*.
14. R. Rosenberg, *Divided Lives: American Women in the Twentieth Century* (New York: Hill & Wang, 1992).
15. W. Chafe, *The Paradox of Change: American Women in the 20th Century* (New York: Oxford University Press, 1991).
16. Evans, *Born for Liberty*.
17. Rosenberg, *Divided Lives*.
18. Ryan, *Womanhood in America*.
19. Rothman, *Woman's Proper Place*.
20. Rosenberg, *Divided Lives*.
21. O. Banks, *Faces of Feminism* (Oxford: Basil Blackwell Ltd., 1986).
22. Evans, *Born for Liberty*.

23. Chafe, *Paradox of Change.*
24. W. Healy, "The Newer Psychiatry," *American Journal of Psychiatry* 82 (1926): 391–401.
25. W. L. Russell, "The Place of the American Psychiatric Association in Modern Psychiatric Organization and Progress," *American Journal of Psychiatry* 89 (1932): 1–18.
26. E. S. Abbott, "What Is Mental Hygiene?" *American Journal of Psychiatry* 81 (1924): 261–84.
27. N. A. Dayton, "The First Year of the New Standard Nomenclature of Diseases in Massachusetts Mental Hospitals," *American Journal of Psychiatry* 92 (1935): 589–613.
28. J. V. May, "The Dementia Praecox–Schizophrenia Problem," *American Journal of Psychiatry* 88 (1931): 401–46.
29. W. Overholser, "The Desiderata of Central Administrative Control of State Mental Hospitals," *American Journal of Psychiatry* 96 (1939): 517–34.
30. S. W. Hamilton and G. A. Kemp, "Trends with Activities of Mental Hospitals," *American Journal of Psychiatry* 96 (1939): 551–74.
31. H. Adler, "A Note on Admissions to State Institutions," *American Journal of Psychiatry* 89 (1933): 1339–43.
32. W. C. Garvin, "The Influence of Modern Psychopathology in State Hospital Practice," *American Journal of Psychiatry* 85 (1929): 661–68.
33. C. B. Farrar and R. M. Franks, "Menopause and Psychosis," *American Journal of Psychiatry* 87 (1931): 1031–44.
34. E. B. Allen and G. W. Henry, "The Relation of Menstruation to Personality Disorders," *American Journal of Psychiatry* 90 (1933): 239–76.
35. C. Hymowitz and M. Weissman, *A History of Women in America* (New York: Bantam Books, 1978).
36. Cott, *Grounding of Modern Feminism.*
37. Ryan, *Womanhood in America.*
38. Cott, *Grounding of Modern Feminism.*
39. W. Freeman and J. W. Watts, "Prefrontal Lobotomy in the Treatment of Mental Disorders," *Southern Medical Journal* 30 (1937): 23–31.
40. W. Freeman and J. W. Watts, "Prefrontal Lobotomy," *American Journal of Psychiatry* 101 (1945): 739–49.
41. Ibid.

42. Freeman and Watts, "Prefrontal Lobotomy in Treatment."
43. P. Hoch, "Treatment of Schizophrenia with Prolonged Narcoses," *Psychiatric Quarterly* 9 (1934): 386–90.
44. M. Sakel, "The Methodical Use of Hypoglycemia in the Treatment of Psychosis," *American Journal of Psychiatry* 94 (1937): 111–29.
45. L. B. Kalinowsky, N. Bigelow, and P. Brikates, "Electric Shock Therapy in State Hospital Practice," *Psychiatric Quarterly* 15 (1941): 450–59.
46. L. B. Kalinowsky and J. H. Worthing, "Results with Electric Convulsive Therapy in 200 Cases of Schizophrenia," *Psychiatric Quarterly* 17 (1943): 144–53.
47. C. J. Gamble, "State Sterilization Programs for the Prophylactic Control of Mental Disease and Mental Deficiency," *American Journal of Psychiatry* 102 (1945): 289–93.
48. H. S. Sullivan, "The Modified Psychoanalytic Treatment of Schizophrenia," *American Journal of Psychiatry* 88 (1931): 519–40.
49. Ibid.
50. A. A. Brill, "Schizophrenia and Psychotherapy," *American Journal of Psychiatry* 86 (1929): 519–41.
51. A. P. Noyes, "Psychotherapy in State Hospitals," *American Journal of Psychiatry* 91 (1935): 1353–66.
52. T. A. C. Rennie, "Psychiatric Rehabilitation Therapy," *American Journal of Psychiatry* 101 (1945): 476–85.
53. H. A. Steckel, "The Need of Sheltered Workshops in the Community Rehabilitation of Mental Patients," *Psychiatric Quarterly* 3 (1929): 404–8.
54. H. A. Pooler, "The Application of Occupational Therapy in the Treatment of Mental Illness," *Psychiatric Quarterly* 9 (1934): 400–11.
55. H. B. Molholm and W. E. Barton, "Family Care, a Community Resource in the Rehabilitation of Mental Patients," *American Journal of Psychiatry* 98 (1941): 33–41. S. W. Bisgrove, "Family Care of Patients at the Marcy State Hospital," *Psychiatric Quarterly* 11 (1937): 296–304.
56. Bisgrove, "Family Care."
57. "Mental Hospital Survey," *American Journal of Psychiatry* 93 (1936): 470–76.
58. H. Lutgens, "Administrative Conditions and Problems of the California Mental Hospitals," *American Journal of Psychiatry* 95 (1939): 1113–18.

59. R. G. Fuller and M. Johnston, "The Duration of Hospital Life for Mental Patients. I—Preliminary Paper," *Psychiatric Quarterly* 5 (1931): 341–52.

60. R. G. Fuller and M. Johnston, "The Duration of Hospital Life for Mental Patients (second paper)," *Psychiatric Quarterly* 5 (1931): 552–82.

61. A. Myerson, "Theory and Principles of the 'Total Push' Method in the Treatment of Chronic Schizophrenia," *American Journal of Psychiatry* 95 (1939): 1197–1204.

62. M. H. Erickson and R. G. Hoskins, "Grading of Patients in Mental Hospitals as a Therapeutic Measure," *American Journal of Psychiatry* 88 (1931): 103–9.

EPILOGUE

1. K. Millet, *The Loony-Bin Trip* (New York: Simon & Schuster, 1992). B. Noel, *You Must Be Dreaming* (New York: Poseidon, 1992). S. Kaysen, *Girl, Interrupted* (New York: Turtle Bay, 1993).

Appendix

*Bibliography of Firsthand Accounts by Women
with Psychiatric Institutional Histories
in the United States Between 1840 and 1945*

Entries with an asterisk (*) are excerpted in this book.

*Agnew, Anna. *From Under the Cloud or, Personal Reminiscences of Insanity.* Cincinnati: Printed by Robert Clarke for the Author, 1886.

*Anon. "Scene in a Private Mad-House." *Asylum Journal* 1(1): 1, 1842.

Anon. "Letter by 'A Friend of the Insane.' " *Asylum Journal* 1(5): 2, 1842.

Anon. "The Ohio Lunatic Asylum." *The Journal of Psychological Medicine and Mental Pathology* 3: 456–90, 1850.

Anon. Case VIII. *American Journal of Insanity* 1: 52–71, 1844.

Anon. "Illustrations of Insanity." *American Journal of Insanity* 3: 212–26, 333–48, 1846.

Anon. "Illustrations of Insanity Furnished by the Letters and Writings of the Insane. *American Journal of Insanity* 4: 290–303, 1848.

Anon. "A Letter from a Patient." *The Opal—A Monthly Periodical of the State Lunatic Asylum, Devoted to Usefulness* 2: 245–46, 1852.

Anon. "A Chapter from Real Life. By a Recovered Patient." *The Opal—A Monthly Periodical of the State Lunatic Asylum, Devoted to Usefulness* 4: 48–50, 1854.

Anon. Life in the Asylum. *The Opal—A Monthly Periodical of the State Lunatic Asylum. Edited by the Patients* 5: 4–6, 1855.

Anon. *A Palace-Prison: or, the Past and the Present.* New York: Fords, Howard & Hulbert, 1884.

Anon. "The Confessions of a Nervous Woman." *Post Graduate Monthly. Journal of Medicine and Surgery* 11: 364–68, 1896.

Anon. "Wondering. The Impressions of an Inmate." *Atlantic Monthly* 145: 669, 1930.

Anon. "They Said I Was Mad." *The Forum and Century* 100: 231–37, 1938.

Anon. "Insulin and I." *American Journal of Orthopsychiatry* 10: 810–14, 1940.

Anon. (Mrs. F.H.) "Recovery from a Long Neurosis." *Psychiatry* 15: 161–77, 1952.

*Beecher, Catherine. *Letters to the People on Health and Happiness.* New York: Harper & Brothers, 1855.

Bly, Nellie (Elizabeth Cochrane). *Ten Days in a Madhouse; or, Nellie Bly's Experience on Blackwell's Island. Feigning Insanity in Order to Reveal Asylum Horrors.* New York: Norman L. Munro, 1887.

Bogan, Louise. *Collected Poems 1923–1953.* New York: Noonday Press, 1954.

*Brinckle, Andriana P. "Life Among the Insane." *North American Review* 144: 190–99, 1887.

Channing, Walter. "The Evolution of Paranoia—Report of a Case." *Journal of Nervous and Mental Disease* 19: 192–214, 1892.

Coleman, Emily Holmes. *The Shutter of Snow.* New York: The Viking Press, 1930.

[Cottier, Lizzie D.] *The Right Spirit.* Buffalo: The Courier Company, Printers, 1885.

*Davis, Phebe B. *Two Years and Three Months in the New York Lunatic Asylum at Utica; Together with the Outlines of Twenty Years' Peregrinations in Syracuse.* Syracuse: Published by the Author, 1855.

Denny, Lydia B. *Statement of Mrs. Lydia B. Denny, Wife of Reuben S. Denny, of Boston, in Regard to Her Alleged Insanity.* N.p., n.p., 1862.

Eliot, Jane. "My Way Back to Sanity." *Ladies Home Journal* 63(10): 54–55, 242–50, 1946.

*Farmer, Frances. *Will There Really Be a Morning?* New York: G. P. Putnam's Sons, 1972.

Fischer, Augusta C. *Searchlight. An Autobiography.* Seattle: n.p., 1937.

Gilman, Charlotte Perkins. "The Yellow Wallpaper." *New England Magazine* 5(5): 647–56, 1892.

*———. *The Living of Charlotte Perkins Gilman.* New York: D. Appleton-Century Co., 1935.

Harlan, Olivia. "Minds in the Mending." *Atlantic Monthly* 168: 330–34, 1941.

*Hillyer, Jane. *Reluctantly Told.* New York: Macmillan Co., 1927.

Jefferson, Lara. *These Are My Sisters: An "Insandectomy."* Tulsa: Vickers Publishing Co., 1947.

Kinder, Elaine F. "Postscript on a Benign Psychosis." *Psychiatry* 3: 527–34, 1940.

*King, Maria. *The Recovery of Myself: A Patient's Experience in a Hospital for Mental Illness.* New Haven: Yale University Press, 1931.

Kirk, Anne. *Chronicles of Interdict No. 7807.* Boston: Meador Publishing Co., 1937.

*Lathrop, Clarissa Caldwell. *A Secret Institution.* New York: Bryant Publishing Co., 1890.

*Lee, Kate. *A Year at Elgin Insane Asylum.* New York: Irving Co., 1902.

*Lunt, Adeline T. P. *Behind Bars.* Boston: Lee & Shepard, 1871.

*McCall, Lenore. *Between Us and the Dark.* Philadelphia: J. B. Lippincott Co., 1947.

*McGarr, Margaret Aikins. *and lo, the STAR.* New York: Pageant Press, 1953.

*Metcalf, Ada. *Lunatic Asylums: and How I Became An Inmate of One. Doctors, Incidents, Humbuggery.* Chicago: Ottaway & Colbert, Printers, 1876.

Milici, Pompeo, and Von Salzen, Charles. "Situational Schizophrenia." *Psychiatric Quarterly* 12: 650–68, 1938.

[Packard, Elizabeth Parsons Ware.] *Mrs. Packard's Reproof to Dr. McFarland for His Abuse of His Patients, and for Which He Called Her Hopelessly Insane.* Chicago: Printed by Times Steam Job Printing House, 1864.

[———.] *The Exposure on Board the Atlantic and Pacific Car of Emancipation for the Slaves of Old Columbia, Engineered by the Lightning Express; or, Christianity & Calvinism Compared. With an Appeal to the Government to Emancipate the Slaves of the Marriage Union.* Chicago: Published by the Authoress, 1864.

[———.] *Great Disclosure or Spiritual Wickedness!! in High Places. With an Appeal to the Government to Protect the Inalienable Rights of Married Women.* Boston: Published by the Authoress, 1865.

———. *Marital Power Exemplified in Mrs. Packard's Trial, and Self-Defense from the Charge of Insanity; or Three Years' Imprisonment for Religious Belief, by the Arbitrary Will of a Husband, with an Appeal to the Government to so Change the Laws as to Protect the Rights of Married Women*. Hartford, Conn.: Published by the Authoress, 1866.

———. *Mrs. Olsen's Narrative of Her One Year Imprisonment, at Jacksonville Insane Asylum; with the Testimony of Mrs. Minard, Mrs. Shedd, Mrs. Yates, and Mrs. Lake, All Corroborated by the Investigating Committee of the Legislature of Illinois*. Chicago: A. B. Case Printer, 1868.

———. *The Prisoners' Hidden Life, or Insane Asylums Unveiled: As Demonstrated by the Report of the Investigating Committee of the Legislature of Illinois*. Chicago: Published by the Author, A. B. Case Printer, 1868.

*———. *Modern Persecutions, or Insane Asylums Unveiled, As Demonstrated by the Report of the Investigating Committee of the Legislature of Illinois Volumes I & II*. (Vol. II entitled *Modern Persecutions, or Married Woman's Liabilities, as Demonstrated by the Action of the Illinois Legislature*.) Hartford, Conn.: Case, Lockwood, & Brainard, Printers and Binders, 1874.

———. *A Bill to Remedy the Evils of Insane Asylums, and Mrs. Packard's Argument in Support of the Same*. Presented to the Massachusetts Legislature, April 28, 1874. Boston: n.p., 1874.

———. *The Great Drama: or, The Millennial Harbinger*. Hartford, Conn.: Published by the Authoress, Printed by the Case, Lockwood & Brainard Co., 1878.

———. *The "Women Hating Party!" in the Idaho Legislature, Exposed!* Boise City, Idaho Territory: Republican Print, 1881.

———. *The Mystic Key or the Asylum Secret Unlocked*. Hartford, Conn.: Published by the Author, Press of the Case, Lockwood & Brainard Co., 1882.

Pennell, Lemira Clarissa. *The Memorial Scrap Book. A Combination of Precedents*. Boston: n.p., 1883.

[———.] *Another Section of the "M.S.B." by L.C.P. A Boomerang for a Swarm of B.B.B.'s*. Boston: n.p., 1884.

[———.] *Prospectus of Hospital Revelations. How Opinions Vary*. N.p., n.p., 1885.

*———. *This Red Book Is Partly a Reprint of What Was Published in 1883, and Later. And Earlier Letters from Prominent Men. Instructions to Dr. Harlow, from Springfield, His Letters from the Hospitals, and Much Else*. Boston: n.p., 1886.

[———.] *Hospital Revelations*. N.p., n.p., 1888.

———. *An Explanation to the Public as to Why Mrs. Lemira Clarissa Pennell*

Was Confined in the Insane Hospital and the Portland Poor House. Augusta, Maine: n.p., 188[?].

———. *New Horrors.* N.p., n.p., 1890.

———. *Leave to Withdraw.* Boston: n.p., n.d.

*Pierce, S. W., and Pierce, J. T. *The Layman Looks at Doctors.* New York: Harcourt, Brace & Co., 1929.

Pollack, Benjamin. "Schizophrenic Thought." *Psychiatric Quarterly* 11: 337–55, 1937.

Putnam, Daniel. *Twenty-Five Years with the Insane.* Detroit: John MacFarlane, 1885.

[Reid, Eva Charlotte.] "Autopsychology of the Manic-Depressive." *Journal of Nervous and Mental Diseases* 37: 606–20, 1910.

*Russell, Alice Bingham. *A Plea for the Insane by Friends of the Living Dead.* Minneapolis: Roberts Publishing Co., 1898.

Ruvtz-Rees, Janet E. "Hospitals for the Insane. Viewed from the Standpoint of Personal Experience, by a Recovered Patient." *Alienist and Neurologist* 9: 51–57, 1888.

*Smith, Lydia A. *Behind the Scenes; or, Life in an Insane Asylum.* Chicago: Printed for the Author by Culver, Page, Hoyne, & Co., 1878.

*Starr, Margaret. *Sane or Insane? Or How I Regained My Liberty.* Baltimore: Press of Fosnot, Williams & Co., 1904.

*Stone, Elizabeth T. *A Sketch of the Life of Elizabeth T. Stone, and of Her Persecutions, with an Appendix of Her Treatment and Sufferings While in the Charlestown McLean Asylum, Where She Was Confined Under the Pretense of Insanity.* N.p.: Printed for the Author, 1842.

*———. *Remarks by Elizabeth T. Stone, upon the Statements Made by H. B. Skinner, in the Pulpit of the Hamilton Chapel, on Sunday Afternoon, 18th of June 1843, in Reference to What She Had Stated Concerning His Being Chaplain in the Charlestown McLean Asylum: and Also a Further Relation on Her Suffering While Confined in That Place for 16 months and 20.* N.p.: Printed for the Author, 1843.

*———. *Elizabeth T. Stone, Exposing the Modern Secret Way of Persecuting Christians in Order to Hush the Voice of Truth. Insane Hospitals Are Inquisition Houses. All Heaven Is Interested in This Crime.* Boston: Printed for the Author, 1859.

[———.] *The American Godhead: or, the Constitution of the United States Cast Down by Northern Slavery, or by the Power of Insane Hospitals.* Boston: Published by the Author, 1861.

Titus, Ann H. *Lunatic Asylums. Their Use and Abuse.* New York: n.p., 1870.

Ward, Mary Jane. "Out of the Dark Ages." *Woman's Home Companion,* August 1946: 34–35, 91–92.

*———. *The Snake Pit.* New York: Random House, 1946.

*Wilson, Margaret Isabel. *Borderland Minds.* Boston: Meador Publishing Co., 1940.

Wilson, Wilma. *They Call Them Camisoles.* Los Angeles: Lymanhouse, 1940.

About the Authors

Jeffrey L. Geller, M.D., M.P.H., is Professor of Psychiatry at the University of Massachusetts Medical School. He was a Robert Wood Johnson Health Policy fellow in Washington, D.C., during 1993–94. Dr. Geller lives in Worcester, Massachusetts.

Maxine Harris, Ph.D., is a clinical psychologist with a private practice in psychotherapy, and the cofounder and codirector of Community Connections, a nonprofit community-based health agency in Washington, D.C. Author of *Sisters of the Shadow* and *Down from the Pedestal: Moving Beyond Idealized Images of Womanhood*, she lives in Chevy Chase, Maryland.